Forbidden Lessons in a Kabul Guesthouse

Forbidden Lessons *in a* Kabul Guesthouse

THE TRUE STORY OF A WOMAN
WHO RISKED EVERYTHING TO
BRING HOPE TO AFGHANISTAN

Suraya Sadeed

WITH DAMIEN LEWIS

voice

HYPERION
NEW YORK

Library of Congress Cataloging-in-Publication Data

Sadeed, Suraya.
    Forbidden lessons in a Kabul guesthouse : the true story of a woman who risked everything to bring hope to Afghanistan / Suraya Sadeed with Damien Lewis. — 1st ed.
        p. cm.
    ISBN 978-1-4013-4131-2
    1. Sadeed, Suraya.   2. Afghanistan—History—2001—Biography.   3. Afghanistan—History—1989–2001—Biography.   4. Women social reformers—Afghanistan—Biography.
5. Social reformers—Afghanistan—Biography.   6. Afghan American women—Biography.
7. Help the Afghan Children (Organization)   8. Children—Afghanistan—Social conditions.   9. Afghanistan—Social conditions—20th century.   10. Afghanistan—Social conditions—21st century.   11. Afghan War, 2001—Social aspects.   I. Lewis, Damien.   II. Title.
    DS371.43.S23A3 2011
    958.104'7092—dc22
    [B]

                                                                              2010053485

Hyperion books are available for special promotions and premiums. For details contact the HarperCollins Special Markets Department in the New York office at 212-207-7528, fax 212-207-7222, or email spsales@harpercollins.com.

Design by Susan Walsh

First Edition

10   9   8   7   6   5   4   3   2   1

THIS LABEL APPLIES TO TEXT STOCK

We try to produce the most beautiful books possible, and we are also extremely concerned about the impact of our manufacturing process on the forests of the world and the environment as a whole. Accordingly, we've made sure that all of the paper we use has been certified as coming from forests that are managed, to ensure the protection of the people and wildlife dependent upon them.

To the
Children of Afghanistan

—SURAYA SADEED

For Hamid Huneidi,
for the gift of life

—DAMIEN LEWIS

Contents

Author's Note

This is a true story. It took place between the year of my birth, 1952, and the present day. Afghanistan has been at war for decades. My home city, Kabul, has been particularly badly devastated. I have changed some people's names to protect family, friends, and communities.

Acknowledgments

Very special thanks to Frances Connell, for her sincere and continuous support; to Lois Schakenhawer, for believing in our cause; to Randall Scerbo and Christine Burrill, for their determination to bring awareness to my work; to Omar Malikyar, for his unconditional support throughout the years; to Stephen Perlman and Jo Anne Nakagawa, for their encouragements to write my memoir; and to Damien Lewis, my coauthor, for his dedication and genuine interest in my story. Special thanks to my indomitable American literary agent, Jesseca Salky, and my enthusiastic UK-based agent, Felicity Bryan. Thanks also to my foreign rights agent, Andrew Nurnberg Associates. Very many thanks to my U.S. publisher, Voice, for their enthusiasm and support for the telling of my story from the very start.

Very special thanks to my daughter, Mariam, for her belief in my work and unconditional support through difficult times, and my husband, Aziz R. Qarghah, whose devotion to helping others is my inspiration.

And many thanks and much gratitude to those Afghans and Americans whose trust in my mission, and commitment to helping Afghanistan children throughout the years, have made my work possible.

I learned that courage was not the absence of fear, but the triumph over it. The brave man is not he who does not feel afraid, but he who conquers that fear.

—NELSON MANDELA

Forbidden Lessons in a
Kabul Guesthouse

PROLOGUE

Lessons by Lamplight

1997

I HAD NO TROUBLE FINDING A STORE THAT SOLD BURKAS IN PESHA-war, Pakistan. I'd started to hear stories about the Taliban's excesses in Afghanistan since their explosion into power started in Kandahar Province in 1994, and I wanted to blend in and go about my work unmolested once I crossed the border from Pakistan into my home country. All the burkas I could find were the same powder blue color and one-size-fits-all. They were too long for me, but the shopkeeper suggested I cut one off at the hem.

Later, in the privacy of my hotel room, I tried the burka on. I wasn't able to get my head into it. The gauze window remained stubbornly stuck on my forehead, and I couldn't see out. I went back to the shop and told the shop-keeper that I needed a burka with an extra big head. He found one that I could just about squeeze into. I figured it would give me a headache, but I'd make do.

The route I planned to take to Kabul was the same that I'd taken for the last three years, bringing money and supplies for medical and humanitarian relief into Afghanistan. Except for my route, though, everything had changed. This time, the entire journey would be in areas under Taliban control.

I exchanged our $35,000 for a sackful of local currency. I had hoped to hide the money beneath my newly acquired burka during the trip to Kabul, but there was no way I could strap that much cash beneath even the world's most voluminous tent. Dr. Abdullah, Nawabi, and Sekander, my three trusted Afghan colleagues, had agreed to accompany me, so they would be able to share the burden of carrying the money.

The four of us caught a taxi from Peshawar to the Afghanistan border, where I donned my burka. As soon as the garment was on me, I could sense the difference. I could go freely wherever I chose without being stared at as a "foreigner." At first the front kept twisting around to the back, bringing my eyeholes along with it, so I couldn't see. And whenever I wanted to eat or drink, I had to hook my arm up like an elephant's trunk and pass the food under the burka, feeling for my open mouth. But I could live with that. For now, at least, the burka was a welcome refuge.

On the Afghan side of the border we joined a crowd of others who'd just passed through the frontier post. We all boarded a battered Soviet-era bus together, our fellow passengers carrying every sort of cargo you could imagine: suitcases, pots and pans, chickens tied up by the feet. I guessed that some of them had to be Afghan refugees returning home to chance their lot under the Taliban. A thick and heavy curtain hung halfway down the bus. Under the Taliban's rules, the bus had to be segregated: men in front, women in back.

The Taliban had strung roadblocks along the route where they stopped the bus and checked that their rules were being adhered to. If a woman was sitting in the wrong section, or if she wasn't properly covered, then the men traveling with her would be punished. No woman was allowed to go anywhere without a male companion, so the Taliban always had a man they could give a good beating to.

As we set off down the potholed road, the bus creaking and groaning at every bump, I wondered why the women were holding pillows on their heads. Almost immediately, the bus cannoned into a massive pothole, and we shot off our seats. Of course the women with the pillows were pretty much okay, but my head hit the roof with an almighty crack.

"Shit! Goddamn it!" I yelled out in Dari. "Tell the goddamn driver to slow down!"

Everyone turned and stared. I was so glad that I was enveloped in my burka. They must have guessed that I was a "foreigner" from my accent, but they still couldn't see me. I turned to the woman next to me.

"At this rate I'm gonna have a bump on my head the size of a pomegranate," I joked.

I couldn't tell if she smiled or not because I couldn't see her face. It was like talking to a mask.

"Here," she said, passing me a bundle. "Take this child's jacket. It's not a pillow exactly, but it might help."

"What do I do with it?" I asked her.

"Stuff it inside your burka. The hood should keep it in place."

I fed the kid's jacket up under my burka and wedged it into the head-piece. When I pulled the burka down again I had a weird lump on top of my head.

"I'm sorry," the woman giggled, staring at me. "It just looks so funny."

"I bet it does," I replied, laughing too.

As we drove on, the blinding sun beat down on us from the bright azure sky. The back of the bus grew horribly stuffy, embalmed within my burka as I was. We finally stopped at a place where a cool stream ran down from the mountainside, and the men got out to drink and to relieve themselves. I leaned forward and pushed the curtain aside so I could speak to Dr. Abdullah.

"I need to go pee," I whispered.

"Sorry," he whispered back. "There's nowhere for a woman to go."

"But I need to," I hissed.

"You can't. Women aren't allowed to get out."

"So under the Taliban, women can't pee? *I need to go!*"

"Just wait awhile. There's a restaurant a little farther on. You can go there."

The men soon climbed back in the bus and started lighting up these horrid cigarettes. Whether they were opium joints or not, I didn't know. But whatever they were, the acrid smoke soon drifted to the back of the bus and started pooling behind the curtain in a thick gray haze.

I leaned forward again and caught Dr. Abdullah's attention. "Can you tell them to stop smoking? We don't have a window back here."

"The women are having a hard time breathing because of the smoke," Dr. Abdullah announced. "There's no window in the back of the bus."

No one seemed to pay him any heed, and the smoke grew thicker and thicker. A few minutes later, as we approached a Taliban checkpoint, I leaned forward for a third time.

"Tell those bozos if they don't stop smoking, I'll unveil myself," I hissed again. "And then the Taliban will beat the crap out of all of you."

All three of my colleagues—Dr. Abdullah, Nawabi, and Sekander—turned to me and stared.

"You can't do that," Dr. Abdullah objected. "You never know what might happen."

"I'm warning you guys—tell them to stop smoking, or the burka comes off."

Dr. Abdullah nodded his head and smiled, figuring that I was joking. Nawabi tried not to laugh. But Sekander was horrified. Sekander knew that I was born and brought up in Afghanistan, but as far as he was concerned I came from a different planet. In his experience, no Afghan woman would act as I did; the only way he could rationalize my behavior was by labeling me as a "foreigner."

"Suraya-*jan*, Afghanistan is not like it was when you lived here," Nawabi remarked. "You've been away in the U.S. and things here have changed. We're in a time now where women can't—"

"That's baloney! Can't do what?" I demanded. "It's precisely because I've lived in the U.S. that I can't put up with this crap."

"See, that's what I mean. You're impossible. We can't reason with you at all."

By now the rear of the bus was a dense fog of smoke. I felt nauseated and dizzy and I was quickly reaching the end of my rope.

"You men in the front!" I yelled out. "I swear to God if you don't stop smoking I'll unveil in front of the Talibs, and they'll beat the crap out of every last one of you!"

Dr. Abdullah sunk lower into his seat. Nawabi did his best to hide his face, but his shoulders were rocking with laughter. Sekander stared out of the window with a stone-still face.

The men at the front turned to one another in consternation. "Who is this crazy woman? Is she with you?"

"It doesn't matter who I'm with!" I yelled. "Stop the smoking, or I'm gonna unveil!"

A moment later the men started chucking their butts out the windows. The woman who had lent me the kid's coat leaned across to me.

"Thank you for doing that," she whispered. "I was about to die."

Dr. Abdullah's restaurant with the pee stop still hadn't materialized, and I was damned if I'd quietly sit in the back of the bus and wet myself. In the Taliban's world, we women were supposed to hold it in for the entire twelve-hour journey. We weren't even allowed to function like human beings. It was completely insane.

At the next stop, I marched down the aisle and went and had a pee in the bushes. In spite of the dangers of getting beaten or worse, the rebel within me just couldn't stomach the Taliban's mindless rules. All of a sudden a row of women were beside me. They'd been dying to go, but none of them had felt they could break the rules until someone else did first.

We reached Kabul by sundown without the slightest hint of any trouble along the way. The Taliban seemed to have the country under control, at least where security was concerned. They had to be a powerful movement, for in a matter of months they had defeated the warring Mujahideen factions, and spread a blanket of iron control over this battle-weary and anarchic land. After my previous experiences in Afghanistan, I had to admit it was an impressive feat.

Dr. Abdullah, Nawabi, Sekander, and I had a private house at our disposal in Kabul that was owned by one of the patients from our Peshawar clinic. It was an upscale, modern property set in the Wazir Akbar Khan district, once the upmarket part of Kabul. Wazir Akbar Khan was now a ghost town, for all but the poorest inhabitants had fled. Still, the house made an ideal base from which to organize our relief mission.

Kabul looked almost exactly the same as when I last had been there three years before, in 1994. It was still a blasted, empty ruin of a city. But there was one crucial difference: there were no more terrifying rocket barrages or snipers trying to shoot those collecting their dead. In fact, Kabul was utterly silent. The more I tried to tune in to the pulse of the city, the more I sensed that something was wrong. The next morning when I got up it struck me what it was. The noise of fighting had been replaced by utter stillness. Apart from the five daily calls to prayer, there was practically no noise, or music, or life at all.

Convinced that Kabul was the embodiment of every sin known to man, the Taliban had descended on the city with their "vice squads." These vice police roared around the streets in their white pickup trucks and set upon anyone they judged to be breaking the rules. People were being punished for everything—and for nothing. The men, for not having long-enough beards. The women, for having white-heeled shoes that the Taliban deemed a "provocation." The vice police had long batons with heavy copper balls on the end. If a woman was spotted showing just a fraction of her ankle, they smashed her shins with those clubs. Elders were beaten and belittled in front of their families. No one seemed safe from the Taliban's efforts to break the will of the city.

That first night I heard the only "music" that existed now—a Taliban dirge played repeatedly on the radio.

> *I am a Talib.*
> *I will spread Islam.*
> *I will hate the infidels.*
> *I will destroy the infidels.*
> *And so I will spread Islam.*

Again and again the Taliban played that dirge, as if they were brainwashing the city's inhabitants with the Taliban's hatred and intolerance. I went to sleep with that mantra running leaden through my mind.

The following morning Sekander hired a taxi to take us to the old Security Service building, which now housed the Taliban's secret police headquarters. I wasn't allowed out of the car. Nawabi was a Pashtun, as were many of the Taliban, and I let him do the talking. When we arrived at the headquarters, he went inside to explain the nature of our mission. Nothing happened in the city without the Taliban's knowledge or blessing.

They seemed happy enough that we had come to give out aid to displaced people in Kabul, but they wanted to oversee the operation. Four Taliban readied a pickup, and we set off in a convoy toward the old Soviet Embassy. The sight of seventeen thousand displaced people in the midst of Kabul city was disturbing enough. But to see them camped out in the skeleton of the wrecked embassy, the gray smoke of their cooking fires lying like a blanket of fog among the twisted ruins, was profoundly unsettling.

It was like a scene from a movie set in the aftermath of nuclear war, when all normal order and life had broken down. As we got out of the car, the women gathered around us and told us their heart-rending stories of being trapped in the middle of the vicious conflict between the Taliban and the Northern Alliance. Many had seen family and friends torn apart by bullets and bombs as the two warring groups pounded each other into oblivion.

I asked the women what they needed most, and how the money we had brought might help. They told us they were surviving on three rations of halva—a kind of hard cake baked from flour, sugar, and oil—per day. They desperately needed salt, fruit, and vegetables. And they asked if there were any doctors who might tend to the injured and the dying.

We decided to give a set amount of cash to the head of each household so they could buy the food they so desperately needed. Dr. Abdullah would tend to those who had been injured in the fighting or hurt during the long march south from Northern Afghanistan to Kabul. I asked the Taliban to unload the sacks of money and help divide it into small bundles to give away. I was intrigued to see how they would react to all that cash.

The leader of the four Taliban was older than the others, somewhere in his midforties, I guessed. He was dressed in a typical Arab-style Muslim outfit, a long black robe that falls from shoulders to feet, almost like a dress, and a small white skullcap. He directed the others to sort the cash, and I was amazed at how honest they appeared to be.

They were strict and fair with the displaced people, giving priority to the older women and the grandmothers who had young kids to care for. I hadn't expected to see such respect from the Taliban "women haters." And they never once asked for anything. I cast my mind back to my earlier trips, when lawless militias demanded—and took—whatever they wanted at gunpoint. Dealing with these guys was quite a contrast.

At the end of the distribution we had a little cash left over. "You guys worked very hard," I said to the Taliban commander. "Will you please take something?"

I'd removed my burka because we were inside the embassy compound, where it was mostly women and children. The Taliban commander stared at the ground. He couldn't look into my unveiled face.

He shook his head. "We don't want anything. These people are the ones in need."

"But you worked hard. You earned it."

"Are you saying this because you're afraid of us?" he queried.

He wasn't being aggressive or threatening. He just seemed curious.

"I'm not afraid of you. Why should I be? I'm not afraid of anyone, apart from God." I smiled and started handing them the remaining cash. "*Basmela rahman rahim*—in the name of God the most merciful . . ."

I could see the shock on their faces. "She knows Holy Koran!"

"I'm a Muslim," I told them.

"You are?" the commander asked.

"Yes, I am."

They still looked as if they didn't believe me. To them a Muslim woman would have acted differently than I did. But I couldn't change the way they saw things, and in any case it wasn't what I was here for.

The women must have felt they could confide in me, for they told me that the Taliban had forbidden them from seeing a male doctor. But under the Taliban's rules, women weren't allowed to work, so they were effectively barred from seeing a doctor at all.

I checked with Dr. Abdullah. Unbelievably, what the women had told me was true. The entire female population of Afghanistan's capital city was effectively deprived of access to medical care. Right then and there, I knew that I had to start an underground women's clinic in Kabul.

Dr. Abdullah had once been a very wealthy man, and he still owned a couple of properties in Kabul. He reckoned we could fix up one of them fairly easily so it could serve as a clinic, and for now we would purchase whatever medical supplies we could find locally. His property had the great benefit of having two separate entrances. We could run it as if it were operating according to Taliban rules, but the back entrance would be the secret one for the women. Female patients could sneak in and out of that entrance, and the men and women would never run into each other.

Over the next few days we hired some male doctors and nurses whom Dr. Abdullah knew well, plus some female doctors who were brave enough to carry on working in the face of the Taliban. And we sent out word for the women patients to come.

Incredibly, once word got around about our clinic, the wives of the Taliban started coming, in secret, for treatment. We learned from them that the senior Taliban were sending their wives to hospitals in Peshawar, or even as far away as Dubai. What vile hypocrisy. While thousands of women remained trapped in this wreck of a city with zero access to medical aid, the Taliban bigwigs sat back and took care of their own.

At the clinic I met a women patient called Masouma. We got to talking, and she asked me where I was from.

"America," I told her.

"But you speak such fantastic Dari."

"Well, I was born in Afghanistan."

"You know, there's another American woman working here in Kabul," Masouma remarked.

I thought I must have misheard her. Surely no foreigners had remained in Afghanistan during the Mujahideen years or under the Taliban. But Masouma was adamant: there was an American woman living just down the street from our clinic. Masouma offered to take me to meet her. We donned our burkas, snuck out of the clinic, and approached the door of a residence that looked pretty much like Dr. Abdullah's apartment. Masouma knocked, and we stood back to wait.

"Who is it?" a voice called out in broken Dari. "What do you want?"

"It's Masouma," Masouma replied.

"Masouma-*jan*," said the voice, "I'm still waiting for the money to buy the raw materials. I'm so sorry."

"No, it's not that," Masouma called back. "I'm here with a lady from America."

"Oh my God! Oh my God! From America?"

The door flew open. A face peered out and glanced around, searching for someone not draped from head to toe in a burka.

"Masouma-*jan*, where is this American lady?"

"Hi," I said, in English. "I'm here."

"Oh my God! Well, hello! Why don't you come in?"

I went inside, and as soon as I removed my burka, the woman enveloped me in a bear hug. She had to be in her late seventies, but her tall frame was ramrod straight, her blue eyes sparkling with life under a fine head of white hair.

"Are you really an American?" she exclaimed.

"I'm Afghan-American," I replied.

"Well, thank you. Thank you for coming. I'm Mary. Mary McMaken. Come on, let's go into the kitchen."

Mary bustled ahead, talking incessantly. I guessed she hadn't spoken English for a long time.

"Now, forgive me for the appearance of the place. If I'd known you were coming . . . But I can offer you homemade cookies and some tea. Zainab! Sara! Fetch the cookies, please," Mary called to two young Afghan girls she had working for her. "And do we have any dried fruits? No? They've all gone? Never mind. Just cookies and tea then."

I took a good look at Mary McMaken as she scurried around the kitchen. For a moment I wondered if she might be CIA. Who else would be here in war-torn Kabul? But something told me that wasn't the case.

She joined Masouma and me at the kitchen table. "I'm so sorry but we're all out of money. That's why there's no dried fruit. The money doesn't always come easy, you know."

"Well, I have some money," I remarked. "Maybe I can help?"

"Oh no, I couldn't . . . ," Mary began. "Well, maybe just a few afghanis . . ."

I smiled. "The cookies are delicious. But hey, *what are you doing here?*"

"Well, you know, I kind of like this life. It's so simple. You don't have a lot of bills to pay. In fact, I guess I like it here all around. I mean, it's a crazy country, don't get me wrong, but underneath these people are so genuine. Plus there's real need here among the women, and that means I can do a little to help."

Mary explained that she ran a tiny charity helping Afghan women develop income-earning projects. She had a weaving program and an embroidery workshop, and she sold the handicrafts in America. She traveled back and forth, carrying the raw materials and then returning with the finished goods. She was the only woman who went around Kabul without a burka, and she managed to get away with it because she was this old, white-haired grandma.

In short, Mary was incredible. Once she'd finished telling me about herself, she refilled my teacup and asked me why I was in Kabul. I told her about my charity, Help the Afghan Children (HTAC), and everything we'd been doing up until now. And then I told her about the secret women's health clinic that we'd just started in Kabul.

Mary clapped her hands together in delight. "That's fantastic! You know, there is so much suffering under these stupid Taliban and their insane rules. . . . But it's great your clinic's so close to here. I can let my women know."

"Spread the word, Mary, spread the word."

"Suraya, there's such great talent here that's being wasted," Mary remarked. "All the girls' schools closed down, and the Taliban banned women from working, so there're teachers and school principals just sitting at home with nothing to do."

I paused for a second, thinking over what Mary had said. "You know, my real passion is education, and making girls a part of Afghan society again. . . . You know what I'd really love to do?"

Mary fixed me with a look. "What do you have in mind, Suraya-*jan?*"

"I want to start a school."

"Well, it's a fine idea," Mary remarked, slowly. She was obviously thinking it through. "But it's not going to be easy. . . . I do know this lady who was the principal of a Kabul school, and now she's sitting around doing nothing. I guess you could start by talking to her."

"Well, get her here! And we can meet."

I left Mary with a bundle of afghanis, so she could buy some ingredients and bake us some more of her delicious cookies. In return, she agreed to get her teacher friend to come around to her house. The next day I was at the clinic when one of Mary's girls arrived.

"The teacher lady is here with Mary-*jan*," she whispered. "Her name is Sabera."

Sabera means "the person who is very patient." It was the perfect name for a teacher and for the person with whom I might be setting up my first Afghan school.

Sabera was the spitting image of Rahela, one of my own teachers at my Kabul high school. Rahela was my literature teacher, and she'd nurtured my love of reading. I'd had a lot of respect and affection for Rahela, and I just knew I was going to feel the same about Sabera. She'd worn a burka to get to Mary's place, but underneath was a smart suit and long pants. She had a real presence, and exuded both character and cultivation.

We made small talk for a while and then got down to business. "I hear you were a school principal. I'm thinking about opening a girls' school."

Sabera gave me a confused look. "A girls' school? Are you new to this city?"

"I know what's happening. That's exactly why I want to do this—girls are being excluded from education."

"It will be very difficult," Sabera remarked, hesitantly. "You know how the Taliban are." She glanced at me, inquiringly. "But what can I do?"

I held her gaze. "I want you to help me start the school."

I went on to outline my idea in greater depth—of starting a girls' school under the very noses of the Taliban. As I invited Sabera to be the principal of the first HTAC school, I detected a mix of hope and fear in her eyes. She asked me for a couple of days to think about it.

That evening I decided to share my idea for starting a girls' school with Dr. Abdullah and Sekander. It was far from definitely happening, but I knew I would need their help if it was to succeed.

"It is a fine idea, but it may prove a little dangerous," remarked Dr. Abdullah with typical understatement.

"Well, if I worried so much about danger I wouldn't be here, would I?"

Sekander shook his head in dismay. "This is no good at all. In fact, it is extremely dangerous. The Taliban are watching everyone. I'm advising you not to have anything more to do with this, or that American Mary woman."

"What is it, Sekander, you don't want girls to get educated?" I countered. I knew he was trying to protect me, but sometimes I had to balance the danger with what was needed to counter the Taliban's blind madness. Getting girls into schools was one of those times. "You're just like the Taliban if you're so against it."

"No, I'm not!" Sekander retorted, angrily. Being accused of being like the Taliban was about as bad as it could get for him. "But I *am* concerned for your safety, Suraya-*jan*. That's all there is to it."

"We came here to do what's needed, and this is something I really want to do. I'm going ahead, Sekander. And I need you guys to help me."

Two days later I met up with Sabera again at Mary's place. She looked happier and more upbeat than when we first met.

"I've thought about it," she told me, barely able to suppress a smile, "and I've talked to some of my teacher friends. And guess what—we are willing to give it a try! But we can't do it somewhere public, otherwise the Taliban will know. We'll have to do it secretly."

"That's great!" I exclaimed. "But how will it work? How can we have a secret school?"

"I can offer up my house," said Sabera. "It's an old guesthouse, so there's lots of rooms. It's even got a big basement. We can hold lessons down there by lamplight. That way no one will see us or hear us teaching the girls."

"But an underground school in a disused guesthouse . . ." I shook my head. "The impact will be so minimal."

I'd had visions of us opening up a huge school, and somehow getting away with it, as we had the clinic. This home-based education initiative felt so small. It wasn't what I had imagined at all.

"We can start with my house and see how it works," Sabera remarked. "If it does, I think I can get twelve teachers to open up their homes. All they'll need is a few basic school supplies."

"Well, that's easy," I told her. "And I can pay their salaries too. But even if it's twelve, the impact will be so small. It's not like our health clinic, where we can treat thousands. I mean, what would it be—maybe two hundred girls in total?"

"You think two hundred girls aren't worth it?" Sabera asked me, quietly. "That's still two hundred girls who would otherwise have no education. And remember, Suraya-*jan*, *quatra, quatra darya mesha*—drop by drop a river forms."

I felt chastened by her words. Of course she was right. I smiled. "*Quatra, quatra, darya mesha*. Fair enough. I agree."

"So, we'll do it?" Sabera asked.

"We'll do it," I confirmed. "I just hope I can come back and really grow these schools, that's all."

"Who knows, maybe God will be kinder next year," Sabera replied. "Next year maybe the Taliban will be gone, and we can open a proper school."

PART I

Finding Hope in a Lawless Land

1993–1995

ONE

Help the Afghan Children

IN DARI, WHICH IS MY LANGUAGE, THE NAME DASTAGIR MEANS "THE person who is always helping others." It was the perfect name for the man I had fallen in love with and married against my parents' wishes during the wild days of my Kabul youth.

Dastagir adored all kinds of music. He loved the way different songs and instruments caressed the senses and lifted or lowered the mood. And he was particularly in love with Indian classical music. As smoke from a Sunday afternoon barbecue drifted across our sunny terrace in June 1993, the lilting tones of Ravi Shankar's sitar floated from speakers Dastagir had set up in a second-story window of our home. The music sent a tiny shiver up my spine. My husband had a way of conjuring atmosphere and magic from nothing, and today he had created a small piece of heaven in our Virginia backyard.

That Sunday afternoon I basked in the spring sunshine and laughed and chatted with Dastagir's sisters. He served us delicious American burgers and spicy Afghan kababs from the barbecue. It was a perfect day: perfect weather, perfect company, perfect eating.

By nine that evening I was anxious to get some rest.

"Guys, let's wrap up," I announced. "Tomorrow is work, and I need to be at the office by eight sharp."

His sisters said their farewells. Dastagir and I cleared away the barbecue things. Yet once we'd retired to bed he still didn't seem to want to call it a day.

"Let's watch a Ravi video," he suggested. "Just one before we sleep."

"Are you crazy? It's Sunday night. We have work tomorrow."

"Just this one," he pleaded. He held up a video of Ravi Shankar doing a live performance. "Please."

With Dastagir I never could find it in myself to say no. So we plumped up the pillows and sat up in bed, watching that Ravi Shankar performance.

It was nearly midnight when he gave me a pained look. "You know, I feel like vomiting."

He hurried into the bathroom. I went after him, but as I reached the door he fell backward into my arms. I lowered him onto the floor, and his eyes met mine.

"Can you fetch me a pillow?" he murmured. "I feel kind of odd. I need to lie here a moment."

I went to grab a pillow from the bed. But by the time I was back his face had gone a deathly white, and he was gasping for breath.

"Oh my God!" I cried. "Mariam! MARIAM! Dial 911!"

Our eighteen-year-old daughter, Mariam, came dashing out of her room. She took one look at her father and made a grab for the phone. Three minutes later there was an ambulance at the door. The medics glanced at Dastagir, his head cradled in my lap.

"We need to get him to a hospital," one remarked. "Like now!"

In the back of the speeding ambulance I stared at the man I loved with a drip in his arm and an oxygen mask on his face. I told myself that this could not be happening. Dastagir was in his midforties, and a month earlier he'd had a full physical. "Your husband's as healthy as a horse," the doctor had told me.

Twice during that ambulance ride Dastagir let out a terrible scream, one that pierced the rasping, alien suck and blow of the oxygen mask. My husband was as healthy as a horse, yet here he was, white-faced and screaming.

On reaching the hospital the medics hustled him onto a gurney and rushed him toward the emergency room. I tried to go with them, but an orderly steered me to one side.

"It's best you wait here," he told me. "They might be busy in there, okay?"

I nodded, dumbly. Busy doing what? They wheeled Dastagir—"the person who is always helping others"—toward the double doors. Just before he went through I saw him raise his one free hand and wave at me. I felt a warm blast of reassurance. He was waving. It was nothing serious. He was going to be all right.

"You're gonna be fine," I called after him. "You're gonna be fine."

A doctor approached me. "Ms. Sadeed? Suraya Sadeed?"

I nodded.

"Ms. Sadeed, I need you to tell me how old your husband is."

"He's midforties. Forty-seven."

The doctor shot me a look, then shook his head nearly imperceptibly. Before I could ask anything, a voice started yelling from the direction of the emergency room.

"Code Blue! Code Blue! Code Blue!"

The doctor whirled and was gone. I glanced around myself, bewildered, then a nurse approached me.

She bent toward me. "You'd best take a seat."

"I'm okay standing," I told her. "I'm fine just here."

"Ma'am, please take a seat," she repeated. "Your husband's not feeling well. And, ma'am, maybe you should call your family."

"My family? But Mariam's got school tomorrow, and graduation Tuesday."

"You might still want to call. I think it's best to."

I telephoned Mariam and told her to take a cab to the hospital. I told her that her father was ill, but not to worry, it was just that the staff had said it was best she come.

The same doctor returned and took me into a side room. I had little sense of time now. He sat me down, just the two of us, me facing him. My mind was blank. I had no idea what was coming.

"There's no easy way to say this," he began, "but I'm afraid your husband didn't make it."

I stared at him with total incomprehension. "What do you mean— *didn't make it?*"

"Ms. Sadeed, I'm sorry to say your husband has passed away."

Didn't make it . . . Passed away . . . I shook my head, refusing to believe what I was hearing. "Doctor, how do you *know* these things? You're not God. . . ."

"Suraya, I know I'm not God," he replied, gently. "But I am a medical doctor. I'm afraid your husband has suffered a massive heart attack. We did everything we possibly could, but he didn't make it. I think it might help if you saw him."

The doctor led me to a side room. Dastagir was lying on the same gurney. He looked so calm. I couldn't believe for one moment that he was dead.

The doctor withdrew. I sat on a chair at my husband's side and reached for his hand. I would just talk to him and touch him and stop all this nonsense. I'd hum him a Ravi Shankar tune, and in no time he'd be smiling and singing along. Who the hell was that doctor to tell me that the love of my life was gone?

The hand I touched was cold. I held it, trying to warm it with my body heat and my love, but the hand just kept getting icier and icier. I knew this wasn't right.

Gradually I felt Dastagir's presence in one corner of the room. I glanced over and smiled at him uncertainly, as if to ask what on earth he was doing standing there, and not lying here by my side. He pointed at his body. I heard his voice in my head.

"Stay away from the body, Suraya. You need to leave the body, now. It's time. This is our parting."

A horrible chill ran down my spine, as if someone had injected ice into me. Perhaps the doctor was right. He wasn't God, but perhaps the impossible truth was that my husband was gone. I slid the wedding ring off his finger and onto my own.

DASTAGIR'S DEATH WAS DEVASTATING AND TOTALLY UNEXPECTED. Many times since then I've wondered about seeing him like that, standing apart from his body. It was as if he were alive and speaking to me, and I think he was trying to help me let him go.

I did let him go. But in the aftermath of his dying I felt as if I had nothing left to live for. The hardest part was Mariam's high school graduation, two days after his death. She had reserved seats for us, right at the very front. My brother-in-law offered to go in Dastagir's place, but Mariam would have none of it.

"No way," she told me. "No way is anyone going to sit in my father's place."

She put a single white rose there instead. And she insisted that I not come in my mourning clothes—I was to dress and wear makeup like normal. Well, it wasn't normal. It was the darkest time of my life. But I did what she asked of me, and somehow I got through that day.

Many times in the months that followed Dastagir's death I asked God, why *me*? We knew so many couples who fought like cats and dogs, so why us? *Why us?*

I was angry for a long time: angry at God; at fate. I felt as if God had cheated me. I was angry at the world for letting something so dark destroy our perfect lives. I was even angry at Dastagir for deserting me.

A black depression swept over me like a huge and crushing wave. On many dark and lonely nights I lay awake despairing, thinking over our lives together in America and of all that we had lost.

Dastagir, Mariam, and I had come to the United States as penniless Afghan refugees in the spring of 1982. The Soviet Union had invaded our country, and as the daughter of one of Kabul's ruling elites, there was no way that I could survive the pogroms. Because my father was a prominent politician, I would be targeted. So we fled to the land of the free, convinced that in this nation of opportunity we could build a new life for ourselves.

My younger sister was living in Virginia at the time, and we went to stay with her while we tried to find work and a place to live. In America you can't get by without a car, but we had no idea how we might acquire one. My sister advised us to get a car loan. Get a loan with what? I asked her. We had no jobs, no money, and our only ID was our I-94 papers, which showed we were legal and allowed to work.

My sister knew of a car dealership in Arlington called Bob Pick Chevrolet that might help us. Bob Pick was a tall, besuited, gray-haired gentleman who was friendly and welcoming, even when he learned that we had no cash and were seeking a loan. He asked us if we were working, and we told him that we were looking for work. He asked if we were legal, and we showed him our I-94 papers.

He glanced at them, then eyed us over his glasses. "You guys have someone to cosign for you?"

"We don't," I replied. "We're just arrived in America, and we're trying to get on our feet."

He paused for a second, as if lost in thought. "You know, you remind me of my youth. I came here myself with nothing. Look where I am now."

He glanced around the gleaming showroom. We were hanging on his every word. I'd expected him to throw us out, but here we were, still talking.

He smiled. "You know what I'm going to do—I'm gonna give you guys a chance."

I couldn't believe what I was hearing. He was going to take a chance on us—with no money, no jobs, and only our I-94s to prove who we were.

He reached under his counter for a calculator. "Normal rate is fourteen percent. I'm adding one percent on top 'cause you've got no employment; one percent because you've just arrived; one percent 'cause you've got no deposit. . . ."

We ended up shaking on an 18 percent interest rate on the loan. Luckily, Dastagir had gotten his driver's license the year before in Germany, where we stopped over as refugees en route to America. As we drove away from Bob Pick Chevrolet in a brand-new blue sedan, I marveled at this country and its generous, open spirit.

Because of his post as governor of Kabul, my father was entitled to have impressive cars and drivers. The one car that I truly loved was his 1957 Chevrolet, black with sweeping white wings. We called it Motor Balsafaid, a car that flies on white wings. Inside it were leather seats and polished wood; and my father's driver, Karim, sat ramrod straight at the wheel in his peaked cap and uniform. In comparison, that little blue Chevy that Bob

Pick had sold us was a pretty average vehicle, but the welcoming hand that he had extended to us was nevertheless extraordinary.

A few weeks after Bob Pick sold us that Chevy, I got my first job in America, working as an administrative assistant at Georgetown University. In my spare time I studied for my real estate exams. Everyone kept telling me that an Afghan refugee couldn't become a Realtor, but I was determined to make it as a real estate agent in America. I'd have the freedom to be my own boss, and I could earn real money.

Two years later I qualified for my Realtor's license, and we purchased our first family home. It was 1984, and by then we had fallen in love with our adopted country. Nothing came easily, but if you worked hard you could make it.

By 1987 I'd gotten my broker's license and founded my own real estate company, DMS—Dastagir, Mariam, Suraya—Realtors, Incorporated. I soon had a dozen Realtors working for me, and the fat checks on sales commissions started piling into my bank account.

I reinvested the money in real estate, and by the early 1990s Dastagir and I owned six houses, condos, and a stretch of waterfront land. I had a whole drawer at home reserved for the files on the properties. One day I was sorting through the drawer and doing some paperwork when Dastagir found me.

He took my hand in his. "Suraya," he said. "How much is ever enough?"

What did he mean, How much is ever enough? I'd never even considered the question.

We were from very different backgrounds. Dastagir hailed from a poor, working-class family, while I was the daughter of the governor of Kabul. *How much is enough?* The simple answer was that there was never enough. I was always seeking a bigger house, a fatter property portfolio, a glitzier car. There was never enough, for those material goods were the markers of success in America, the things that gave life meaning.

After I lost Dastagir, none of our material wealth meant a damn thing anymore. My craving for more—more money, more property, more, more,

more—died with his passing. A couple of months after Dastagir's death, my broker's license came up for its three-year renewal. I stared at that license for a moment, then locked it away in a drawer. My money lust was gone.

I closed down the real estate business and let my workers go. My life slipped into a formless limbo. One evening six months after losing Dastagir I had dinner with two close friends, Anisa Durrani and her husband, Musleh. With Dastagir gone I'd sold our big Virginia house, and Mariam and I had moved into an apartment. It was a rare occasion these days when I left the apartment, but Anisa had enticed me out to their house in Fairfax with the promise of some spicy Afghan food.

We left the TV on in the background while we ate. A report came up on CNN about the conflict in Afghanistan. After the Soviet Red Army's withdrawal from the country in February 1989, the Mujahideen had started a murderous war for control of the country. Various armed factions had converged on Kabul, and the fighting continued to tear the city apart.

The CNN reporter was in a refugee camp on the Pakistani border, one of many camps trying to cope with the exodus of Afghans escaping the fighting. Men, women, and children were fleeing Kabul, the city of my birth, in droves. The scenes were horrifying, and as I watched those shocking images I was struck by how empty my life had become. During the decade that we had lived in America, I rarely followed the news from Afghanistan. It was too depressing, and I was far too focused on getting ahead. Now, staring at those TV images, I felt drawn to the suffering.

"Suraya? Suraya? Do you want some more kabab?" Anisa repeated. I'd been lost in the bloody, hungry, dusty world of that CNN report. "There's a couple more chicken and some beef."

"My God, it's horrible," I interrupted, gesturing toward the TV. "You reckon we could do something about it? I mean, there's got to be something we can do, right?"

Anisa raised her eyebrows. "You want to do something about the *camps*?"

My friend had every right to be skeptical. I'd rarely shown the slightest interest in the humanitarian crisis unfolding in Afghanistan.

"Well, just look at all those people," I told her. "I mean, they're from Kabul, just like us. Imagine being in that place so close to hell."

"It is pretty terrible," Anisa agreed.

She was choosing her words carefully. It was common knowledge among our friends that I'd pretty much cracked after losing Dastagir. I'd gotten rid of our beautiful house and folded my money-making machine of a business; I'd locked myself away and let my appearance go.

"We've got to be able to raise some money, or get donations of clothes, or do *something*," I told her.

"I guess," Anisa replied.

Over the remnants of that meal in Fairfax, the germ of the idea for a charity to help the Afghan people was born. Our priority was to work with the children, for it was their pinched and hungry faces that had so touched us on TV. We racked our brains for a name: Feed the Children; Help the Children; Care for the Children. The morning after the dinner, I telephoned the Virginia State Corporation Commission, which registers charity names. They checked the not-for-profit register, but all the names we had thought of were taken. Yet if we inserted the word *Afghan* they were all free. We chose Help the Afghan Children, for it said exactly what we wanted.

In the next weeks I threw myself into starting the charity with the same obsessive energy that I had applied to my real estate business. We started looking for support at the local mosques where the Afghan-American community congregated. I gave a short announcement after Friday prayers, asking for donations to help the people in the refugee camps. Our aim was to provide the absolute basics for survival—food, shelter, blankets, and clothing.

Of course, it was daunting. We were complete novices, so why would anyone put their faith in us? But most people in the Afghan community knew me, which made it a little easier. They knew that I could be making a fortune as a Realtor instead of begging for donations from a largely impoverished immigrant community.

There were some twenty thousand Afghan-Americans in Virginia, most still struggling to make something of their lives. Many were still on welfare, a step I'd never taken, or they were taxi drivers or factory workers. At the time there were few organizations raising money in America to help Afghan refugees. People wanted to give what little they could, but until the creation of Help the Afghan Children there was no conduit for doing so.

The first donations were handfuls of dollar bills stuffed into the little wooden charity boxes in the mosques. Then the checks began arriving in the mail. A few weeks into our fund-raising efforts I attended a prayer meeting in a private home that doubled as a mosque. A little old lady approached me. She was hunched over her walking stick, and her movements were stiff, but her eyes were piercingly sharp.

She fixed me with a quizzical look. "Are you Suraya Sadeed? Help the Afghan Children?"

"I guess," I said. "Yes, I am."

She thrust an envelope into my hand. "I want you to take this. It's only seventeen dollars, but it's all I can afford."

"Thank you. Thank you. Every little bit helps."

She glanced at my face. Her eyes were watery.

"I had two sons who fought against the Soviets. I have been waiting for someone who was willing to go back and help." She wiped the corners of her eyes with her scarf. "I would like you to take this money and go inside Afghanistan and give it to those most in need, in the memory of my two sons. . . . Will you do that for me?"

I was struggling to hold back my own tears. "Yes, I will. I will."

"Do you promise? And you will come back and tell me?"

"Yes, I promise with all my heart."

From the moment we started Help the Afghan Children at her dining room table, Anisa and I had pledged to go where the need was the greatest, and that meant venturing deep inside Afghanistan.

It was December 1993, and the cold war was over; the Soviet defeat in Afghanistan had tolled the death knell for the USSR. With the withdrawal of the Soviet Red Army, the world's media had lost interest in Afghanistan, and the international community had all but disengaged from the country's plight. The Mujahideen factions had started to fight among themselves for control of the country, plunging it into anarchy and bloodshed.

By the time Anisa and I founded Help the Afghan Children, Afghanistan was a closed and forbidden land. No aid workers were working inside; it was too dangerous for them to do so. Despite this, the devastating violence inside Afghanistan was so great that many people had a burning desire to help however they could.

In just a few weeks Anisa and I managed to raise over $35,000 from our local Afghan-American community. It was an extraordinary effort from a group with so little to give. And having raised so much money, there was now no turning aside from our mission to take much-needed aid into war-torn Afghanistan.

The Pakistanis used the border with Afghanistan like a valve. They opened it to Afghan refugees only when the international community promised more money for the refugee camps on their soil. Right now the border was closed, and an estimated one hundred thousand people were trapped in Hesar Shahee, a temporary camp for displaced persons set in a barren desert plain on the outskirts of the Afghan city of Jalalabad. Terrible stories were filtering out of there about women and children dying in droves. If we wanted to help those most in need, our initial aid trip would have to take us to Hesar Shahee.

In a sense, ours was an impossible mission. Anisa and I were two women traveling from America with a big bundle of cash and no experience in relief work. Afghanistan was a lawless land torn into countless fiefdoms controlled by warlords. But I told myself that it couldn't really be as bad as people said. I told myself that it was Hesar Shahee or bust.

I didn't know it at the time, but I had another reason for going to Afghanistan. After losing Dastagir, I needed to go to a land of pain and learn how people survived their losses—and by doing so, I might learn how to deal with my own trauma and mend my own hurt. But I didn't fully appreciate at the time how this trip could help me heal myself.

The only viable starting point for our journey into Hesar Shahee was the Pakistani border town of Peshawar. I would be traveling with Anisa and her husband, Musleh—she to help with the aid work, he to take care of some business in Pakistan. We planned to stop off first at a refugee camp on the outskirts of Peshawar to distribute half the money.

That way if anything did happen on the journey inside Afghanistan—if we were robbed, or kidnapped, or worse—at least half of the $35,000 would have reached people in need.

TWO

The Beginning

THREE MONTHS AFTER THE DINNER WHERE I REALIZED I HAD TO help the Afghan people, Anisa and I flew out of Washington, D.C.'s Dulles Airport headed for Peshawar, the wild Pakistani frontier town along the northwest border with Afghanistan. On the outskirts of Peshawar sits the seemingly endless plain of Naser Bagh, site of many refugee camps containing hundreds of thousands of destitute Afghans.

We'd found an intermediary based in Peshawar to organize a visit to one of the camps and to link us up with Ali, this camp's administrator. A short taxi ride out of town brought us right to the place. It lay before us like a vast tented sea bathed in golden afternoon sunlight, velvety gray mountains rising in the distance in rumpled lavender folds. But the harsh beauty of this place belied its utter hopelessness.

As Anisa and I threaded our way through the crowds, I couldn't help but notice the vacant looks on the women's faces and their straggly, knotted hair. Not a tree or a blade of grass was left standing in any direction. The grass had been trodden away under the feet of a hundred thousand refugees, and the trees had been torn down to feed cooking fires. The lucky families had white canvas tents donated by the United Nations, but an equal number of families hunkered down under flimsy plastic and cardboard shelters.

Even though it was only May, I could see the heat from the burning sun pooling and boiling in those tents like an oven. There wasn't the slightest breath of wind, and people lay in the open, gasping for breath. We followed a narrow stream of snowmelt from the distant mountains, one that had turned a murky gray-brown by the time it reached the camp. It was an open sewer, and the stench was overpowering. Raggedy kids splashed in the shallows. Mothers beat and scrubbed clothes against rocks. An old woman with a metal cooking pot bent to scoop up water.

Ali, the refugee camp administrator, was waiting for us at the center of the camp, beneath the only two surviving trees. In the shade cast by their branches were a clutch of new tents and a scatter of plastic tables and chairs. Ali rose to welcome us, and in spite of myself I recoiled instinctively from his figure. He had a huge, bristling mustache, dirty yellow teeth, and hair that was so heavily oiled that it almost seemed to be dripping onto his shoulders.

A crowd of children had followed us through the camp, but now they held back, fearful and uncertain at the border of Ali's domain. I saw him lift a hand toward them, and the kids flinched and cowered. In that one moment I had seen all that I needed to see. Ali tried a smile, but it came out as a twisted grimace.

"No, no, come, come," he tried again, gesturing for the kids to approach. "I have some sweeties for you. Come. Come and get some boiled sweeties."

Not a child moved. Ali took a handful and threw them into the crowd. The kids erupted into a wild melee as each tried to get a hand on one of the candies.

Ali turned away and gestured to the chairs. "So, welcome, welcome. You are from Help the Afghan Children? A new organization from America, I think? You are most welcome, as is the helping you bring."

He offered us tea, then pulled out a piece of paper from inside his dirty robes. He slid it across the table.

"I have prepared a list of the families most in need. I am thinking this is what you are needing, so you know exactly who to help."

"Well, thank you." I pushed the piece of paper back at him. "But we'd like to talk to the refugees directly, so we can get our own sense of their needs."

Ali gave me an oily smile. "But there is no needing for this. I can tell you all that the peoples need. I am the camp administrator. My list is the best one. If you try speaking to the peoples directly, they may trick you. They are no angels, Mrs. Sadeed, no angels at all."

As he was speaking I couldn't help but stare at his hair. It was scream-ing: *wash me, please!* He kept going on about his list of "most needy," and I kept countering that we needed to speak to the refugees ourselves. I had thought the hardest part of this mission would be raising the money, but Anisa and I were starting to realize that giving it away could prove equally challenging.

Eventually we called Ali's bluff: without speaking to the refugees, we wouldn't distribute a single dollar of aid. Ali offered a grudging compromise. We could speak to the refugees, but only if we did so in the company of the camp guards and started with his "most needy" list. And so, in the company of those guards—Pakistani policemen in sloppy uniforms assigned to the camp by the local government—we headed into the midst of the suffering.

I gazed out over a sea of people, desperate, haunted faces stretching as far as the eye could see. It was overwhelming. Even if we distributed all of our $35,000 it would barely buy each of these families a crust of bread. Many of the refugees were on the official United Nations list, and they did get regular rations. But there was an equally large number who weren't. Logic dictated that it was those families—the ghost refugees—who needed help the most. And that, after all, was the heart of our mission: helping those most in need.

I turned to the guards. "I need to compile a list of those families who aren't on the UN program," I announced. "Widows first, and then those with the most children."

The guards shrugged. Their faces were impassive, their hands resting on the long wooden batons they carried at their sides. They clearly weren't the slightest bit interested in helping. Their eyes said it all: *you stupid, naive Westerner; you've got Ali's list; whoever you try to give your dollars to, we'll still be getting our share.*

I faced the crowd again. "*Salam alaikum*," I began, Arabic for "peace be unto you." Although we Afghans speak mostly Dari, we use some Arabic phrases for greetings and prayers.

"My friends and I have come from the United States of America to be here with you today." I switched to speaking Dari, so that the Pakistani guards wouldn't understand. "We have brought help from Afghans in America. Now, we can't help everyone, but we can help some of you, and I need to work out who needs help the most."

"Not those on the list, sister!" a voice cried out from the crowd.

"Not those ones!" another voice added. "Not the list families."

"Help us! Help us!" a third voice yelled.

"Well, okay," I responded. "But I don't know which of you are most deserving. I want to prioritize those who aren't on the UN register. First the widows, then the grandparents with kids to look after, then those families with the most children. So, if you'll come forward and give us your names—"

Within moments we were all but overwhelmed. Anisa tried to keep a record of names as I asked each family about their circumstances. The crowd kept pressing in from all sides. Among the pleading faces and outstretched hands the most repeated refrain was: *Please don't give to the families on Ali's list. Please don't give to the same people as the foreigners always do.*

I knew then that my instincts about Ali were correct. There was some hidden game going on here. I didn't know quite how it worked yet, but it could only be about power and money.

We left the camp with an alternative list of the "most needy," along with an alternative plan. There was little sense in having our own list if we went ahead and distributed the aid in the camp, for then the guards—and Ali—would simply take what they wanted. We had to circumvent their control. So we sent word for the refugees to come to us at our hotel instead.

For aid workers, journalists, and the like, the only place to stay in Peshawar was the famous Green's Hotel. It was a magnet for all and sundry who washed up on the border of Afghanistan. Thankfully Fateh Khan, the hotel manager, was a tolerant man who appreciated the needs and foibles of Westerners. And as far as Fateh Khan was concerned, the three of us with our U.S. passports were Westerners, no matter what our country of origin.

Early the next morning there was a knock at my hotel door. I opened it to find Fateh Khan standing there in his typical stylish attire. Fateh Khan's business depended upon repeat customers from aid agencies and media networks, so he was polite and courteous at all times. But this morning's developments had stretched even his patience to the limits.

"I'm sorry to disturb you, Ms. Sadeed, but there are so many people asking for you. The hotel cannot cope with this many visitors. Of course, we love having you and your colleagues here, but please don't invite all these people to the hotel. Not all at once, anyway."

Fateh Khan led me to the elevator, and when it reached the lobby I peeked out the door. The refugees from the camp had come to the hotel early. They had crammed the lobby to bursting and were blocking the way outside. For the first time since we'd arrived in Pakistan I felt real fear—not for myself, but of losing the money.

I'd carried the $35,000 in cash from Virginia strapped around my waist in a money belt. On reaching Peshawar we'd changed it into Pakistani rupees. With the exchange rate at one American dollar for fifty-five rupees, we'd ended up with a bundle of cash the size of a small suitcase. Anisa, Musleh, and I had divided it among the three of us, so that if one of us got robbed we wouldn't lose the entire lot.

I asked Fateh Khan to spirit Anisa, Musleh, and myself through the hotel kitchens. There was a parking lot at the rear of the hotel, and he announced to the refugees that we'd do the distribution out there. As I scurried through the kitchens one thought lingered foremost in my mind: *who will ever believe us if we return to America having lost all the money?*

Moments later I found myself gazing out over a mass of powder blue burkas. They stretched before me like the shifting waves of a human ocean. We unrolled the list and started calling out names. As each woman came forward, I asked her to remove her burka so I could see her face and hear her story. Each tale was told in the same flat monotone: the men of the family had been killed or captured; their houses had been burned down; the survivors had fled, the women and children enduring a terrible journey. Finally, they ended up here.

To the refugee women, this was how life was. They lived in a place where everyone had a similar story, and no tale was remarkable. But as the waves of human suffering washed over me, I felt like I was drowning. I tried to gaze into each woman's eyes and to connect deeply with her, but bearing witness to such pain was exhausting.

These women had nothing. They had no soap with which to wash, no clean water, precious little shelter, and starving children to care for. They had been stripped of everything: their self-respect, their dignity, their past, their history, and their humanity, even. When they told their stories, doubt clouded their eyes: Was there ever a life before the camps, or was it all just a dream? Had they ever known a reality other than this one?

The shock of these encounters left me reeling. But somewhere deep inside myself, I had found exactly what I was seeking. Faced with such a tide of human torment, I'd forgotten about my own suffering. I felt as if my own pain in losing Dastagir was nothing.

We gave a fistful of rupees, the equivalent of twenty dollars, to each family. It wasn't much, but it would buy them a little precious food, soap, or clothing. Halfway through the distribution I heard an agonized cry from somewhere in the crowd. I froze. Someone within that sea of powder blue burkas was calling my name.

"Suraya-*jan!* Suraya-*jan!*"

I turned my head this way and that, searching the crowd. Surely I must have heard it wrong, for who in this shifting miasma of suffering could know my name?

"Suraya-*jan!*" There it was again.

"Who called my name?" I cried out.

"Suraya-*jan!*" a voice drifted back to me. "I called you."

"Where are you?" I searched the crowd wildly. "I can't see you. *Who are you?*"

A figure moved; stood; shifted a pace or two forward. "I'm here."

The cry came to me half-muffled by the burka. I took a few steps toward the mystery woman. The sea of powder blue figures parted before me. I tried to imagine who she might be, trying with all my will to penetrate the burka's anonymity.

"How do you know me?" I asked.

"From school."

How could she possibly know me from school? I had gone to Rabia Balki High, one of the best girls' schools in Kabul. How could anyone from my school have ended up here?

"Rabia Balki?" I asked the faceless woman. "You know me from there?"

"Not there. College. We were classmates."

College? Only the wealthiest, smartest students had ended up going to Kabul University. I couldn't fathom how anyone from there could possibly have ended up here. With their fine educations most Kabul University graduates had left Afghanistan and were doing well overseas. Images from my college days spooled through my mind. As each figure flashed before me I wondered, *could it possibly be her?*

I settled upon Parwin. There were days when Parwin hadn't made it to class because her cruel stepmother had beaten her so badly. At times she was in such pain she couldn't study properly. Maybe Parwin's stepmother had thrown her out, and somehow she had ended up here.

I went to ask her if she was Parwin, but I stopped myself. Perhaps she was, and she didn't want people to know. Perhaps she didn't want to be recognized. I tried to pierce through the pepper-dust holes of her burka, to see into her eyes, but all I saw were shadows.

"Can I see your face?" I asked her.

She shook her head. "I used to sit next to you in psychology. Dr. Sadeq was our lecturer."

"My God . . . psychology . . . Can I please see your face?"

She shook her head, more powerfully this time. "No. I'm not who you think I am. I've changed so much. But you—you haven't changed at all."

She seemed somehow ashamed of her appearance in front of me, and for a moment I felt a stab of guilt for looking so young and free and blessed by all that my life in America had gifted me.

"Please lift your burka, just so I can see who you are. Please."

"I can't," she murmured. "But, Suraya-*jan*, can I please have some money to buy a little milk for my child?"

For your child, I found myself thinking. *What on earth are you doing having a child in a place like this?* And then I stopped myself. Whoever she was, she'd probably had the child long before she ended up here, or maybe she'd had no choice. I was thinking like a typical American—assuming that all women had the means to prevent pregnancy if they so desired. Over the past decade I'd grown utterly removed from the reality of life for so many women in Afghanistan.

I delved into my money belt and took out a thick bundle of rupees. But when she reached out to take the money I noticed her hand. We froze, the bundle of cash held halfway between us. I stared at the wrinkled claw of her hand in shock. She knew that I was staring, but I couldn't help it. Her hand looked so hard and so wrinkled and so *old*.

Surely she couldn't be a woman of my generation, not with a hand like that. Perhaps she wasn't who she said she was; maybe that's why she wouldn't show me her face. But she had to be genuine, for she knew the name of my psychology lecturer.

I passed her the money but I kept hold of her hand. I traced the deep cracks and lines and calluses with my own manicured fingers. I glanced at her feet. She was wearing a pair of worn-out men's shoes, the pants beneath the burka a ripped and dirty gray. I tried to visualize the face behind the mask—a face from my college days that would go with such ruined hands and clothing.

"What are you doing here, sister?" I whispered.

She shrugged. "That's what I ask myself every day."

"But how come you don't have a job?"

"You don't know this place, do you?" she replied, an edge of bitterness to her voice. "There's no jobs for those like us. No work at all."

"Well, can I have an address? A phone number maybe?"

There was a snort of derision from beneath the burka. "There's nothing like that here."

"At least let me give you mine, so we don't lose each other again."

She tucked the money beneath the folds of her clothes. She raised her head and looked at me in silence for a second, and then she turned and walked away.

I called after her: "I don't even know your name! Can I have something, anything, just to get ahold of you? Please!"

I followed with my eyes as she threaded her way through the crowd, but there was no response. Eventually I lost her in the shifting sea of burka-clad women.

I asked around. I tried to discover who she might be. I was told that I would need to be patient. It would take time to track her down.

In spite of the shock of my mystery encounter, I still felt buoyed by our aid distribution. We had managed to help five hundred urgently needy families with no disasters, and we had frustrated Ali's corrupt system. Half the money had already gone to the right people, just as we'd promised our donors in America.

But now it was time to start the journey into the Hesar Shahee camp, deep inside Afghanistan.

THREE

The Camel Road

T HE GREEN'S HOTEL WAS SWARMING WITH AID WORKERS WHO BOM-
barded us with dire warnings about what we were trying to do. The
refugees were tricksters who hid behind their burkas to get repeated aid deliveries. We were complete novices, and right now not even the most experienced went inside Afghanistan. If we tried to get to Hesar Shahee, we had
a death wish.

The rumor had spread through the aid community like wildfire—that
we'd come here with hundreds of thousands of dollars and no experience or
proper plans. Veterans of the aid business tried to convince us to hand over
our cash to them, for distribution through their trusted networks in the
Pakistani refugee camps. I figured their concern was probably genuine, listened to them politely, and then told them: "Well, maybe not this time."

Anisa and I sought guidance from Dr. Abdullah, the director of the
Afghan Medical Committee in Peshawar. He was the son of an Afghan
politician, and our families had known each other well during the Kabul
years. I felt that I could trust him. He was a tall, craggy-faced, white-haired
man with a noble commitment to the cause. With his family connections,
he could easily have made it to America. Instead he had opted to stay and
help the Afghan refugees who were flooding into Pakistan.

I met Dr. Abdullah in the company of his right-hand man, Nawabi.
Nawabi was as tall as Dr. Abdullah, and with his sharp white beard and
spotless Afghan *peran tunban*—a kind of sweeping robe—he had real presence and bearing. Nawabi had been a senior police officer in Kabul before
working for Dr. Abdullah, and he came from a distinguished family. Yet he

was modest, ordered, and disciplined, traits that he retained from his police years.

I outlined our plans to go to Hesar Shahee and asked for their best advice on the route in. The two men glanced at each other—*Do you want to tell them or shall I?*

Nawabi went first. "*Saheb*—ma'am—you really shouldn't do this. You really shouldn't go."

"Nawabi's right," said Dr. Abdullah. "It really isn't a good idea to go inside."

"Well, I'm going, no matter what you say." I glanced at Anisa for support, but she was saying very little, and she looked worried. "We promised people in the U.S. that we'd go inside. And if the camps in Peshawar are in such awful shape, we need to see how bad it is on the other side. The cameras are not there, and I can only presume it's infinitely worse."

"Well, if you are going to ignore our advice, what do you want from us?" Nawabi asked. "For what it's worth, our advice would be that you use your money to build a clinic here in Pakistan, to help the refugees. Isn't that right, Dr. Abdullah?"

Dr. Abdullah nodded. "Exactly. A clinic near the camps to provide medical care would do more good than anything."

"Then I'll do it," I interjected. "If a clinic will really help those women I met yesterday, let's build one. Whatever it takes, let's get one up and running."

I had spoken those words almost before I'd considered what I was saying. A clinic would mean regular monthly costs, and after we distributed aid to the displaced people in Hesar Shahee, all the money we'd raised would be gone. When I'd set out on this trip I'd imagined doing just the one mission. But after meeting my college friend in the first camp, everything had changed. Even if I had to sell some of my American properties, I'd make that clinic happen.

"Just like that—you'll help us?" Dr. Abdullah queried. "A clinic would truly work wonders."

"Like I said, let's do it. But Dr. Abdullah, Nawabi—there is a trade-off. We help you with that clinic; you help us go inside."

Nawabi shook his head. "It is extremely dangerous, especially for you. You are women and you come from the U.S. Everyone will see you as Americans. No matter what you do, people will realize you've been away from Afghanistan for years. It is crazy even to try."

"Please don't go," Dr. Abdullah added. "I am begging you. Stay here and help us with the clinic. It's much better for everyone that way."

For a moment my conviction wavered. I was afraid: for myself; that we two American women would be kidnapped somewhere inside; of losing Mariam and of Mariam losing me. It would be so much easier to stay and build the clinic here, and these two men, whose advice I instinctively trusted, insisted we'd do far more good that way. Then I thought of the old lady who had given me the seventeen dollars in the name of her two sons, and all the other tiny but heartfelt donations. I couldn't turn away from this mission.

"I will help you build a clinic, but first we have to go inside. We're going to Hesar Shahee, and what we'd like from you is your help getting there."

Dr. Abdullah gave a resigned shrug. Nawabi stroked his beard pensively. It looked as if they were resolved to my willfulness.

"If your mind is made up," Dr. Abdullah said, sighing, "we know someone who does go inside. You'll need to speak to a colleague of ours, Dr. Mangal."

Dr. Abdullah and Nawabi took us to meet Dr. Mangal in his cramped Peshawar office. He ran a small clinic in the Afghan city of Jalalabad, and he was forced to travel between there and Peshawar regularly. He was a short, chubby guy who clearly made it his business to know everything about everyone; that was perhaps the only way he managed to survive the journeys inside, which passed through some of the most dangerous territory on earth. I knew Dr. Mangal's type. He was an operator, and he would carefully guard his own self-interests.

Dr. Mangal was an odd duck. He was married, but he flirted shamelessly with his secretary. He was dripping in gold. He had a gold watch strapped to his wrist, and gold around his neck and on his plump fingers. I found it offensive that a man dealing with refugees could be wearing so much gold. It was also very un-Afghan. Afghan men do not wear gold. It is seen as being effeminate. If an Afghan man wants to show off his wealth he will have several wives, many kids, and a huge house with high walls, and his wives will wear the gold. But if he could take us into Hesar Shahee, who was I to complain? As I outlined our mission, I sensed Dr. Mangal's reluctance to take two Afghan-American women into the lion's den.

"Right now is a very bad time," he announced in his unusually high-pitched voice. "It is the height of the Mujahideen's power. The Soviets are gone, and the Mujahideen are fighting for control of the country. It is a very bad time for anyone to try to venture inside—"

"I know," I cut in. "But we have to take this money to those we promised to help, and that means Hesar Shahee."

Not for one moment had I forgotten the plight of the displaced people trapped on the barren desert plain of Hesar Shahee, deep inside Afghanistan where no aid workers could reach them. It was in their name that we had raised money in America, and no matter what the warnings I couldn't turn aside from the path of helping them.

"There is something you should understand," Dr. Mangal remarked. "Hundreds of thousands of people have fled Kabul and are trapped in Hesar Shahee. But to the Mujahideen, these are the people who stayed in Kabul under the Soviet Communist rule. They see these people as Communist collaborators, as their enemies. So, if you are going to Hesar Shahee, the Mujahideen will see you as someone who is helping their enemies."

"All the more reason to help them," I replied. And then, in a calculated appeal to his own self-interest: "And, of course, once we've seen your clinic, we'll be able to help you too—perhaps on an ongoing basis."

His eyes lit up. "Well, I do know and work with all sides. Perhaps I am the right person for you to travel with."

Back at the hotel, Anisa and I sat down with with Musleh, her husband, to consider our options. As far as I was concerned, if Dr. Mangal could get us into Hesar Shahee, then I'd turn a blind eye to his venal self-interest. But Anisa and Musleh didn't seem to agree.

"It's really not looking very good, is it?" Anisa remarked. "Everyone's advice is the same—that this Hesar Shahee trip is crazy. I really don't think we can go."

"Well, what did you expect?" I said. "Afghanistan's no tea party. We knew that before we came. We promised all those people back in America that we were going *inside*. That's what made them believe in us. That's what made them give."

"But everyone says we can do more good here, and they should know," Anisa argued. "Surely you're not going to continue, not after hearing all those warnings."

I glanced at Musleh.

"You should listen to Anisa," Musleh remarked. "You can do more good here in Peshawar. Return to the States with photos of the clinic you started, and tell people the truth—that it was too dangerous to go inside. Where's the harm in that?"

Anisa and Musleh had clearly made up their minds. I was disappointed, though Anisa's disquiet and her concern had become increasingly obvious over the last couple of days. It was their decision, and I had to respect it. But most of all I had to steel myself to go on. I'd heard more and more stories about the horrors unfolding in Hesar Shahee, and someone had to break the logjam and venture inside. I told Anisa and Musleh as much, and they promised to wait in Peshawar until my return.

The one thing that I needed for the Hesar Shahee mission was blankets—thousands of them. Hesar Shahee was set on a bare and open plain, and at night it was bitterly cold for the people in the camp. I'd heard stories of babies freezing to death in their mother's arms, and I wanted to spend our remaining money on blankets for them, keeping only enough cash to cover the costs of the journey into Hesar Shahee. I toured the Peshawar markets, haggling for the best quality at the best possible prices.

With Dr. Mangal's help, I hired three ancient Bedford trucks plus drivers. The morning of our departure, I kept a careful eye as our ten thousand blankets were loaded on the trucks. I couldn't help but admire the paint jobs of those trucks. The lead vehicle had a huge black eye spray-painted above the cab. This was the "all-seeing eye," and it was supposed to defend us against the "evil eye," a malevolent power in which many cultures believe.

The second truck had the figure of an enormous bodybuilder spray-painted across the cab in lurid colors. The third sported a romanticized, dreamy, kitsch waterfall scene. And then there were sayings, poetry, and prayers. On each truck there were several "God be with you" phrases. The bodybuilder truck also had this: "In reality everything belongs to God—we just own it for a few days." And the waterfall truck had a verse of Urdu poetry.

> *What a great and noble country Pakistan is.*
> *What a perfect and beautiful place to be . . .*

We climbed up into the trucks, Dr. Mangal and myself in the front seat of the lead truck, and his wife on the bench seat behind. With a grunting of the tired engine and a belching of thick black smoke we jolted ahead. I waved good-bye to Anisa and Musleh, who had helped load up blankets. They looked a little guilty, but I harbored no ill will toward them. They had each other to live for.

Our three-truck convoy crawled through the busy, chaotic streets of Peshawar. We exited the city via the refugee camps. In no time we seemed to have left the modern world behind and journeyed back through time. The road ahead was scattered with broken-down stalls made of mud bricks and straw, with a patchwork of tiny fields growing wheat and vegetables on either side.

I was dressed like any American woman, in black pants and a blouse. I had a *chadar*—a traditional Afghan scarf—draped around my shoulders, leaving my face showing. We passed through the infamous Northwest Frontier Province, local Pashtun men pausing in their fields. Eyes peered out from faces with wild, hennaed beards beneath dark and twisted turbans. I could sense their incomprehension and hostility, and I began to appreciate the warnings I'd been given about a "Western" woman traveling into such a closed region.

I did my best to ignore the looks. I was excited and nervous to be getting so close to my country—a country that I had fled some fifteen years before—and I wasn't about to let anyone spoil this moment. Each turn of the truck's wheels was taking me closer, and in spite of the dangers, I couldn't wait to cross the border into Afghanistan. Dr. Mangal pointed through the windshield at a sight I knew so well—the glistening, knife-edge peaks of the Shamshad Mountains.

A moment later I felt tears streaming down my face. I was crying uncontrollably, and it was the sight of those towering peaks that had set me off. A rush of memories and emotions crowded in on me. I was getting closer to the dark and suffering land, yet to me, those mountains conjured up images of laughter and light. I was crying for both the happy memories of the past and the tragedy of the present.

I'd last seen the Shamshad Mountains from the Afghan side when I was in my teens. My family would take its winter vacation in the Afghan city of Jalalabad. Back then it was known as the "Garden City," and we used to flee the snows of the Kabul winter to bask in its steamy, flower-scented sunshine. We owned a fine house from where we would head out for family picnics in the nearby mountains.

Our Jalalabad home had an orchard of beautiful, spreading orange and grapefruit trees. I loved playing hide-and-seek with my sisters in that enchanted woodland. By the time we were teenagers, we had started hanging out at Jalalabad's Behsood Bridge. From there you could watch the most spectacular sunsets, the giant ball of fire slipping into the swirling confluence of the Kabul and Kunar rivers. It was such a romantic setting, and we girls would dress in our smartest, sexiest outfits.

The boys would park at the riverside, the music from their car stereos blaring out over the river. Invariably, it was the newest Beatles hit, or something by our own pop sensation, Ahmad Zahir. We knew him as the Elvis Presley of Afghanistan, and his songs were all about heartbreak and romantic love. That suited us girls just fine, for we were all in love and nurturing secret desires. Even if we weren't allowed to be close to boys, we were still free to fantasize and dream.

We Kabul girls used to think we were better than the girls from Jalalabad. It was a time of flared bell-bottoms, turtlenecks, and thick shiny belts, and we never wore the same outfit twice. The boys sported long hair and sideburns down to their chins. When I was feeling particularly daring I'd dress in a miniskirt, which drew horrified gasps from my mother. My brothers were equally scandalized, but I didn't care. I always had been the family hothead, and my parents were forever trying to drag me into line.

Spring in Jalalabad was magical. Almost overnight, the orange trees would flower in a carpet of shimmering white, the rich and heady scent filling the air. Ancient palaces left over from the time when Jalalabad was the playground of kings had crumbled into ruins and were overtaken by a riot of gorgeous flowers. It was such a wild, romantic city, and in the winter months we'd set up our home there.

But that was then and this was now. A somewhat discomfited Dr. Mangal thrust a scrunched-up tissue into my lap, as if that was going to stem my tears. I took my Afghan scarf and covered my face, using the soft folds to dry my eyes. I sobbed a little more, then told myself to pull myself together. Our journey was only just beginning, and I sensed I would need all my strength for the miles that lay before us.

"Ah, you are feeling better," Dr. Mangal remarked once I had emerged from the folds. "That's good. I think it would be better now if you sat with my wife, in the back."

"Why?" I asked.

"This is a very odd region," Dr. Mangal replied, his eyes darting about nervously. "It's officially part of Pakistan, but in reality Pakistan has no presence here. The local Pashtuns make their own rules, and it's best if we pass through unnoticed. And it's perhaps best to cover your face too."

I squeezed myself into the rear of the cab alongside the doctor's wife, pulling my *chadar* closer around my features until my eyes alone were showing. I figured it was best to follow the doctor's advice, for he was a veteran traveler here.

Our journey through the Northwest Frontier Province was taking us ever closer to the Khyber Pass, our passageway into Afghanistan. This lawless area was supposed to harbor every vice known to man. You could buy and sell anything here. An antitank missile? No problem. A kilo of heroin? No problem, if you had the cash. A thirteen-year-old virgin? Done deal. Priceless Afghan antiquities? Easy. Just follow the smuggler to his den. A contract to assassinate someone? Fine; just tell the killer how you wanted them killed.

The road into the chasmlike valley of the Khyber Pass is like no other on earth. It snakes ever upward, every now and then seeming to fling itself toward a precipice, our ancient truck wrenching back from the drop at the last moment, stones skittering and tumbling into the abyss. Mysterious, ominous mountains loomed above us. With each painful turn of the Bedford's wheels the sheer rock sides of the pass crowded in. It felt as if we were being sucked into a giant void that had banished the sun and the sky, drawing us onward into the very crack of doom.

We'd been on the road for three hours when finally we came to a wheezing standstill on a small patch of flattish ground. On one side of the road was a row of low, blocky buildings, dwarfed by the obsidian black of the sheer mountain walls above us. Those were the Pakistani police and customs posts, Dr. Mangal explained. On the opposite side was a row of stalls selling *Doodh Pati Chai*, tea Pakistani-style—hot, milky, and sugary sweet. A row of drivers, all men, sat outside the tea stalls. The few women were left to stew in the vehicles.

The air through the truck's open window was thick with a dizzying scent. It was an exotic, heady blend of snuff, hashish, camel dung, grilled meat, diesel oil, and gunpowder. It was around three o'clock by now, and the plan was to do the entire journey in one day. From the map it didn't appear to be more than eighty miles to Hesar Shahee, so it should be easily doable. I wasn't supposed to dismount from the truck, so I let Dr. Mangal do the talking and the bribing of the Pakistani police and army. I saw the flash of banknotes, and we were waved through the Pakistani side of the border and were poised to enter Afghanistan.

A moment later our driver drew to a halt in the no-man's-land between the two borders.

"This is as far as I go," he muttered, speaking more to Dr. Mangal than to me. "We start unloading here."

Dr. Mangal glanced nervously over his shoulder. "The driver says he can't go on. He says we'll have to unload—"

"I heard what he said," I interjected, "but there's ten thousand blankets. They've been paid to take them to Hesar Shahee. That was the deal."

"We can't go on," the driver repeated. "We don't have the papers to enter Afghanistan."

I glared at him in his driver's mirror. "But you knew that back in Peshawar. Why didn't you say so?"

The driver shrugged, doing his best to ignore me. I turned to Dr. Mangal. "Why didn't you warn me? You must have known."

He grimaced. "Well, I thought you'd be upset."

"I'm upset now, so what's the difference? What are we going to do stuck at the border with ten thousand blankets and surrounded by thieves?"

Dr. Mangal tried a smile. "Not to worry. Let me see what I can do."

He tumbled down from the truck, returning a minute or so later.

"There's good news and bad news," he announced. "At four o'clock the border will be closed. But not to worry. There is an alternative: we can go by the camel road."

"Okay. No problem." I gestured at the driver. "So at least get him to drive us via this camel road."

"Well . . ." Dr. Mangal bobbed his head, nervously. "I'm afraid it's not quite that simple. You see, the camel road means we'll have to travel by camel."

"By *camel?*" I exploded. "You're going to load ten thousand blankets onto camels! And where exactly do we get the camels to carry ten thousand goddamn blankets?"

Dr. Mangal held up his hands in an effort to calm me. "Not to worry. I will find the camels."

"So what happens when we reach the Afghan side? Or is this camel train going all the way to Hesar Shahee?"

"When we get to the Afghan side we will sort something out. Insh'Allah—God willing."

I slumped back in my seat. I had a very strong suspicion that this was a total setup. Dr. Mangal must have known what awaited us at the border, and doubtless he'd be taking a cut of the fee paid to everyone along the way.

Dr. Mangal seemed to know everyone here, and from somewhere he rounded up a one-hundred-beast camel train. He'd clearly been through this rigamarole before, but that didn't make it any less unsettling. I have always hated camels. I'd learned in my youth that a camel will remember anyone who was bad to it and wait to seize the moment to take revenge.

As the line of ungainly, humped beasts assembled, a crowd of people came shuffling out of nowhere. I guessed these were the guys who sat here all day, waiting for convoys like ours.

"You need help?" one asked.

"You need to load the camels?" another cried.

"Blankets onto camels?" called a third.

From my place at the window I tried asking how much they charged, but no one paid me the slightest heed. They bunched around Dr. Mangal, and he set them to work. I was frustrated and angry, and tired of being cooped up in the truck like a chicken in a cage. And after buying those ten thousand blankets I was painfully aware of how little remaining cash I had.

I'd paid the truck drivers half the money up front, but that was to take us all the way to Jalalabad. With the extra costs of the camel train, not to mention the blanket loaders, I was damned if I was going to give the drivers the remainder of their fee. I climbed down from the truck and told Dr. Mangal as much. He looked worried.

"Well, the problem is, if you go back on your word in this part of the world there may be trouble and—"

"But I'm not going back on my word," I cut in. "*They are.*"

"Well, I don't think they'll see it that way," he whispered.

Cursing under my breath I peeled off a wad of rupees and handed it to him.

"You pay them then," I snapped. "Generally, I don't enjoy being robbed."

By the time the blankets were loaded aboard the camels it was getting dark. Dr. Mangal and one of the camel drivers levered me onto one of the beasts. I'm only a little over five feet tall, and from there it was an awfully long way to fall. I was utterly terrified. I knew what camels are like. One moment they'd be walking with that horrid, swaying, seasick motion of theirs, the next they'd decide to plump themselves down, and you'd go flying over their heads.

With a groaning of leather and a series of burping, spitting camel grunts, we set off into the shadows. I held tight to the camel's saddle with one hand, the other gripping the *chadar* close around my eyes. I was cursing away behind its folds, hoping my camel didn't understand English, and not giving a damn whether Dr. Mangal did.

The camel route followed a faint path that snaked off to one side, disappearing into a cleft in the mountains. Despite the danger, I was glad of the gathering darkness. It meant that I couldn't see just how far there was to fall.

After fifteen minutes atop the camel we reached an area where the narrow crevasse widened out just a little. To either side the soft yellow light of oil lanterns flickered in the shadows. There were a series of what had to be caves clustered along the sheer rock walls of the camel route. Shapes glittered and danced in the lanterns' flames, their forms seductive and graceful. *What is this place?* I wondered.

"Come see, madam," a voice called from the shadows. "Come see our beautiful wares."

I glanced at Dr. Mangal. He shrugged, then gestured with his hand for us to dismount the camels and go inside. I stepped across to the nearest cave opening. Before me were a series of beautiful tables, each a slab of polished marble carved into an exotic shape. I ran my hand across the cool surface of the nearest one. There was something oddly familiar about their forms, but I couldn't quite place it.

The shopkeeper—for shop this had to be—approached me. He had a string of *Tasbih*—Muslim prayer beads—in his hand, and he kept clicking them through his fingers. He glanced at the table under my touch, eyeing it proudly.

"Quite beautiful, isn't it," he remarked. "And very old. A genuine piece of Afghan history. I will make for you a very good price. A special price for a lady from . . . Where is it you come from, ma'am?"

"Hold on a minute," I murmured. "Just let me . . ."

I reached beneath the "table," feeling with my fingers across the smooth cool of the undersurface. It just couldn't be. . . . And then my fingertips dipped into the first of many indentations, the first of what I'd feared I might find there. Struggling to keep my anger in check I asked Dr. Mangal to help me lift the table onto its side, so I could see properly.

Once we'd turned it over, all was revealed. The "coffee table" was made from a polished marble tombstone. Few Afghans could afford such headstones, and as I read the inscription on it, and then on another of those tombstones, I realized that I knew each of the families whose names were carved thereon. And now I knew that law and order had broken down to such a degree in Afghanistan that people were actually robbing graves.

Invariably, it is a specific verse of the Koran that is carved in Arabic upon a Muslim's tombstone.

> *Bismallah illah Rahman Rahim* . . .
> *In the name of God the kind and the merciful,*
> *Say it that God is just one,*
> *And that no one has been born from him nor he born from anyone.*

As I mouthed those words I felt hot tears of rage upon my face. What was happening to my country, and to the city of my youth? What could possibly justify the looting of those graveyards? I couldn't believe that we Afghans were actually selling our dead, and that even the sanctity of the grave was being violated.

I glanced at the shopkeeper's prayer beads—his *Tasbih*—then directly into his eyes.

"How could you do this? That is a Koranic verse. A *verse of the Holy Koran*. You've turned it into a coffee table!"

"Well, we didn't go to Afghanistan to fetch them!" the trader objected, trying to avoid my gaze. "It was Afghans who brought them here to us!"

"Is that all you have to say? Is everything reduced to survival and greed? Is there no respect for anyone, not even the dead?"

"It's just a dumb piece of stone," he muttered. But I could tell he knew in his heart of hearts that what he was doing was wrong.

"What kind of Muslim are you?" I demanded.

"It's not a living thing," he grumbled. "It's just a lump of stone." He turned and stumped off into the shadows. "I didn't kill or hurt anyone. . . . It's just a lump of stone."

I felt Dr. Mangal's hand on my shoulder. "Come. We should go. The camels are getting restless."

I followed his form into the slice of darker shadow that traced the path between the cliffs up ahead. To the trader it was sheer stupidity to worry about a piece of inanimate stone. To him the value of that stone was just the stone, not the history or the human misfortune that it embodied. To me this was a terrible betrayal of my country, symbolic of all that we had lost.

∞∞∞∞∞∞∞∞∞∞∞∞∞∞∞∞∞∞∞∞∞∞∞∞∞∞∞∞∞∞∞∞∞∞∞∞

FOUR

The Devil's Flowers

SOME TWENTY MINUTES LATER WE REACHED TORKHAM, THE AFGHAN border post. In my childhood memories Torkham was a neat and pretty place with a smart, tarred road and well-tended flower gardens. Now there was just a dirt path leading into the middle of nowhere, with a few wooden shacks clustered along it. The stalls were mostly selling candles, matches, and rope—the kind of things you might need to negotiate the camel road.

The camel drivers stopped in an open space and unrolled their prayer mats. Women were not allowed to pray with the men, so the doctor's wife and I sat in a corner, watching. Once the prayers were done, the camel men started calling out in the general direction of the shops.

"Bring the trucks! Bring the trucks! We're ready!"

Three battered vehicles came chuffing out of the gathering darkness. They were still swathed in khaki green from when they had been part of the Soviet Red Army. I paid off the camel men and began haggling with the Afghan truck drivers, but I had precious little leverage. Here I was stuck in the middle of nowhere with ten thousand blankets. What else was I going to do but hire them?

Eventually we had our cargo loaded and were on our way. In my mind I still envisioned a two-hour drive to Hesar Shahee. In my day it had been a fine road and I still hadn't fully realized quite how things had changed.

The first sight that met my eyes were the ugly, burned-out shells of Soviet tanks. I stared at those blasted metal carcasses and noticed the lithe forms of raggedy children dashing in and out of them. For a generation born into war, this was their playground.

We rounded a bend in the road, and below us opened out a sweeping valley. It was strikingly beautiful in the fading light of dusk. I inhaled deeply as I gazed out over a rippling sea of flowers. The whole of the valley floor was carpeted in a light, almost translucent green, peppered with red, purple, and orange blooms. Glistening slivers of water snaked through the flower garden, and the very sight of it lifted my spirits. I had been expecting only burned-out buildings and deserted villages. This was a lovely surprise.

The flower fields were iridescent with health and vitality. For a moment I wondered how they managed to maintain such a garden in the midst of a bloody civil war, when everyone was starving or a refugee. But thank God, I told myself. Thank God there still was beauty here in the land of my birth, and water and trees and flowers.

I turned to Dr. Mangal. "Wow. It's beautiful. Just a carpet of beautiful flowers."

Dr. Mangal gave an odd smile and stared out the window.

For a moment I thought about my daughter, Mariam, and the single white rose that she had left on Dastagir's chair at her graduation. I felt an urge to touch the earth and pick one of those flowers. I would put it inside one of the books that I had with me, so that I could give it to Mariam when I got home.

I told Dr. Mangal what I wanted to do. He exchanged glances with the driver. "I really don't think you should."

The driver nodded. "You don't want those flowers," he stated, matter-of-factly.

"The driver's right," said Dr. Mangal. "You see, they're not really flowers."

"How can they not be flowers?"

Dr. Mangal shrugged. "Well, it's drugs. They're opium flowers."

"But opium's an ugly, sticky brown stuff."

The driver pulled his truck to a halt, climbed down, and grabbed one of the flowers. He showed me the little wooden cup attached below the flower head, so the sap could bleed into it. He explained how the sticky brown liquid would be collected, then taken over the border into Pakistan by donkey train. The no-man's-land of the Khyber Pass was home to many hidden laboratories where the raw opium would be refined into heroin, at which point the drug's value would have increased a hundredfold.

"That's what paid for the war against the Soviets," the driver continued. "It was drug money that bought the weapons for the Mujahideen."

"It's a big problem today," Dr. Mangal added. "Some farmers grow nothing but opium poppy, and they're hopelessly in debt to their landlords."

"*Warlords*, not landlords," the driver corrected. "The warlords own the land, and the farmers rent it. If there's a drought, the crops fail and there's no money. They even sell their own daughters to be able to pay the warlords."

"We are a nation ruled by a beautiful but deadly bloom," Dr. Mangal remarked.

"No, no, no—there's nothing beautiful about it," the driver objected. Then, to me: "You know what they call this? It is *Gol-e Shaitan*—the Devil's Flowers."

In spite of all they had told me I fell in love with that name—the Devil's Flowers. It painted a thousand different pictures—of indolence, beauty, charm, and menace; of sin and pleasure. For a moment I wondered what it would be like to pitch a tent in the heart of that field of Devil's Flowers and spend a night bathed in their heady, exotic scent.

We left the valley of the Devil's Flowers and came into a high pass. We crawled around a sharp bend and found a group of three pickup trucks blocking the road ahead of us. As we slowed I heard the sharp crack of rifle fire. More gunmen opened fire from the pickups, tracer rounds flashing like fireworks into the night sky above us.

Dr. Mangal turned to me, a note of urgency in his voice. "Stay in the truck! And keep an eye on the blankets. . . . Let me do the talking."

We pulled to a stop, and he clambered down from the cab. A young boy with a Kalashnikov assault rifle approached.

"What are these?" the young boy demanded, pointing with his weapon at the cargo in the rear of our vehicle.

"Blankets," Dr. Mangal replied. "All three trucks are carrying blankets only."

"Where are you taking them?" asked the boy.

"Hesar Shahee camp. It's a delivery of aid."

The boy didn't appear the slightest bit interested in our humanitarian mission. He gave a signal, and a group of teenage militiamen came forward, each with a glinting bayonet attached to his rifle. I peeped from the cab as they clambered onto the rear of the trucks and started thrusting their razor sharp bayonets into our precious cargo.

With each knife thrust I imagined a freezing mother in Hesar Shahee camp, and I felt my anger and my bile rising. The militiamen must have noticed my anguished looks, for they started laughing at me. They drove in their long knives repeatedly, hooking out blankets and hurling them to the ground.

"This is the tax you pay us to pass," the militia leader announced, indicating the growing pile of blankets. "I have a proposal for you. Why not give all the blankets to us? Then we can do the aid distribution for you."

Dr. Mangal gave an ingratiating smile. "Well, sadly—"

"No way is that happening!" I cut in, speaking through the cab's open window. "I came from the other side of the world to get these blankets to the people who need them, and I'm sure as hell going to make sure they get there."

Dr. Mangal gave me a look. "You see, as the lady says, we do need to deliver the blankets ourselves."

"She is from where?" the militiaman demanded. "America? London? Where?"

"America," Dr. Mangal conceded.

"Then she must have a lot of money, and can afford to pay more tax."

"Unfortunately, she spent everything on the blankets and hiring the trucks," Dr. Mangal countered.

The boy shrugged. "If she has no money, you must hand over the cargo. Then we will decide the correct tax to take from an American—"

"No way!" I cut in, angrily. "*No way* are you taking those blankets."

"If we want to take them, we take them," the militiaman snapped, for the first time looking at me directly. "Or how will you stop us?"

"You'll take them over my dead body!"

"You're willing to die to get your blankets to a bunch of refugees?" he demanded, incredulous. "You're willing to die for that?"

"You're damn right I am!"

Dr. Mangal gathered together a handful of extra blankets. He thrust them toward the militiaman. "Here, have these as an extra tax. Then we've paid double what you first demanded."

There was a tense silence before finally the militiaman nodded at one of his henchmen to take the proffered bundle.

He gave me a murderous look. "You are lucky you're a woman. It is against our tradition to kill women."

Engines growling, the pickups moved into formation, two ahead of us and one at the rear. And in that fashion the militiamen "escorted" us across their terrain until we reached the next checkpoint. The same process of bargaining and "tax" taking repeated itself as we were passed from one militia to the next along the road to Hesar Shahee.

By the time we were approaching the fifth checkpoint, I was boiling over with frustration and anger. At this rate we'd get to Hesar Shahee with no blankets remaining. I announced that I was getting down from the truck.

Dr. Mangal flinched. "Ms. Sadeed, you really should stay inside."

"Oh no." I shook my head. "Not this time. Now is the time for me to talk, not you."

"This is not the United States," he objected. "Here a woman cannot talk like you do, or tell these men what to do."

The truck ground to a halt. I jumped down, my feet making a jarring impact on the hard earth. I turned and straightened my clothes. Pulling my *chadar* closer around me, I marched ahead until I was face-to-face with the lead militiaman. The only light came from the vehicle's headlights, which danced and flickered in the fine dust thrown up by the truck's wheels. The militiaman peered at me, searching for a man to speak to, but Dr. Mangal was hanging well back.

"We're an aid convoy taking a cargo of blankets to Hesar Shahee camp." I spoke into the silence. "We need you to let us pass and to give us safe passage."

"We take a tax of a dozen blankets," the militiaman announced, trying to recover his composure.

"No blankets," I countered. "They're for the displaced people. You're not getting a single one."

He stared at me, his eyes wide with disbelief. "You say very foolish things for a woman. We make the rules around here. And we take whatever we want."

"Oh no you don't! In fact, if you were man enough you'd buy the blankets needed to cover your mothers and sisters, so we don't have to bring them all the way from America! And if you were man enough you would accompany us and ensure safe delivery of our cargo to those who are freezing to death in the cold."

I felt the militiamen bunch up closer together. They were looking to their leader and waiting for his signal. Well, I was in too deep now. In any case I was angry at these teenage bandits for stealing all our blankets. Not one of them had it in him to lend a helping hand to those truly in need. If they weren't stopped we'd have no blankets left to give out in the camp, and all of our efforts would be in vain.

The militia leader couldn't have been more than seventeen. I was hoping that he didn't have it in him to shoot an unarmed woman, one who was old enough to be his mother. In Afghan tradition a man would never do so, especially if she was asking that man for his help and protection. But that was the Afghanistan of my youth. I just hoped and prayed that some of those good, honorable values had survived since then.

"If you're man enough you'll come and sit in the truck with us as an escort," I told the militia leader. "And you'll help save the lives of your suffering mothers and sisters."

The militiaman was hissing with a barely suppressed rage. "If you were a man, by now I would have killed you," he grated. "But since you are a woman—"

"Yes, I am a woman," I cut in. "And an honorable Afghan man would come sit in the truck and protect a women in need."

The militia leader silenced me, issuing a stream of orders in Pashto to his fellow fighters. We'd been conversing in Dari, and I'm by no means fluent in Pashto. I wasn't sure exactly what he'd said, but in an instant they were mounting up their vehicles. Without a word or a look to me he strode across to our truck and ripped open the door.

"Start the engine," he rasped.

He hauled himself inside and took a place on the front seat, his assault rifle lying across his knees. I hurried after him.

"In the back," the militiaman snapped. "I am not sitting next to a woman."

I slid into the seat next to Dr. Mangal's wife. She looked utterly terrified.

The militiaman stabbed a finger at the windshield. "Drive. *Drive.*"

As the truck pulled away he leaned out of the window and yelled some orders at his men. The pickups closed in around us, the gunmen holding their weapons at the ready. I wondered where they were taking us, whether we had been kidnapped or if the militia leader had actually heard my plea for help. I was terrified. I felt my heart beating fast, my pulse booming deafeningly in my ears.

We drove onward in a horrible, tense silence. For an instant Dr. Mangal caught my eye. His expression said it all: *you stupid, stupid, stubborn American woman! What have you done?* I tried to ignore him. Eventually the headlights picked up a glint of white ahead. It was another group of vehicles. The militia leader leaned out of the window and greeted those before us.

"This is our stuff," he added, jerking a thumb behind him at the cargo of blankets. "So let us through."

There was a nod from the gunmen at the checkpoint. Engines snarled, and the pickups moved to the side of the road. We were waved on without so much as one blanket being handed over. Our militiaman's words, backed up by his firepower, had gotten us through.

By the time we had sailed through another half dozen checkpoints, I started to believe the unbelievable—that the militiaman was trying to help us. The challenge that I had thrown down appeared to have hit home. Perhaps all was not lost in my country. Perhaps the values of honor and welcome and respect were still alive here.

The militiaman and our driver were smoking like chimneys, passing a roll-up back and forth between them. I wanted to break through to this guy, to make a human connection beyond him not being able to shoot me because I was a woman. Hidden beneath all of his teenage gunman posturing I sensed there was a core of good in this young man, and I wanted him to use that to spirit us safely to Hesar Shahee.

"Where are you from?" I tried asking him.

"Why is she asking me this?" he demanded of the driver. "How would she know where I am from?"

The driver's only answer was to shrug and to continue driving. In the militiaman's experience, no Afghan woman would ever have acted as I had—hence I had to be a foreigner.

"I know this country as well as you," I told him. "I'm an Afghan. I was born here."

"Where were you born?" he demanded, still not looking at me.

"Charikar."

"Which part of Charikar?"

"Actually, I was born in the governor's compound."

He glanced at me. "The governor's compound? What were you doing there?"

"My father was the governor. But you wouldn't know him. You weren't even born at the time."

"I know all the governors."

"Okay, well, my father's name was Mir Abdul Aziz."

"I don't know him," he muttered. "Well, maybe you are an Afghan, but now you come from America. So, do you have a lighter for me? All people from America have good lighters."

"I don't. I don't smoke."

"Well, okay, do you have a pen for me?"

"Maybe. But can you read and write?"

"No," he conceded. "But my uncle can." There was a short pause. "So, what's going on in America? Like, how many days does it take to get there?"

"From here, three or four days. You have to take a truck, a taxi, and then a couple or more airplanes."

"It's a long way? Much farther than going to Iran or Pakistan?"

I nodded. "It's a long, long way from here, that's for sure."

The militiaman's name was Naqibullah, which means "the one who is honored by God." He had huge hazel eyes, but they were horribly red and inflamed—presumably from all the drugs he was smoking. The contrast between the deep chocolate brown center and the raw and angry red was a little frightening. And beneath the jet-black hair that peeped out from under his turban, I noticed he still had the odd few pimples of youth.

We'd been on the road for six hours or so since crossing the border when I heard the noise of dogs barking in the distance.

"We're getting close to Hesar Shahee," Naqibullah remarked.

"How do you know?" I asked.

"You hear those dogs? There's these nomads from Pakistan camped up around Hesar Shahee. It's their dogs you can hear."

We couldn't do the aid distribution in darkness, so we planned to spend the remainder of the night at Dr. Mangal's clinic, a few miles farther on, in Jalalabad. Even so, I felt relief flooding through my veins. I had been so tense and fearful throughout the journey from the border, which had lasted most of the night, and my entire body ached. But here I was at last, passing by Hesar Shahee.

As we approached Jalalabad, Dr. Mangal and my militiaman friend pointed out that the city lay all before us, but it was shrouded in darkness as deep as the grave. We crawled along deserted streets where here and there a tiny *gais*—a kerosene lantern—threw its feeble light out of a door or window. Afghanistan's second city had no electric power at all. The *gais* was the only source of light in a city that was eyeless and entombed, its streets silent and deserted.

Dr. Mangal directed our driver along darkened roadways until we reached the small house that doubled as his clinic. We had to feel our way inside. Once I'd been shown to my room, I realized just how emotionally and physically drained I was. There was a mattress on the floor and a tiny lantern, which was all that I needed.

I closed the door, lay down, and fell asleep without even bothering to remove my shoes.

FIVE

The Edge of Darkness

I AWOKE TO A VOICE CALLING ME FROM OUTSIDE THE DOOR IN MY room in Dr. Mangal's clinic. "Morning prayers," the voice called to me again.

I glanced at my watch. It was five o'clock. I'd barely slept and now they were waking me. I'm not a morning person, but I roused myself, washed my face, hands, and feet in the ritual cleansing for prayer, and went to join the women of the house.

As I prayed I reflected upon the Islam of my childhood. My father's faith was gentle and tolerant. It had much in common with Sufism, the philosophical, mystical branch of Islam that developed in the second century and flourished throughout Afghanistan. It espouses a collective good that goes beyond religion, something that is antithetical to the rigid Islamism that is predominant today. By nature Afghans are nonextreme in belief, and beneath the surface lies a deeply ingrained tolerance of others—as long as they come to our country in peace. Only comparatively recently did radical, political Islam come to Afghanistan, and even then it was brought by outsiders.

After college, in the late 1970s, Dastagir and I had traveled to Lebanon for further study. At the time, Lebanon was tearing itself apart in a horrific civil war. The fighting pitted Christians against Muslims, and at its most basic the bloodshed was all about which God one claimed to believe in. Dastagir and I had few friends in Beirut, so I sought out Dari literature to keep my mind occupied. The only Dari books that I could find were about Sufism. I started reading the writings of Rumi, a thirteenth-century Afghan poet. I learned many of Rumi's verses by heart, and his beautiful, lyrical words came back to me as I recited my dawn prayers in Dr. Mangal's Jalalabad clinic.

> *Come back, come back, whoever you are.*
> *If you have no belief, or if you are a Buddhist or a Christian,*
> *Whoever you are, come back.*
> *This place is not a place where you go back hopeless.*
> *If you have sinned and have said one hundred times you would not sin*
>   *again but you did,*
> *Still, you can come back again.*

Somehow Rumi's words had come alive for me in Naqibullah, my erstwhile killer-turned-protector on the road from the border. Naqibullah had remained with us all the way to Jalalabad, and he had taken it upon himself to keep guard over the cargo by sleeping in one of the trucks. Out on that dark, chaotic road I had challenged him to do what was right, and it seemed that nothing was about to make him shy away from that task.

Naqibullah joined us for breakfast. It consisted of a big pot of sweet green tea and delicious freshly baked Afghan bread.

"*Salam,*" I greeted him. "You slept well?"

"*Salam alaikum, Madar-jan.* Yes, very well," he replied. Then, jokingly: "The front seat of a truck is far better than your average Afghan cave!"

Naqibullah had used the term *madar-jan*—dear mother—to address me. It was the first time that he'd done so. He was dressed in the same robes and turban as the night before, and of course he had his Kalashnikov at his side. But there was something different about him now: he'd scrubbed his face and his hands and his fingernails until they were glowing clean.

He took some tea and bread, and sat a little behind me, his weapon lying across his knees. I sensed a benign presence there, as if this young militiaman had become my great protector. It struck me then how easy it was to start to unravel whatever bad had been done to the boy's mind. Doubtless Naqibullah was capable of the many dark things he had threatened, but just below the hard surface lay a bright spirit. All Naqibullah needed was the opportunity and the inspiration to allow his good nature to shine through.

Once we were done eating, Dr. Mangal and I started planning the day's work. I drew Naqibullah into the conversation, asking him about any security issues that we might face.

"The people in Hesar Shahee have suffered much, but they have good hearts," Naqibullah replied. "They will cause you no trouble, *madar-jan.*" He patted his weapon. "And there is no need to worry, for I will be beside you at all times."

I smiled. "Naqibullah, I feel a lot better knowing that."

He gave an embarrassed grin and pulled out his tobacco pouch. He started to roll what looked to my unpracticed eye like a joint.

"You know, Naqibullah, you're too young to be doing that. It'll only do you harm."

Naqibullah slipped the half-rolled smoke under his robes. "Okay, *Madar-jan,* I'll try to stop." He got to his feet and nodded respectfully to Dr. Mangal and me. "When you're ready, I'll be waiting by the trucks."

I guessed he had gone outside to have a quiet smoke, but at least he had listened to me.

Around seven o'clock we were readying ourselves to leave when we heard a harsh rap on the compound's metal gates. Four armed men appeared. There was something distinctly officious about their bearing.

"What's going on?" I asked Dr. Mangal when he returned from speaking with them. "Who are the four gunmen?"

"The local governor sent then. He wants to know what you're doing here."

"Well, I guess I'm a guest of the governor, as I'm in his city. So tell him to come and visit himself if he's interested!"

Dr. Mangal rolled his eyes. I was joking, really. Why would the governor of Nangarhar Province, of which Jalalabad was the capital, bother himself with me and my blankets? I knew what Dr. Mangal was thinking: *here we go again, she's trying to cause more trouble.* He went to have a last word with the governor's men, and they left.

I thought nothing more of it, but a few minutes later there was a crunching of gravel outside, and a convoy of vehicles pulled to a halt. There were two Jeeps crammed full of men bristling with guns, and sandwiched between them a sleek top-of-the-line metallic silver Mercedes. It looked so utterly out of place here.

Dr. Mangal turned to me. "It's the governor!"

"You didn't really invite him, did you?" I had to bury my face in my *chadar* to stop myself laughing.

"Of course I did. You told me to. But I didn't exactly expect him to come."

A huge guy dismounted from the Mercedes, his billowing robes struggling to hide his massive stomach. His spotless white *peran tunban* fell from his shoulders to his feet and was topped off by an enormous white turban.

"*Salam alaikum*—peace unto you," he announced, in a deep, rumbling voice. "Welcome. I am Haji Qadir, the governor of Nangarhar Province."

The import of the governor's name—*Haji*—didn't escape me. *Haji* denotes someone who has undertaken the *Haj*, the holy pilgrimage to Mecca, something that all Muslims are supposed to do during their lifetimes if they can afford it.

"*Salam*—peace," I returned the greeting. "Thank you for coming. I am Suraya Sadeed of Help the Afghan Children."

I couldn't quite believe that the governor was here. What could possibly interest him in my cargo of blankets?

Haji Qadir glanced at the trucks. "You bring a cargo of blankets for the refugees? Thank you for doing this. Now you can leave it to us to distribute them."

I sighed. I felt my spirits sink. *Here we go again.* "Thank you for the offer, Governor, but I'm afraid I can't allow that. You see, I gave assurances to people in America that I would deliver the aid in person."

He fixed me with a look. "But now that you are here in Jalalabad, you are under my protection and my authority. You are a woman. You should trust us to undertake this last part of your mission."

I felt my anger start to rise. "Well, if someone *were* looking after the

Afghan people then maybe they'd have blankets in the first place, instead of freezing to death as they are."

"And that means what exactly?" he demanded. "You don't trust us?"

"If you can afford to drive that fantastic Mercedes I guess you could afford to provide a few blankets to the people. So no, Governor, I don't really trust in your priorities."

There was a stunned silence. The governor swiveled his eyes across to Dr. Mangal, who was standing beside me, and stared.

"A woman, saying this to me!" he announced, angrily. "A woman challenging the governor of Nangarhar Province! A *woman*." He turned his glare on me. "What makes you think you have the right to say such disrespectful, arrogant things to me?"

"I'm trying to explain why I need to deliver the aid myself," I replied, evenly. "That's all. After coming all this way it's not so much to expect, is it?"

He waved his hand at me in angry dismissal. "I do not argue with women. But if you were a man, have no doubt I would show you otherwise—"

"Well, that's fine," I cut in, before he could change his mind. "I'm not asking you to argue with me. So, we can go ahead and distribute the blankets?"

The governor shrugged. "Fine. I will assign you some soldiers as escorts. But if I find just one of those blankets for sale in the market tomorrow, I will blame you for it."

"Look, if they sell the blankets to buy milk for their kids then that's up to them," I shot back at him. "As far as I'm concerned it's whatever the refugees most need."

He glared at Dr. Mangal. "Did you invite her here? There is no talking to her. I have always said there is no point talking with women. This one proves it." He clicked his fingers. "Captain Saleem, take five of your soldiers and escort this woman to Hesar Shahee. Makes sure everything happens just as I have said it should."

With that the governor lowered himself into the plush leather interior of his Mercedes. He signaled to the driver, who gunned the engine, and he was gone.

Dr. Mangal stomped off inside. He was speechless with anger, but I didn't particularly care. My priority was the mission, and I'd gotten what I wanted. We were going to Hesar Shahee to deliver the precious blankets, and no one was going to stand in our way, or steal them for themselves.

A half hour later our trucks pulled away from Dr. Mangal's compound, heading for Hesar Shahee. But if I hadn't known I was in Jalalabad, I would never have believed it. There didn't seem to be a tree or shrub or garden anywhere. The entire city had been ground into dirt and dust.

Two decades of fighting—first the Soviet Red Army against the Mujahideen, then the Mujahideen among themselves—had torn this ancient city to pieces. Roads had been ground into rubble by the Soviet armor, leaving potholes the size of cars that our convoy had to dodge around. The Soviets had decreed that all orchards had to be destroyed, to stop the Mujahideen from hiding in them. They had been ripped up and torn down. Jalalabad the Garden City was no more.

We left the deserted townscape and made our way toward Hesar Shahee. After an hour's drive a treeless plain opened out before us as far as the eye could see. Scattered across the empty, windswept vastness was a sea of tiny white specks. Tents, I realized, each of which had to house an entire family.

Hesar Shahee is a Dari name meaning "the edge of the kingdom." But as I gazed out over that dustbowl shimmering in the baking heat, I knew that the people here were in a place close to hell. I couldn't believe that the governor of Nangarhar Province was happy to shunt hundreds of thousands of women and children into a place like this. Thank God I hadn't let him get his way with the blankets.

On the left side of the dirt road there was a field of tiny, humped mounds, some of which appeared to be freshly dug. I glanced at Dr. Mangal, inquiringly.

"The graveyard," he told me.

"But so many?" I whispered. "And so small?"

Dr. Mangal gave a sad shrug. "The children and the babies."

I forced myself to look again. My God, there were thousands. I was gazing out over a field of thousands of dead infants. Nothing that I had heard about Hesar Shahee had prepared me for this. I felt my shock turning to rage. How could the governor drive around in his plush Mercedes, when just a few miles away he knew—*he knew*—there was this.

I thought back to the lush, well-watered fields of Devil's Flowers that we had driven through the previous evening. I couldn't believe that a poppy flower and the drug it produced were valued above the vulnerable women and children left to live in such a place as this. As I climbed down from our truck I cursed the governor of Nangarhar Province, for it was his responsibility to find a place that would offer at least a modicum of sanctuary to the people here. And this blasted moonscape was definitely not it.

People had gathered here at Hesar Shahee in the hundreds of thousands, for there was no way through to Pakistan. The authorities there had closed the border to any more refugees, and who knew when it might open again. It was still early, but the temperature had already crept over eighty-five degrees Fahrenheit. I dreaded to think what the heat would be like at midday, even though the temperature would plummet to below freezing overnight. A crowd gathered, pressing in from all sides with desperate eyes and nervous faces.

No one knew what we were there for, but I sensed something different here compared to the camps in Pakistan. There everyone knew the system. Foreigners brought aid, and only those who shouted the loudest might get some. But here the crowd had gathered in respectful, quiet order as they waited to hear why we had come.

I turned to Dr. Mangal. "How do we work this? How do we make this fair?"

He glanced around at the crowd. "We have to find those most in need."

"There are families here without even tents," Naqibullah volunteered. "The newest arrivals, those who've only just made the journey from Kabul."

"Right. Let's start with them," I said. "At least they can place the blankets on the ground to sleep on. Two blankets per family. Even then, I doubt there'll be enough."

I made a short announcement to the crowd, explaining what we had to give and who we would prioritize. No one complained. No one jostled for places or accused one another of sneaking ahead. They waited patiently until their names were called. Even though they had virtually nothing, the people here still had their dignity and their respect.

"Come and help," I told Naqibullah, "and give two blankets to each family."

For a moment I watched over Naqibullah as he handed out the precious blankets. The sympathy he felt for the plight of these families was written all over his young features.

I turned to deal with my own line of supplicants. A young woman stepped forward. I froze, staring at her in open-mouthed amazement. She gazed back at me with huge brown eyes, her dark hair bound up in a ponytail, her head half covered in a *chadar* of rainbow colors. I couldn't tear my gaze away from her beautiful, despairing eyes.

She looked at the ground, embarrassed. Of course, she couldn't know why I was staring—but she was the spitting image of my daughter, Mariam. In fact, it was as if someone had taken my daughter out of America, dressed her in Afghan clothing, and transported her here.

Seeing "my daughter" here had shaken me to the core. I could just about deal with a faceless multitude, but seeing this young woman who was the double of Mariam had forced me to contemplate what it would be like to have one of my own loved ones consigned to a place like Hesar Shahee. Each person suffering here had been rendered an individual in my mind, someone whom I might love and cherish and care for, as I would for my own daughter. It was shattering.

I tried to pull myself together. I handed her the blankets. She had an infant child tucked under one arm, a beautiful little girl. As she took the blankets I noticed that her stomach was swollen. I guessed she had to be several months pregnant. I wondered how on earth she had managed to flee the fighting in Kabul in that condition.

"When did you get here?" I asked her.

"Three days ago," she answered.

"You don't have a tent?"

"No. Not yet, *Khala-jan*. I think they're going to give us one soon."

Khala-jan is Dari for respected auntie. "What's your name?" I asked.

"Fatima," she said.

"Where's your family?"

She shook her head. Glanced down at her child. "I don't have one. This is it."

"Where's your husband?" I asked.

"They killed him."

She started to cry. I reached out and placed an arm around her, and I found myself crying with her. I used my *chadar* to wipe away her tears, drying the fine porcelain skin beneath her hypnotizing eyes.

"Tell me what happened."

"We were living in Macrorayan," Fatima began. "It's a part of Kabul. Perhaps you know it?"

I nodded. I did.

"One evening we were having dinner and a rocket hit the apartment," Fatima continued. "My husband was blown up and his body fell into my arms. My parents asked me to flee Kabul with them, to make for Pakistan, but I said no. I couldn't just leave my husband like that. I had to give him a proper burial."

She glanced at me, her face appealing for support. In my mind's eye I saw Fatima's husband, a crumpled, bloodied corpse. The image morphed into that of Dastagir, lying cold and lifeless on the gurney in that Virginia hospital.

I held her. Rocked her in my arms. "I know," I said. "I know."

"I left Kabul a few days later with my child. I caught a bus. It was crammed full of people trying to flee Kabul. All I could carry was my wedding ring and one picture album. But halfway to Jalalabad we were stopped by the militia, at a place called Sarobi. They were bad, bad men. They took everything."

Fatima glanced at her bare hand, and the tears began to fall again. "They even took my wedding ring."

When I was a child my family used to go for picnics on the shores of the beautiful lake at Sarobi. It was now a place menaced by a cruel militia who even robbed young mothers of their wedding rings. How my country had changed.

"You know, I have a daughter your age," I told Fatima. "She is the spitting image of you. And you know something else, she's only just graduated from high school."

"She's so lucky," Fatima whispered. "I wish I were your daughter."

As she said those words I felt as if my heart were breaking. If there was a God, how on earth could he have visited all of this on Fatima?

I felt a presence at my side. It was Naqibullah, and he was standing there very much on guard. I caught his eye, but he averted his gaze, bringing up a corner of his sleeve to dry his face. I realized then that Naqibullah—the hardened, gunslinging militiaman of yesterday—was crying too. By hearing Fatima's story, Naqibullah was learning how war pummels the innocents, grinding their lives into dust and ruin. Before now he had been the engine of that destruction, and now he was face-to-face with its devastating human consequences. It was as much of a shattering experience for him as it was for me.

"How are you now?" I asked Fatima.

"I have some pain, here, *Khala-jan*," she told me, indicting her right side. "When the rocket exploded it showered me with metal. I think some of it is still inside."

I held her at arm's length so I could look into her eyes. "You were injured by the rocket? And you are pregnant. How on earth did you make it here alive?"

"I had lost my husband," she replied. "I had only space inside myself for the pain of losing him. I think maybe I didn't know how badly I was hurt."

"It's a miracle you made it."

I glanced at Naqibullah. He stared at the ground. "It was by the grace of God," he muttered. "By the grace of God."

"*Khoda mehraban as*," Fatima echoed. "God is kind."

A part of me wanted desperately to take Fatima and her daughter back to Pakistan, to America, even. Anywhere that wasn't here. But as Naqibullah and I returned to handing out the blankets, I came across so many others in need. I was torn. How could I single her out above all others? I kept returning to Fatima, and it reached the point where Dr. Mangal took me to one side.

"You're here to help everyone," he told me. "Please, you need to stick to your task. Otherwise, when we go this girl will be targeted if she receives more than the others. You think you're helping, but you might be doing her harm."

Our ten thousand blankets didn't even come close to satisfying the needs at Hesar Shahee. There were anguished looks from those we'd failed to help, which just served to reinforce my sense of guilt at not having brought more. But I still felt such a strong sense of gratitude from those that we had helped, and it bore me up. It made the dangers and fears of the journey in here more than worthwhile.

The more I saw of this camp, the angrier I felt myself becoming. Little kids ran around barefoot, treading on the scorpions and snakes, which were everywhere. We didn't find a single aid worker or medic in the entire camp. Hesar Shahee was seen as being too dangerous for the aid agencies. Every day there were more deaths: from cholera; from dehydration; from diarrhea; from scorpion stings; from the freezing cold of the desert nights.

But the very worst was the lack of water. There was no water whatsoever—not even a trickling stream—in the whole of Hesar Shahee. The people here depended entirely on UN water trucks that were supposed to come every other day, but which were often delayed.

A woman told me that there wasn't even enough water for her to bury her dead child. I didn't understand why she needed water to bury the dead. Perhaps it was to cleanse the body before burial.

"You know, this isn't a normal situation," I told her. "You don't have to wash the body. Not here, where there isn't even enough water to drink."

She shook her head. "It's not that."

"Then what?" I asked.

"We need the water to pour on the ground, to make it soft enough to dig a grave. Otherwise, you can't even scratch a hole big enough to bury a child. We had to wait three days for the water truck. Then everyone donated a little of their water ration, and with that I made the ground soft enough to scratch a hole with my bare hands."

I didn't know what to say. In this place, even the dead could not find dignity or rest.

"You've seen the graveyard?" she added. "The rows of tiny graves? Each is just a pile of dirt the length of your child, with a stone placed above the head. Every day it keeps growing."

I found myself repeating long-forgotten prayers as I pleaded with God to help all the mothers of Hesar Shahee camp. Please God, find them a way to Pakistan, to the camps across the border. Even those terrible places were a kind of relief after Hesar Shahee. The rivers might flow like open sewers, but at least there was water.

The mother within me couldn't do the "right" thing and give Fatima no more than the countless others in need. In a private moment I drew her aside and handed her a wad of rupees.

"For your child," I told her. "And for your *children* soon, I hope. And for you, because I love you as my daughter."

She smiled, shyly. "In my heart I am your daughter, *khala-jan*."

All through the day Fatima had kept repeating the same phrase to me: "*Khoda mehraban as*—God is kind." Her faith was humbling, and I saw how it comforted her, even here. Fatima had so much faith; faith that I had lost. Deep inside me I hadn't forgotten God, but the years of materialism had taken me a long, long way from belief. I'd spent a decade or more in America during which I'd learned to worship another god—Mammon, the god of riches and greed.

I had thought of myself as the master of my own universe in the greatest country on earth. Yet when I saw these people, so resilient and so full of hope, I felt foolish and empty. In reality I had only been the master of material possessions. These people had mastered the human spirit, finding the strength that lies within.

That evening we left Hesar Shahee and returned to Dr. Mangal's clinic.

Over tea I reflected upon what I had heard in the camp. Everyone had told me these terrible stories of how Kabul was being torn to shreds by the fighting. The fairy-tale city of my youth was in meltdown, its inhabitants fleeing in droves.

Thousands of rockets just like the one that had killed Fatima's husband were being fired into the city daily. I couldn't imagine what that would be like, what it would do to Kabul. I kept thinking about the old film clips that I'd seen of World War II, of the bombing of London and Berlin. Would it be like that?

Naqibullah appeared, breaking me out of my bleak reverie. He sat down beside me and poured himself a glass of tea.

"So what now for you, Naqibullah?" I asked him. "You're not going back to what you were doing before?"

"No, I'm not."

"Where do you live, anyway?" I asked him.

"In a village nearby."

"Where are your folks?"

"I don't know, *Madar-jan*. I guess they were killed in the war. I never knew them. I was brought up by my uncle."

It was common enough in Afghanistan for an orphaned child to be taken in by relatives. Naqibullah wouldn't see himself as being particularly unlucky, for there would be many other kids like him. At the end of the war against the Soviets, there were 2.5 million orphans in Afghanistan, nearly all of them living with their extended families.

Like countless other Afghan boys, Naqibullah had had no schooling, and he could read only the Koran. He was fit for little in life, apart from being a gunman or a farmer. He'd told me he wasn't going back to the militia life, so I asked him what he planned to do instead.

"Well, maybe, *Madar-jan*, you might want to take me with you?" he suggested, haltingly.

"Take you where? To America? To Pakistan?" I shook my head. "Both are impossible."

In my mind if there was one person I should have helped, it was Fatima.

She was completely alone and vulnerable, while Naqibullah had his village just nearby. He had a support network and fallback options, while Fatima had none of that.

"I have another idea," Naqibullah suggested. "I'm going to check with the people who bring water to the camp. I want to see if I can help with the deliveries, and earn a little income that way. I think it would be a good thing to do, *Madar-jan*."

"That's a great idea," I enthused. "You do that, Naqibullah, and I will be so proud of you."

I was all out of money now. I went and found Dr. Mangal and asked him to lend me a thousand rupees, the equivalent of twenty dollars. I gave the cash to Naqibullah, and with it my blessings and my thanks.

"One day you will be a great man," I told him. "You have helped a lot of people already. And I have faith that you'll help others in the future."

"Pray for me, *Madar-jan*," he said.

"I will," I told him.

We dropped Naqibullah off at Hesar Shahee camp the following morning, on our way to the border. As the convoy pulled away, I turned my head to get a final look at him. He stood there, alone, his figure surrounded by the boiling dust thrown up by our parting, his rifle slung across his shoulder. He lifted his hands, waved, then rubbed them vigorously across his turbaned head in a gesture that somehow spoke to me.

Madar-jan is gone, it said. *I'm alone again, living on my wits. There must be a future out there for me somewhere.*

Eventually his tiny figure was lost in the dust and the shimmering heat behind us. I knew instinctively that I was never going to see Naqibullah, or Fatima, again. I settled into my seat in the stiflingly hot cab and tried the window to see if it would roll down any farther. I was on the brink of tears and I desperately needed the air.

I thought back over the months that I had spent in Virginia, wallowing in pity and depression at losing Dastagir. Fatima's husband had been killed before her eyes, and she was bereft of family in an utterly hopeless place, yet she endured. What was my loss in comparison? In Fatima I had met a young mother so brutally dispossessed, yet she had the quality of an angel whose faith gave her an inner strength and peace. And in Naqibullah I had known an angry young gunman who was really just an orphan boy struggling to be valued and to be free. I had nothing to complain about. My life was blessed.

I realized something else then. Either I could go back to America and feel sorry for myself some more, or I could take up the challenge of helping the millions of Fatimas and Naqibullahs here in Afghanistan. I could wallow in pity, or I could go do something that was vital and meaningful and real. There was no choice, really, and I knew that my life would never be the same again.

On the lawless road to Jalalabad, and in the waterless death camp of Hesar Shahee, I had finally found my calling.

∞⊂∞⊃∞⊂∞⊃∞⊂∞⊃∞⊂∞⊃∞⊂∞⊃∞⊂∞⊃∞⊂∞⊃∞⊂∞⊃∞⊂∞⊃∞⊂∞⊃∞⊂∞⊃∞⊂∞⊃∞

SIX

The Widow Camps

SOME NINE HOURS AFTER SETTING OUT, WE WERE BACK IN PESHA-
war. In my absence, Dr. Abdullah and Nawabi had gone about forming
the HTAC clinic. It was to be called the Aria Clinic, "Aria" being the
shortened version of "Ariana," the name of the ancient Persian Empire that
had lasted for a thousand years in the region. We chose this name because
it was neutral to Afghans: it has no ethnic, tribal, or religious affiliations, so
it would be acceptable to everyone.

Dr. Abdullah was the clinic director, and Nawabi was appointed the
clinic manager. They had found premises that we could rent close to the
refugee camps. There were a good number of Afghan doctors and nurses in
those camps, and Dr. Abdullah and Nawabi had hired a dozen of them to
staff the clinic. Nawabi kept coming to me with list after list of costs, so I
could approve them. The building rental, salaries, medical equipment—
none of this was going to come cheap.

But after my experiences in Hesar Shahee, I couldn't for one moment
imagine not going ahead with the clinic. Like every other refugee in that
camp, Fatima was hoping to make it to the safety of Pakistan—and that
meant a camp closer to Peshawar. By the time she got there, I was determined to have the clinic up and running. I didn't care about the cost. I'd
sell some of my properties in America if I had to, but I would make this
happen.

One of the biggest challenges was turning out to be medical supplies. In
my enthusiasm for starting the clinic, I'd promised we'd stock it with only

the best Western medicines. But purchasing these medicines from the United States was proving to be a nightmare. I decided I'd deal with that when I got back to Virginia, and for now we'd make do with locally sourced drugs. We opened the clinic two weeks after my return from Hesar Shahee, and on that first day Dr. Abdullah admitted over one hundred patients. As word spread, the demand from the refugee camps mushroomed.

A few days later I was preparing for my departure to the United States when Dr. Abdullah sent one of the clinic staffers to find me. I was in the Green's Hotel, writing up a report on my trip and trying to dodge all the aid workers and journalists who were desperate to speak to me. None of these grizzled reporters and aid workers could quite believe what I had done, and it was only now that I truly appreciated the dangers I had exposed myself to.

Dr. Abdullah had sent me a note: *We have tracked down your college friend, the one who hid behind the burka. She is here waiting for you.*

I immediately jumped into a cab and headed for the clinic. I hadn't for one moment forgotten my college friend from the camp. That chance encounter was burned into my mind. Now that I was about to see her again, all the conflicting emotions of our previous meeting came flooding in on me. I just wanted to have an answer, to know who she might be.

I caught sight of her hunched figure sitting on a bench in the waiting room, but there was a difference now. There were only women patients present in the clinic, and my unknown friend had felt comfortable unveiling. As she turned to greet me, I found myself staring into the face of a haggard old woman. I was speechless with shock.

I rushed over and held her in a tight embrace, struggling to recover my composure. "Oh, thank God," I murmured. "Finally I've seen you and I know who you are."

It was a lie, but I couldn't think of anything else to say. Uttering the truth—that I couldn't recognize her at all—would have been unforgivable. As I hugged her, I wracked my brains for a way to work out who she was without asking her name.

Then, a flash of inspiration. "Have you registered with the clinic?" I asked.

She shook her head. "No, not yet."

"Oh, but you must. Come, I'll help you."

Before she could protest I half-dragged her over to reception. I grabbed the register and placed it before her, putting a pen into her hand. My eyes were glued to the paper as she started to write. By the time she had finished I felt dizzy and sick with shock. I had to get out of the room, and I made an excuse that I needed to use the bathroom.

I locked myself in there and forced myself to face the reality of who she was: *Nasreen Saber*. Nasreen, whose name means "the beautiful flower." At college, Nasreen had been the epitome of everything "proper." I could remember her well-cut clothes and neat looks like it was yesterday. She had worn smart navy business suits, with silky white blouses, and not a hair was ever out of place.

We weren't exactly soul mates—with my red leather miniskirts and my motorcycle-riding boyfriend, Dastagir, I had been the archetypal college rebel. But I'd respected Nasreen, and I had appreciated her intelligence and her beauty. She was about the last person I would ever have imagined ending up in that dirty, overcrowded camp.

Nasreen would be in her early forties, but to me she looked as if she were eighty years old. It was as if someone had taken her and sucked out every spark of joy and life, leaving a dry and shriveled husk.

After recovering a little I rejoined her in the waiting room. Nasreen told me she had two grown daughters, and that the money she had asked for at our first meeting was to buy milk for her granddaughter. All four of them—mother, daughters, and grandchild—were living in the camp.

"What happened, Nasreen?" I asked her eventually. "How did you end up here?"

"One night the Communists took my husband, my father, and brothers," she whispered. "They took them in 'for questioning.' I never saw them again. A little later our house was burned down. I fled with my daughters and came here. Overnight I became a nonperson. That's what I am today."

"But what happened to your mother?"

She shrugged, averting her eyes. "There's nothing to say. . . . You know, my husband is the lucky one. He died. And my father and my brothers . . ."

"But Nasreen, there must be something to live for. Your daughters. Your grandchild."

She turned her lifeless eyes toward me. "In the camp?" She shook her head. "There is nothing."

It was time for Nasreen's medical treatment. I left her with the nurse and went to find Dr. Abdullah. I asked him how this had happened—that my friend had aged twice her years and seemed to have died inside. Dr. Abdullah could see how upset I was. He asked me to take a seat and to prepare to hear some pretty difficult stuff.

"The camp administrators are running rackets," Dr. Abdullah told me. "I think you detected that yourself. The families on the official lists get all the aid, and the camp administrators take their cut and sell it on. In fact most of them have shops in town and are wealthy men."

"So that's why Ali tried to force us to give to his list of 'most needy.'"

"Indeed. Human nature is not always pretty or kind." Dr. Abdullah paused. "But that is not the worst. In and around Peshawar there are the 'widow camps.' Have you heard of them?"

"No. Never."

"I feared as much." He sighed. "Women without men to protect them, like your friend, Nasreen, are forced to live in an isolated part of the camp. Anyone with money or power—businessmen, policemen, whoever—pays a 'fee' to those in charge, so they can enter the widow camps and use the women at will. That is what I fear has been forced upon your friend all these years. And her daughters, if they are old enough . . ."

"My God, it's unbelievable," I exclaimed. "It's inhuman. It's like the devil's come to earth and is living among us."

"I'm afraid it is. There is so much that is harsh here, and brutal and unjust. We try to do what we can to spread human mercy and kindness, but we struggle to do so among all of this."

I was struck by a sickening thought. "Are you telling me that any woman refugee who comes here can be placed in those widow camps?"

"I'm afraid they can. If they have no man to protect them they are terribly vulnerable."

"So are you telling me that Fatima, the young girl I met in Hesar Shahee, may end up *in a widow camp?*"

"Suraya, she might. But please, don't lose heart. You have done such fantastic work here. Look around you, at this clinic. Look how you're helping. I know how this must make you feel, but don't lose heart."

"What's the point, Dr. Abdullah?" I asked, tearfully. "What the hell is the point of building a goddamn clinic and taking aid to Hesar Shahee if that beautiful girl ends up in a widow camp?"

"Where there is life, there is hope," Dr. Abdullah replied, gently. "We keep them alive in the hope that one day they may go home. And once they are home, then we hope they find the peace and the support in which to heal. That is all we can hope for, Suraya. Without that, none of us would ever do anything."

Where there is life, there is hope. Perhaps in the war-ravaged country of my birth that was as much as we could wish for.

I left Peshawar with many burdens. In addition to having to raise funding to cover the costs of the Aria clinic, I resolved to get Nasreen out of that widow camp. I would find the funds to rent her a small place somewhere in Peshawar.

Not only was Nasreen my college friend, but she was also a manifestation of all that was evil about the war in Afghanistan. She was a person who had lost everything. She was ashamed even to show her face. And how many times must she have wished that she was dead? Before leaving, I tried to really reach out to her, to touch her heart.

"You know, we have common pain," I told her. "A few months ago I lost my husband. He died before my very eyes. I didn't even get to say a proper good-bye."

I hoped that this might melt her, that through my suffering I might connect to her own, but she only stared at me with her dead eyes. I wondered if maybe she hadn't heard me.

"I never got to say good-bye," I repeated. "I never got the chance to wish him farewell."

"You didn't get to say good-bye. . . ." She shrugged. "For me, that was just the start of my journey into this hell."

I SHARED THE FLIGHT BACK TO THE UNITED STATES WITH ANISA AND Musleh, but I sensed a separation between us now. My trip inside had thrown a gulf between us. Without anything being said, I knew that neither of them was going to play an active part in HTAC anymore. I didn't resent it. It was just that they had a different life and different priorities.

All my adult life I had been so wrapped up in gaining prosperity and being the perfect American. Now I felt as if I'd awakened from a deep, deep sleep. We'd had the fine house, the foreign vacations, and the brand-new cars, but I now realized that there had been this enormous void in our lives.

Living in the West had given me every material thing that I could have wished for, but at the same time I had lost so much of what makes life worth living. In America my happiness was determined by the interest rate or the state of the housing market. If the interest rate fell, I was happy because I'd have to pay less on my home loans, and likewise if property prices rose. I had lived by that mantra.

Somewhere on the road to Jalalabad I had come back to myself. I had realized that I couldn't measure my happiness by numbers alone. I had helped countless refugees. And what I had gotten in return—experiencing the joy of helping others—was immeasurable. I could feel a new kind of happiness burning in my heart, and I was impatient to return to Afghanistan to do more.

There were two overriding priorities in my mind. The first was a lesson from Fatima: I had to go and see for myself what was happening in the besieged city of Kabul, and how HTAC might help save lives there. The second was a lesson from Naqibullah, and it was of the burning need for education in my country. Naqibullah had shown me the thin line between light and dark, how a child gunman could so easily be turned around. I had a vision in my mind of countless Naqibullahs sitting in classrooms and learning. That was my long-term promise to Afghanistan: I was going to start building schools.

But that would be impossible to do right now, in the midst of a chaotic and anarchic civil war. My driving priority had to be to save lives.

FOR SO MANY YEARS DASTAGIR HAD BEEN MY SOUL MATE AND MY confidant, but now that he was dead I had no one to turn to but my daughter. While I had been away on my Afghan mission, nineteen-year-old Mariam had been alone in our Virginia apartment. Upon my return I told her all about Fatima—the refugee girl in Hesar Shahee who was her double— and Mariam tried hard to imagine what Fatima's life was like. But I held a lot of other stuff back from her, especially the dangers that I'd run. Mariam was hurting and raw after losing her father, and she was still vulnerable.

I did tell Mariam about my determination to return to Afghanistan, and I could tell that she was torn. On the one hand, she was proud of me. I caught her telling her school buddies all about my trip to Hesar Shahee over the phone. On the other, she was scared of losing me. She didn't want to talk about it; she was pushing twenty and nearly an adult, and she was trying to show how independent she was. But she kept asking me if I was really sure I wanted to go back to Afghanistan. And others in my family were equally concerned.

My mother lived in Virginia, a twenty-minute drive away from our apartment. She'd come to America shortly after my father's death, in the years following the Soviet invasion of our country. One Sunday shortly after I returned from my trip, I went to see her and tell her all about it. Typically she feigned disinterest. It was next to impossible for my mother to show real engagement in anything her daughters were doing. She was far too cool for that. And from my teenage years onward she'd always known that I would do exactly what I wanted to do, no matter what she said.

My mother's name is Homaira. In Arabic it denotes a woman who has very fair skin and red cheeks. Many Afghans prize such looks, and my mother was considered a real beauty. In the earliest years of her marriage she had worn the burka, but by the time I came along, the ruling regime was trying to open up Afghan society. The wives of government officials were being encouraged to set an example by throwing off the burka.

Contrary to what many believe, the burka is not an invention of the Taliban. It has a long history in Afghanistan. Centuries ago the burka was considered a status symbol, for only the wife of a wealthy man could afford one. A woman wore the burka to signify that she wasn't a peasant working in the fields.

I spent a while telling my mother about my trip to Hesar Shahee camp, at the end of which she gave me some typical advice.

"You've done what you needed to do," she told me. "You've been there and seen what it's like. Now it's back to normality. Time to get on with your life."

I knew she meant my previous life—that of the successful, professional businesswoman. In my mother's mind, my madcap Afghan trip was very much a one-time venture.

"But I'm going back to Afghanistan," I told her. "This is what I want to do with my life now."

My mother snorted. "Why do you always have to be so different? I wish you could be like my other daughters. Go to work, come home, take care of the family and throw some nice parties. Why so crazy and so wild?"

I didn't have an answer. My mother and I had always had a fractious relationship. The love was strong, but so too were the confrontations. As a child I was forever having these independent, wild thoughts—especially over religion—and I could never stop myself from voicing them.

Like many youths, I'd questioned my religion. I'd ask my mother if she really believed that all people from all other religions wouldn't go to heaven, just because they weren't Muslims. She was scandalized by such thoughts. Saying "if" or "why" was taboo. In faith, you just accepted what was. My sisters were equally scandalized. They'd invoked God's name against me: *may God forgive you for all the things you're saying.*

My family had always wanted me to conform, but I'd never been able to do so. My older sisters had all left high school and married and settled down. I was the first daughter in the family to break with tradition and go to the university, where Dastagir and I had become infamous for being the love-struck, motorcycling, rebellious couple. I wasn't about to start trying to conform to my family's ideas now, especially if that meant my not returning to Afghanistan.

In fact I felt a driving urgency to get on with my mission, and I had a mountain to climb in terms of need. I started doing the rounds of the Afghan-American radio stations, telling them what HTAC had achieved in Peshawar and around Jalalabad. I put together a short HTAC newsletter called *The Voice of Innocence*, and I started giving it out at Afghan-American gatherings. And all the time I stressed how we'd proven ourselves *inside Afghanistan* and asked people to reach into their hearts again.

Before long I ran into the old lady who'd given me the seventeen dollars in the name of her two sons. She'd probably imagined it helping just the one person, but in fact it had done so much more.

"I bought four blankets with your money," I told her, happily. "That's two families in Hesar Shahee who now have something to keep them warm at night. That's two families helped in the name of your two sons."

She fixed me with her smiling eyes. "God be with you in your work."

I N LOSING DASTAGIR I HAD REDISCOVERED MY HEART AND MY HUMAN soul, and my ability to care for others. And in the wilds of Afghanistan I had found my reason for living again—a reason other than making money. And I guess I had found my answer to Dastagir's question—*how much is ever enough?* There is always enough. In the West we have enough to help others. *Always.*

Dastagir always had been the social conscience of our family. A few weeks after we had first arrived in Virginia we went for an interview with Arlington Social Services. As refugees we were entitled to get benefits—chiefly food stamps, Medicaid, and accommodation vouchers—and the interviewer offered us all kinds of support.

"But we're not living on benefits," I objected. "We came here to work, not to live on charity."

"Look, you've only just arrived," the lady said. "It's to tide you over until you find something."

"Well, don't you have any jobs going here?" Dastagir asked, glancing around the chaotic office.

The lady ran her eye over Dastagir's form. "But you don't have any experience in social work."

"So what?" Dastagir smiled. "I'll get some. Anyway, I've got a master's degree from the American University in Beirut."

The lady shrugged. "Okay, I'll look into it."

Two weeks later Dastagir was sitting in a seat in that office doing the same job as the interviewer. Every day he spoke to those in society most in need, and he was plugged right in to their suffering. By the time I'd gotten busy with my Realtor work, selling property to affluent Americans, it felt as if we were leading two separate lives. We lived and worked in two different worlds, and they rarely, if ever, coincided.

I knew that Dastagir's dream car was a black Honda Accord. He had a picture of one pinned to his office wall. One day I decided to buy him that car. I'd had a good month, with the checks from the real estate business rolling in. I got the Honda delivered to the house, called Dastagir outside, and revealed the gleaming black vehicle to him with a flourish.

We still had Bob Pick's old Chevy. It leaked, and the heater didn't work, and in winter the water would turn to ice beneath our feet. But even after I bought him that gleaming Honda, Dastagir continued to take that wreck of a Chevy to work. I couldn't understand it. He had a lovely new car, yet he kept driving that wreck.

One day I had it out with him. "I brought you a brand-new car, but you refuse to drive it to work. How many other men have wives who can buy them these kinds of things?"

Dastagir sighed. "Look, the parking lot is full of rusty old vehicles. Where am I going to park a brand-new Honda? The Chevy blends in just fine."

One day Mariam and I decided to finish that old Chevy once and for all. We waited until Dastagir had gone to bed, and then we put the garden hose through the car window. I set my bedside alarm to get me up early, and we left the water running all night long. Before anyone was awake I went out and removed the hose.

The instant Dastagir left for work, Mariam and I ran to the window to watch. He opened the Chevy door, and a deluge of water gushed over him. He stood there in total shock and disbelief. I could see the expression on his face: *what the hell?* A moment later he was standing before us, dripping wet and angry.

"You know, this is the nastiest thing that you have ever done!" he announced. "You know that?"

Mariam couldn't hold it in any longer. "But, Dad, your new car has been sitting there for months, and you never drive it!"

Dastagir turned on his heel and left, slamming the door behind him. He hailed a cab and made his way to work that way. Thankfully, by the time he was home that evening, things had calmed down a little.

"What possessed you to do that?" he asked me. "We could have given that car to charity. I mean, do you remember how much it cost us?"

"Sure I remember. Bob Pick Chevrolet. Nine thousand dollars and eighteen percent interest. But it's been a long time."

"Yeah, but you don't change cars like you change shoes. You know, there's people I meet at work who don't have . . ."

I covered my ears. "Look, I don't want to hear about all those people on welfare. They aren't us, okay?"

For a few weeks the Chevy sat outside the house. From the outside it still looked okay, but inside it was getting more and more moldy. Finally this guy came around with a delivery from Pizza Hut, and I caught him eyeing the Chevy.

"You know, that car's been sitting there for months," I told him. "Why don't you take it? Make me an offer."

He circled the car a couple of times, swung the door open, then turned to stare at me in disgust.

"My God . . . what have you done to it?"

I tried not to laugh. "It got wet."

"Well, the most I can offer is one hundred and fifty dollars."

"Deal," I declared. "Tell you what. Next Tuesday, you bring us one hundred fifty dollars' worth of pizza and we'll call it quits, okay?"

The guy grinned. "Sure. You got yourself a deal, lady."

The following Tuesday was a big family gathering. Most of my folks were there, along with most of Dastagir's. At seven-thirty, the doorbell rang. The pizza guy was there with thirty pizzas.

Outside I handed the guy the keys. "Enjoy the car," I whispered. "And do me a favor: drive it away quietly, okay?"

"Sure thing," he replied. "Enjoy the pizza party!"

It was around midnight when people started to leave. Dastagir and I came out to see everyone off, and it was then when he noticed the Chevy was gone.

"Where's the car?" he asked. "The Chevy. You finally gave it to charity, did you?"

"No. I got a load of pizza for it."

Dastagir did a double take. "You swapped the Chevy for some pizza? You sold a nine-thousand-dollar car for thirty pizzas?"

By now everyone but Dastagir had started laughing. He protested for a while longer, but eventually he joined in. He was still trying to be angry, but he just couldn't manage it. Even he could see the funny side of swapping Bob Pick's Chevy for an armful of pizza.

WE'D FOUNDED HTAC IN DECEMBER 1993. NOW, AFTER COMPLETing my first Afghan aid trip, I decided to take the plunge and rent an office in a raggedy old Virginia high-rise. It was ten feet by ten feet, and

I nicknamed it "The Bunker." It didn't have any windows, and you could barely swing a cat in there. There was a table, a chair, and an electric typewriter that switched between English and Dari typeface.

I placed a sign saying HTAC above the door. I didn't want to write the name out in full, for I guessed that no one else in the block would know where Afghanistan was. In any case, I wanted to blend in. "HTAC" could be any kind of small company, and right now it was just a one-person show—me.

The highlight of my day at The Bunker was the mail. I got into the habit of scrutinizing the envelopes to try to work out which contained the checks. Those got opened first, and the last were the bills. HTAC had no regular income, and with the Aria Clinic I'd committed to a $50,000 yearly expense, plus I was also trying to raise funds for my next aid mission.

Small donations trickled in from a community that was far from wealthy. Month by month, I kept dipping into my own savings, and I was painfully aware that I wasn't selling fine properties to rich folks anymore. Once the money was gone, it was gone. I started to lose heart. I was working harder than I ever had at the height of my Realtor days, yet the money I was bringing in was a pittance in comparison. On the anniversary of Dastagir's death, I began to seriously question whether I could carry on.

At times I wondered if I shouldn't go back to working as a Realtor, and then I could donate big chunks of money to needy Afghans. But there was simply no one else doing the kind of work that I was. No one was going inside, to the heart of my country's suffering. Plus I had so many people in Peshawar depending on me—both within the clinic, and within the refugee population that it was serving. Dozens of people were dependent on me for their salaries, and tens of thousands were depending on me for their health care.

It was hard to keep positive and motivated, but I couldn't let people know that I was struggling. I wasn't established enough to show any frailties. HTAC needed me to be absolutely self-assured and resolute. I had to wear a mask of total certainty, for if there was one thing I'd learned during my Realtor days, it was that nothing succeeds like success. But in reality, I was growing more and more fearful of failing.

I T WAS NOVEMBER 1994 AND APPROACHING THE END OF THE month—the time for paying bills. Once again I needed to dip into my savings, but there wasn't a great deal left anymore. I placed a calculator on the desk and decided to crunch some numbers. The clinic was seeing some 2,500 refugees per month. I divided that by the time I spent locked in The Bunker. I calculated that for every hour worked I helped fifteen people.

Fifteen people per hour. I asked myself was it worth it, and I decided that it was. Knowing that made it all seem worthwhile, and I didn't lose heart. Savings or no savings, I would get on with organizing my next mission. I planned to go to Kabul, the war-torn city from where Fatima, and thousands like her, had fled. By doing so I would fulfill the pledge that I had made at the end of my first mission—to see what good HTAC might do there.

No commercial airliners were flying into Afghanistan, so the only possible route in was through Pakistan, via Peshawar, then on to Jalalabad and Kabul. I spread the word among my regular supporters, and I promised to take their donations into the very heart of our nation's pain. They knew that Kabul was a cauldron of terrible suffering, and they redoubled their efforts to give.

Before leaving the United States, I bought a long black coat that fell to my ankles, a pair of flat shoes, and a large black *chadar*. This time I wanted to blend in. That shapeless black trench coat was only one step away from the burka, and it was the armor behind which I intended to hide my "Western" identity, my apprehension, and my fear.

In many ways, during my first trip to Afghanistan, ignorance had been bliss. Now I knew what I was heading into. Kabul was being ground to dust in a paroxysm of mindless brutality and hatred. And when I contemplated the journey before me, a part of me was terrified.

SEVEN

City of Ghosts

UPON REACHING PESHAWAR I HEADED TO THE CLINIC TO SEE DR. Abdullah and Nawabi. I hoped that at least one of them might accompany me on my mission. But my two most trusted advisers were aghast when I suggested going to Kabul. Every sane person was fleeing from that war-torn city, so why on earth did I want to head into the anarchy and mayhem?

No one had accurate figures, but best estimates were that sixty thousand people had died in Kabul under the assault of the warring militias. Dr. Abdullah and Nawabi pleaded with me not to go. A day didn't go by in Kabul without the militias pounding one another with bullets and bombs. Why risk all that? With the $35,000 that I had brought I could found another clinic, and I could do so much more that way.

They'd used the same argument to try to dissuade me from going to Hesar Shahee. I couldn't shake the image of thousands upon thousands of Fatimas trapped in the war-torn city of Kabul. I redoubled my resolve, and I begged them to help me find a way.

"Well, I have heard of people hiring a car to drive the road to Kabul," Dr. Abdullah conceded. "But the risks are simply too great."

"And remember," Nawabi added. "You have thirty-five thousand dollars to take with you. The looting on that road is horrendous, and if anyone so much as suspects what you are carrying. . . . Well, I shudder to think about what will happen to you."

"Okay, so if I hire a car and hide the cash, will one of you at least come with me?" I really did not want to set out on another journey into Afghanistan alone.

"In all honesty I can't say that I'd like to," Dr. Abdullah answered. "But it isn't even an option. Nawabi and I are busy every day running the clinic."

I knew he was right. Running the clinic was taking up all of their time, and it was wrong for me to ask them to turn away from their work here.

"If you are determined, you will need protection," said Nawabi. "And there are two people here we trust absolutely. Perhaps they can see you safely to Kabul."

Nawabi called the two men in to see us. One, Farid, looked to be in his midtwenties, and he was a guard at the clinic. Crucially, he was Pashtun, which meant he stood a good chance of getting us through the tribal areas. The other, Sekander, was in his early thirties and was in charge of the clinic's security. He hailed from the north of Afghanistan and had served with Ahmad Shah Massoud's Mujahideen fighting the Soviets. Sekander would provide the military expertise in case things went against us.

I could tell from the start that the two men were very different. Farid was fiery and talkative, and within no time he was bragging about our mission taking aid to Kabul. Sekander was the opposite. He was cool and calm, and always on the alert. At all times he carried a concealed weapon, and his presence gave me a certain peace of mind.

I changed the dollars into a sackload of rupees. The only way to carry the money was to hide it in money belts under our clothes. There was too much for me alone, so I split it into three bundles. I wasn't particularly comfortable with having Farid and Sekander each take a third of the cash, but Dr. Abdullah's and Nawabi's trust in them gave me some peace of mind. Still, I knew how easy it would be for them to steal the money.

On the road to Jalalabad, we paid a little "tax" to pass each checkpoint. My experience of being here with Naqibullah helped me deal with the militia. I understood them now, their privations, their blindness, and their hunger. Each was a potential Naqibullah, and I told myself that when the war was over, I would return here and build schools for these teenage gunmen.

The road beyond Jalalabad was a complete unknown. We formed a convoy with others traveling to Kabul, seeking safety in numbers. As with

Sekander, most of the men seemed to be armed. Our route would take us through Sarobi—the place where Fatima had been robbed of her wedding ring—territory ruled by the notorious Gulbuddin Hekmatyar and his militia. This was the one place that the locals warned us about above all others. "God be with you," they said, "but Sarobi is the place where no one is spared."

It was late afternoon by the time we neared Sarobi. The Mujahideen had imposed a curfew, and with the sun sinking behind the mountains this was where we called a halt. The final stretch of road from here to Kabul was known as "sniper alley," and any vehicles traveling after dark would almost certainly get shot to pieces. There was a horrid atmosphere to this place, a dark and suffocating tension. Even so, I must have dropped off, for I awoke around four in the morning to see that figures were stirring all around me.

The men lined up on the roadside, facing west, and in the ominous darkness they went about their morning prayers. Once they were done we reformed our convoy, bunching the cars closer together, and set off into the half-dawn. Hekmatyar's militia base lay just ahead of us, and the entire convoy had decided to run the gauntlet by speeding past without stopping. Whatever happened, we were to keep driving.

Farid and Sekander mumbled their prayers on either side of me, and that alone indicated how worried they were. We rounded a bend in the road, and there was Hekmatyar's base. I stared out at the buildings from which I was certain the attack would come. I tensed, expecting to hear the harsh rattle of gunfire, but the seconds went by, and still no bullets came. We gunned the vehicles' engines, and unbelievably we passed by Hekmatyar's base unscathed.

Unknown to us, Hekmatyar's militiamen had been attacked by a rival faction, and they'd suffered horrendous casualties. Hekmatyar was too busy patching up his wounded men to worry about our convoy, so we passed by his lair unnoticed and unmolested.

We threaded our way along sniper alley and into the tunnels that provide a route through the mountains that encircle Kabul, at the end of which an empty, ghostly vista opened before us. Where once had stood the city of Kabul, barely a tree or wall was left standing. Grand buildings had been reduced to empty skeletons. Whole streets had been pounded into dust. Entire neighborhoods had been flattened into shapeless heaps of rubble. And it was deathly quiet. Not a soul seemed to be moving.

Sekander glanced at me, worriedly. "We will make for my place?" he queried.

I nodded. I had nowhere else to go in this city that had been my home for so many years.

We reached Sekander's house around ten in the morning. It was a low, dun-colored building of mud bricks with a wall around the outer compound. No sooner had we set foot inside than I heard this weird, high-pitched screaming cutting through the air. The noise was terrifying, and instinctively I knew that it spelled danger.

Sekander pulled me onto the floor. "Down! Get down! And stay away from the windows!"

Moments later the air erupted as a series of explosions tore into the city. The rockets—for rockets they were—slammed into streets and buildings all around us. I cowered on the floor, hands covering my ears, as blast after blast tore the air from my lungs. In between the rolling explosions and the ghost train howl of the next incoming barrage, I heard this unearthly screaming as women and children cried out in terror.

For forty-five minutes the rockets rained down. All of a sudden they stopped, and for a moment there was a ringing silence. It didn't last. Sekander's house was situated at the base of a mountain, one that houses the main television and radio stations. A hail of bullets started pounding out of positions all around the summit. The guns boomed and roared, their staccato beat rapping out a deadly rhythm that echoed across the lifeless city.

I was in tears now. I was crying in fear and confusion. But most of all I was crying for all that Kabul had lost. Everything—my childhood freedom and happiness, the harmony and peace—all of it was gone. I felt such an incredible sadness in my heart.

Finally the pounding of the guns petered out into a deathly quiet. I turned to Sekander. "Who are these people?" I whispered. "What in God's name are they doing?"

"In Kabul, there is no place to hide. This is why we tried to stop you. But we couldn't seem to make you understand."

He moved me a little nearer to the window. Thick plumes of smoke and dust hung over those parts of the city where the rockets and bullets had hit.

"Keep back," he cautioned. "But look: Ahmad Shah Massoud is on Koh-e Televisione—Television Mountain. Mr. Sayaaf is in the Silo Area; Silo Street, around there." We shifted slightly so another sector of the blasted city became visible. "On the western side the head of the Hazara group, Mazari. And General Dostum is around the eastern edge, there."

He drew me away from the window. "Those are the four main Mujahideen factions. Then as you know there is Gulbuddin Hekmatyar at Sarobi. Hekmatyar's waiting to clean up, when all the other factions have fought themselves to exhaustion. It's Hekmatyar's rockets that are leveling the city. That's what you heard when we arrived."

I could barely comprehend what Sekander was telling me. Five warlords were locked into a full-scale battle for control of Kabul. They were firing indiscriminately, and anything—schools, hospitals, clinics—could be hit. These were the same Mujahideen leaders who had heroically driven the Soviet Red Army from our land, but now they were bombing Kabul without the slightest concern for civilian casualties.

What could I possibly achieve in the face of such wanton destruction? People couldn't even live here, yet somehow I had imagined I could *deliver aid.* I spent the entire morning paralyzed with fear. I cried for hours. Sekander and Farid must have been wondering what on earth to do with me. I had been horribly arrogant forcing them to bring me here, and I wondered what my hosts must think of me now.

"Here, you'd best take these," Sekander announced, handing me the money belts. "As a woman there's less chance of you being searched."

"It's safer that way," Farid added. "For you and for us."

"There's no point coming all this way to lose the money," Sekander added. He tried an encouraging smile. "Fat lot of good we'll have been as your bodyguards then."

The simple act of them returning the money gave me a huge boost. I knew that I was with people who were utterly decent and caring. It would have been so easy for them to steal the cash and abandon me, and there would have been absolutely nothing that I could have done about it.

"So what should we do now?" I asked Sekander.

"We wait," he replied. "We can't move when there's fighting. For two days we lie low and wait."

"Why two days?" I asked. "What will happen then?"

"There's a holy day coming up. If they stop the fighting, we can get out and see the city, and try to work out what we can do."

"Do you really think we can do anything? Among all of this?"

"I am a soldier," said Sekander. "When it came to defending my country against the Soviets, I killed. I killed the Russians. But when it comes to the sort of killing you are seeing now, I could never do it. I am ashamed of what the Mujahideen are doing. Like many Mujahids, I knew this war for power would tear the country apart. I fought for what I believed in, and I do not believe in this war for power. So now I have to fight against it. And if there is a way in which we can do that, Suraya-*jan*, by helping the victims here in Kabul, then, God willing, we will find that way."

I smiled. For the first time in many hours I felt hopeful.

"In two days," Sekander added, getting to his feet, "I think we can move and see what we may do in this city. My wife is now preparing tea and something to eat. We must stay strong for the days ahead."

I was brought into the largest of three rooms in Sekander's house—a reception area for guests with colorful cushions scattered on the floor. The walls were painted sky blue, and the entire room was scrupulously clean. In the center was a bright red Afghan rug that blazed like the setting sun.

Sekander's wife's name was Surat Begum, which means "the beautiful-faced lady." She placed bowls of fresh bread, salad, and rice on the floor, and as we ate, Sekander told me some of their life story.

In the immediate aftermath of the Soviet withdrawal, Afghanistan had been swept up in a wave of optimism and hope, a moment when everything good had seemed possible. "At that time my father told me it was time to settle," Sekander recounted. "I was the eldest son, and before he died he wanted to see me married. I chose to marry my cousin. We had always been close, and it was a match to which all agreed. We came and set up home here in Kabul, believing that peace had come to our country."

Sekander shrugged. He left the rest unsaid. It had proved to be a hollow hope. Far more people had been killed in Kabul during the few years of Mujahideen infighting than during the long war against the Soviet invaders.

Sekander earned around one hundred dollars a month working in the Aria Clinic. It was a good wage at the time, but was probably not enough, considering what people had to be paying for food in blasted Kabul. After the meal I tried offering Sekander some money to help pay for the food.

"You are our guest," Sekander remarked, simply. "You can stay for as long as you wish, and you will never pay for anything. You will not insult us."

A little later I tried giving the money directly to his wife. She gazed at the cash longingly, but shook her head.

"I can't, Suraya-*jan*. If he found out he would be so angry. It is an embarrassment even to refuse. Please don't tempt me."

This was the Afghan way. It was one that I knew and loved, yet still it amazed me that this family's open generosity had survived in a city torn apart by war. I had feared that the ancient traditions had died. But far from it—or at least not in Sekander's household.

In the Afghanistan of my memory, the graciousness one should show to guests was inviolable. If you went to a place in peace and asked the community for sanctuary, then they would die to protect you. No matter what your religion, color, or creed, if you asked for protection, you would receive it. The dishonor of allowing a visitor to be harmed would be worse than dying.

Just as Sekander had predicted, on our third day in Kabul the guns mostly fell silent. Now and again the odd crack of gunfire rang out across the city, but mostly all was quiet. Sekander explained those occasional gunshots as snipers defending their territory. Not everyone put down their weapons just because it was a holy day.

Sekander suggested we hire a taxi and head for Karte Se and Karte Char, in the southwest of the city, two of the worst-hit areas. As we ventured onto the streets I caught sight of the odd scurrying figure searching for provisions—women trying to stock up before the next bout of fighting began.

We drove along streets that had been so utterly torn apart that one pile of rubble looked pretty much like the next. This wasn't the place where I had grown up. This blasted, cratered emptiness was a million miles away from the city that I had known.

Eventually I spotted something that I did recognize. "Oh my God, that's Kabul University, my old college!"

Sekander glanced at it, then at the menacing mountain heights that lay beyond it. "Well, maybe we shouldn't go there today."

As far as I was concerned, I was under Sekander's orders. He was trying to gauge the threat and avoid the most dangerous areas. We drove on in silence. The quiet settled over us, deep and heavy and suffocating. The voice of the city—the buzz and hum of cars and trucks and people—had been utterly silenced, as if all life had been snuffed out.

We reached an area that looked vaguely familiar, and I realized that we were nearing the house in which one of my older sisters had lived, immediately after getting married. She had fled the country like me, and was now living in Pakistan. I asked the driver to slow the car, and there it was. But now it was a burned-out, gutted ruin, the windows devoid of glass like sightless eyes. I was tempted to ask the driver to stop, but then Sekander stiffened with the crack of a bullet snapping past us.

"Stay in the car!" Sekander ordered. Then, to the cabbie, "Go! Keep driving."

There was an edge of panic to his voice. I glanced around myself, fearfully. The driver gunned the engine, and the growl of the motor all but drowned out the crack of a second bullet zipping past. Something told me that those shots were close, and that they were aimed at us.

We turned a corner. A bizarre scene confronted us. Ahead a pack of dogs was snarling and fighting, dragging something back and forth between them. They completely blocked our way.

"My God, all these dogs!" I blurted out. "What is this? It can't be for real."

"Look, they don't want their enemies to collect their dead," Sekander snapped. His voice was thick with tension. "They shoot at each other when they go out to collect their dead."

He signaled for the driver to turn the car around.

"But what's that got to do with the dogs?"

"They shoot at each other, so no one goes out to collect the dead. The bodies lie in the streets. . . ."

Before Sekander could finish there was a horrible, unearthly howling. I turned my head to look. There were shoes and hats and coats lying in a shapeless heap on the road, among a melee of slavering dogs. And then I realized that the piles of clothing were actually bodies, and that the dogs were yelping as they tore them apart and feasted upon the flesh.

"Cover your eyes," Sekander urged, indicating my black *chadar*. "Cover your eyes, *Saheb*-ma'am. You do not want to see these things."

I started to throw up. I vomited out the cab's open window, retching onto the road. In seconds my guts were empty, and I was heaving up bile.

"Get us away from here," I whispered, pulling my *chadar* over my head.

Sekander told the cabbie to drive. Eventually, I heard him ask: "Is there anywhere you want to go? Your old family home maybe. . . ."

I shook my head, keeping it covered. "No. Just take me back to your place."

At that moment I would have loved nothing more than to be back in my apartment in Virginia, far away from this sick and inhuman hell. I had never imagined such cruelty and horror could exist. I hated the Mujahideen. I hated and loathed them for what they had done to this city—to my city—and its people.

The following day Sekander managed to find us a route through Kabul to my old family home. No one would mistake us for body collectors in this neighborhood, so there was no sniping. We stopped the car just outside the ruins of the gate. I stood there, gazing in, and I felt only despair and bleak desolation. Where once had stood grand walls and beautiful gardens, there was now only a tumbled heap of shattered rubble.

Sekander warned me not to go farther. The warring factions were in the habit of planting mines among the devastation. I glanced up the street to the place where the ice cream shop had once stood. My sisters and I used to sneak out of the house when my parents were napping and make a rush for the ice cream parlor. The owners knew us well, for we were the governor's daughters, and we were some of their best customers. All that now remained of the ice cream shop was an enormous, jagged bomb crater.

As we drove away from the ruin of my old home, I caught that dreaded noise again—a high-pitched screaming that tore the air apart. The taxi driver skidded to a halt as the barrage of rockets started to slam into the city. All around us there was the flash and roar of explosions, as missile after missile tore into whatever they had hit. We had just reached Pul-e Surkh—the Red Bridge—and we were completely in the open.

"You said it was going to be three days with no fighting!" I yelled at Sekander as we jumped out of the vehicle.

"I said the holy day lasts for three days," Sekander yelled back at me. "But I don't know their schedule."

Our only option was to take cover beneath the bridge. The riverbed was dry, its rocky surface strewn with garbage and God knows what else. We crouched in the shadows, flinching with every blast. All we could do was hope and pray that a rocket didn't score a direct hit on the bridge.

As we cowered beneath the explosions, I started to have this bizarre out-of-body experience, as if I were flying above the burning city. I could still see my body crouching in the rubble beneath the bridge, but my spirit was flying high above and somehow immune to everything. I guess this was my mind's way of getting me through the sheer terror of it all.

For three hours the rockets smashed into the city, and the earth shook beneath our feet. At dusk the barrage finally petered out. We made our way back to Sekander's house in a shell-shocked silence. Three times we had had a lucky escape: first, in the rocket barrage that had greeted our arrival in Kabul; second, getting sniped at; and now caught in a rocket barrage again. We might not be so fortunate next time.

All I could now think of doing was getting the hell out of Kabul. Dr. Abdullah and Nawabi had been right: my hopes of taking aid into this city had been naive in the extreme. Anyone trying to undertake aid deliveries here would be lucky to survive just a few days. As it was, I knew the worst images from the Kabul streets would haunt me for the rest of my life.

We left Kabul the following morning. The gods must have been with us, for we made it back to Peshawar without being robbed, kidnapped, or killed. I tried giving Sekander two hundred dollars' worth of rupees, to help cover the costs of hosting me, but he just kept telling me not to insult him. So I gave the cash to Dr. Abdullah, who promised to get Sekander to accept it come what may. I deposited the rest of the money that I had raised into our Peshawar bank account. At least it would finance the clinic for several months.

I had a few days left in Peshawar before my return flight to America, and I wanted to see Nasreen. I wondered if she had recaptured some of her joy in life, now that she was out of the widow camps. I hoped so. After the failure of my Kabul mission, I needed something to lift my spirits. We met at the clinic and took a tray of tea things into the garden. She didn't look particularly different from when last I had seen her, but I hoped in talking she might come alive.

"So, how're you doing?" I asked her. "How's the new place?"

"You know, with this money you send me, three families can survive. Three families could live on it. I tell you, three families."

Nasreen was being very insistent. It was almost as if she was angry with me for sending her the money, for needing to survive on the charity of an old college friend.

I tried to lighten the mood a little. "You remember how wild we were at college? Remember all those crazy things we got up to?"

For a moment the faint flicker of a smile pulsed across Nasreen's features.

"You were the real crazy one," she murmured. "You and Dastagir—you were too wild. You guys were the most notorious couple in college, with your freewheeling romance."

I laughed. "But surely you must've had a man? A guy in secret you never told me about? A handsome college boy?"

"Well, none of that matters now. . . ."

Nasreen's voice tailed off. I could see an indescribable pain in her eyes. The sense of all that was lost was just too much for her. It wasn't as if she was able to cry or grieve, for she was locked in a place beyond mourning. I tried to think of something else to talk about. I tried asking her about life before, but even as I did so I remembered what Dr. Abdullah had told me about the widow camps.

"Things happened in the camp," Nasreen murmured. "To me. To my daughters. Shameful things."

"What things?" I probed, gently. "What happened to your girls?"

She looked at me, then away. No words came. A shutter had fallen across her face, and that small flash of light that I had seen was gone. If I couldn't talk about the past, and I couldn't talk about her present, then she and I had nothing. In spite of our shared upbringings, our lives were worlds apart.

I didn't want Nasreen to see me just as a source of charity. I wanted her to see me as a friend, and I wanted to really help her. In theory, she could still do something with her life. She was a university graduate with a degree in English—a rare and valuable thing here. Yet she was broken and entombed within her shame. She sat in that garden vulnerable and alone, just waiting for a strong wind to take her.

That evening I spoke to Dr. Abdullah about her. Maybe there was some way she could get treatment. Maybe some kind of therapy. It wasn't impossible, Dr. Abdullah told me, but he suspected that there were deeper, hidden traumas that Nasreen might never be willing to reveal. He would do what he could, but he couldn't make any promises.

A victim needs to take the first step, which is wanting to be healed, and Dr. Abdullah didn't think that Nasreen was ready. She had pretty much given up on life, and even Dr. Abdullah's gentle kindness might fail to reach her. Nasreen had a pulse, and she breathed, but she was dead inside. Who had I been kidding when I'd thought I might cure her through our friendship?

I left Peshawar feeling really, really low. My Kabul mission had been a failure. I had gone in with a mission to help the thousands of Fatimas trapped in that benighted city. Instead I had cowered beneath the bullets and the bombs, and run from the dark horrors that I had found there.

By not doing what I had promised to do, I had failed those in America who had given me their money. And if there was one thing that I was unaccustomed to in life, it was failure.

EIGHT

A Promise to Fatima

ON MY LONG FLIGHT BACK TO THE UNITED STATES I HAD PLENTY of time to contemplate my failure. I had made a promise to my donors that I would take hope into the heart of warring Kabul, and I had failed to do so. And deep within myself I had made a promise to Fatima, one that I had also failed to keep.

I wasn't used to failure. Rebellion: yes. Likewise defiance against mindless authority. But even during the wildest days of my youth my willfulness was never compounded by failure. My high school teachers may have cursed me for my rebellious spirit, but I had always managed to distinguish myself academically.

My school—Rabia Balki High—was one of the largest in Kabul, with over four thousand pupils. It was very much like any Western school, with smart, modern buildings, including a pharmacy, science laboratories, a library, and basketball courts. What I had rebelled against was the school system, and the emphasis it placed upon learning by rote.

One day in history class we were learning about an Afghan "hero" called Sultan Mahmood. He had taken an army to invade India and sack Delhi. There he had seized vast quantities of jewelry and gold, and he had desecrated all that was sacred to the Indians—their Buddhist temples and their Hindu shrines. In the previous week's lesson we had learned about Ghengis Khan, a Mongol leader who had invaded Afghanistan. He had been portrayed as a war criminal.

The teacher asked various pupils to repeat what she had just been telling us about Sultan Mahmood. I hadn't bothered to take any notes, and I announced that I had a question to ask instead. I saw her eyebrows knit together in disapproval, but I ploughed ahead anyway.

"Why is it that Sultan Mahmood is a hero and Ghengis Khan a villain, when they both invaded and looted someone else's country?"

"Isn't it obvious?" the teacher snapped. "Sultan Mahmood was a hero because he was spreading Islam."

"Well, Ghengis Khan is someone's hero," I countered. "I bet you see his statue all over his country. And I bet Sultan Mahmood is seen as a murderer in India."

The teacher was incandescent with rage. Such comments were close to heresy as far as she was concerned. All that the teachers ever wanted us to do was to write down what they said, memorize it, and repeat. At Rabia Balki, an independent, inquiring mind was seen as a dangerous thing.

By far my worst confrontations were with my Koran teacher. She and I were at loggerheads from the very start. Our Koran studies were about one thing only—memorizing verses of the Koran in Arabic. The teacher was a short, ugly woman with an evil temper. She carried this thick wooden ruler and was forever beating pupils. I had developed a stutter in my early teens, and the words I found most difficult were those beginning with the guttural "kha" sound. It is common in Arabic, and reciting the Koran was sheer torture for me.

One boiling hot July day I found myself stuck in Koran lessons. I couldn't wait for class to end and to go home. I'd chosen to sit near the back, in the hope that the teacher wouldn't pick on me to recite. I was whispering with one of my friends, and all of a sudden the teacher was beside me.

"Get up!" she yelled. "Get up and read this *Surah*."

I got to my feet, and a row of faces turned toward me. My classmates started making silly faces behind the teacher's back in an effort to make me laugh.

"In the name of God the most merciful and the most wise . . . ," I began. But just as soon as I hit my first "kha" I stumbled. "Kha . . . Kha . . . Kha . . ." I kept trying to say it, but the word was stuck on the end of my tongue.

The entire class was laughing. Teacher stuck her face into mine, her cheeks puffed and red with rage.

"You are making fun of the holy Koran!" she screamed. "How dare you? For this you will burn in hell, you hear me?"

I nodded. I was trying not to laugh. I could feel the rebellion and the mirth bubbling up inside me, especially as my classmates kept making silly faces over the teacher's shoulder.

"Get up!" she ordered.

I glanced around me. "Up where? I'm already standing."

"Up on your desk!" she cried.

I did as ordered. "Not good enough," teacher snapped.

"Well, where else do you want me to go?" I countered.

"Up on one leg! Now!"

I got onto one leg, the whole class rocking with laughter as I did so. I was wearing what we girls called a "miniskirt," but it actually ended just above the knee. Teacher rapped me across my bare knees.

"Oh, so you have all this high fashion showing off your legs," she raged, "but you can't learn the holy Koran!"

One of my friends began imitating me, going "Kha . . . Kha . . . Kha . . ." The refrain was taken up by more of the students, and soon the entire class was barking away. Teacher whirled around in an effort to nail the culprits, but just as soon as she did so, everyone fell silent. She whirled back again, her face twisted with fury.

"If you think because you're the governor's daughter you can get away with this, think again!" she spluttered. "I don't care who your father is!"

What's this got to do with my father? I thought. The Koran teacher made me stand on one leg until the bell rang at the end of class. It was such a relief to escape from such utter mindlessness and go home.

My father's workload was heavy, and more often than not my mother was busy with her social activities. Consequently I spent a lot of time with my nanny. In fact I even called her *"moma,"* the word for "mom" in Dari. Nanny hailed from a wild and rugged part of northern Afghanistan called the Panjshir—Lion—Valley. She was fearless, and my parents used to complain that I got my rebellious ways from her. In secret, Nanny used to approve of my being naughty. "That's my girl," she'd tell me.

One day Nanny took me to her rural home, where we were welcomed like royalty. A river ran through the village, the banks of which were lined with weeping willows. It was such a romantic, magical setting. Of course, I was a city girl afraid of everything, but Nanny was completely in her element. She trapped a snake and whirled it around and around her head. She caught scorpions by the tail and thrust them in my terrified face.

By the time I was in my teens my rebelliousness was at its zenith. I'd started to steal my father's cigarettes. Whenever he went to the bathroom I'd take one and hide it in my clothing. I'd bring it to school, and some other girls and I would go into one of the smelly old bathrooms to light up. We'd pass the cigarette around, each taking a puff, which was the height of cool.

Of course, Nanny quickly realized what I was up to, and I used to believe that my smoking was a special secret I shared with her. When my younger sisters were old enough, I tried to get them into smoking too. One day I was in the garden showing them how to puff on one of our father's cigarettes. Out of nowhere he appeared, and I had to stuff the lighted cigarette into my pocket.

He offered a friendly greeting, as if he hadn't noticed a thing. But as he went to pass me he bent and whispered: "That thing is going to burn a hole in your pocket."

I was mortified. One moment I'd been laughing and joking with my sisters, and feeling so grown up, the next my father had brought me down to earth with a crash. I'd always thought he was too busy to know what I was up to, and I didn't feel so smart now.

I filled the boredom of my school hours with reading. I'd sit at the back of the class with a book hidden under the desk. My early favorite was Mickey Spillane, who wrote detective thrillers set in the United States. They were boys' books, really, and I thrilled to their action and their drama. But reading trashy novels wouldn't get me through my exams.

I once reached an end-of-year exam time with practically no notes to study from. There was a class grind called Karima, and I noticed she'd left her school bag unattended. I fished out her notebook and dropped it into my own bag. I felt bad at having stolen it, but I told myself it was either that or fail.

I spent the entire night cramming, reading her notes, which she'd written neatly, in two colors: red for the title, blue for the main text. The next morning Karima turned up for the exams with red, puffy eyes. I just knew she'd been crying over her missing notebook.

A few days after the exams I confessed to her. "Karima, I need to apologize. I stole your notebook."

"I knew it!" she cried. "I swear to God I knew it was you! You never pay attention to anything but still you passed. I knew it was you. *I knew it.*"

"Well, what did you expect me to do?" I countered. "I had no notes to study from. And you should have kept your bag safely by your side."

"You mean you have the right to steal it, if I don't look after it!"

"Here's your notebook." I held it out to her, like a peace offering.

"Shove it! I don't need it. I passed anyway, 'cause I knew it all by heart."

"See. I knew you didn't need it. It was so neat it was really easy to use."

"How would you know? You can't even read properly. All you ever read is those dirty books."

By that Karima meant my Mickey Spillane novels. My father was always nagging me to read "proper" books and to behave better at school. But I kept getting called to the headmistress's office due to my aberrant ways, and most times she would pick up the phone to my father.

"*Wali, Saheb*—Governor, Sir—I have your daughter here. I'm sorry to bother you, but Suraya-*jan*—dear Suraya—has been arguing with one of the teachers."

When I came home my father would give me the silent treatment, which killed me more than anything. I used to think: *Talk, won't you? Say something! Let's get it over with.* Finally he'd call me into his study.

"What happened at school?" he'd ask. "Why did I get a call from the headmistress?"

"Her? She's got nothing else to do. Anyway, she hates me."

My father would roll his eyes. "So why among the five thousands kids it's only you that she detests? And why can't you be like the rest of the girls?"

"Because I'm not, that's why."

I didn't want to upset my father or make him angry. I knew that he didn't approve of a lot of the things that I was doing. But deep down I sensed there was a part of him that was proud of my nonconformity. Whatever I was getting up to, I always seemed to do it with a degree of humor and charm. Perhaps that was what redeemed me in his eyes.

By the time I was eighteen I had graduated onto more serious reading and was devouring Afghan literature and poetry. Poetry holds a special place in Afghan culture, being an important part of our storytelling tradition. But my newfound love of high literature hadn't made me any more popular with my teachers.

In our final high school exams, if you scored a passing grade you could apply to go to the university. If you failed, you were barred from doing so. I did achieve a passing mark, and in the university entrance exams that followed I was placed third highest in all of Kabul. No one could believe it, least of all the school principal.

"As far as I'm concerned you didn't deserve to pass your high school exams," she told me. "You never did a day's work, and your behavior and dress have been appalling. As for your university entrance exams . . ." She shook her head despairingly, taking a last disapproving look at my short skirt. "Well it's good riddance. Let's see what college can make of you."

In fact I thrived in the free atmosphere at Kabul University, and I became accustomed to a life in which I didn't fail. I didn't fail academically. I didn't fail professionally. And I didn't fail to make money, particularly once we migrated to America. And so the failure of my aid mission to war-torn Kabul had hit me extra hard.

After Kabul I felt hopeless. I couldn't imagine what difference I could make in the face of the cruelty of the Mujahideen, plus the lack of concern from the world community. Yes, there were millions of innocent people trapped in that city, but not one reporter was in Kabul; not one picture filtered out of the dying city. It was almost as if the scenes that I had witnessed weren't happening on planet Earth.

Afghanistan had sacrificed one and a half million lives in the war against the Soviets. That conflict was the catalyst that brought about an end to the cold war. By December 1991 the Soviet Union collapsed, the Berlin Wall came down, and Germany was reunited. But while the rest of the world enjoyed a massive peace dividend, my country was drowning in blood. The United States had stood shoulder to shoulder with the Afghan Mujahideen while they battled the Soviets, but now America had washed its hands of the Afghan people.

After returning from that Kabul trip I spent weeks living in a kind of limbo. I couldn't shake the horrific images from my mind. Whenever I tried to talk to anyone about what I had witnessed in Kabul, they didn't appear to want to know. Neither my sisters nor my brothers seemed able to hear it. I could tell what they were thinking: *hey, don't even go there.* It wasn't fair to dump such stuff on Mariam, and I didn't even try with my mother. She hadn't approved of my going, and I didn't want to face her censure.

In short, I had no one to talk to or help me carry the burden.

I wrote angry articles for the Afghan-American newspapers. I asked: *How come Afghan-Americans marched in front of the White House against the Soviets, but now everyone is silent?* In reality things are far, far worse. But sadly, the Afghan-American community was starting to fracture along ethnic lines. It mirrored what was happening with the warlords fighting for Kabul. Dostum was an Uzbek; Mazari was Hazara; Massoud was Tajik; and Hekmatyar was a Pashtun.

I had hoped the Afghan-American community would rise above all that. I knew that I had to. HTAC had to be seen as nonpartisan; otherwise, its humanitarian mission was finished. I continued as best I could to raise money, but I was plagued by feelings of failure and betrayal.

In many ways the Mujahideen who were tearing apart Kabul were an American creation. They had been created in Pakistani training camps, using Saudi money plus American weapons and training. The Mujahideen had fought a war that no one thought could be won, and against all odds they had vanquished the Soviets. But then America chose to turn its back on its creation, leaving Afghanistan to implode as the Mujahideen fought among themselves. That was why people would eventually welcome the Taliban. They offered two things for which Afghans were desperate: peace and security.

While I had been cowering under those rocket barrages in Kabul, the Taliban were already on the rise. Their name, Taliban, means "The Students"—as in, students of the Koran. As with the Mujahideen, they were formed and shaped in Pakistan. But while the Mujahideen had been freedom fighters first and foremost, seeking to rid the country of foreign invaders, the Taliban's mission was more avowedly driven by religion. From the very first, their aim was to unite the country in peace, but under harsh Islamic Shariah law.

By the summer of 1995, about six months after my trip to Kabul, the Taliban were seizing their first swath of territory, in the far southeast of the country. Initially their coming was celebrated, for they brought about an end to the anarchy and the bloodshed. Under the Taliban there were no more militia roadblocks and looting, and no more mass killings. No more women were raped, or young girls carried off as warlord brides.

The Taliban moved through the country in a lightning swift advance. In a matter of months they were poised to take Kabul. In the autumn of 1996 the warring Mujahideen were finally driven out, and the Taliban took the city. It hardly seemed believable, but under the Taliban, blasted, war-torn Kabul became an oasis of peace. Refugees seeking sanctuary from the fighting farther north, where the Taliban sought to drive out the remnant Mujahideen forces, began flooding into Taliban-controlled Kabul.

I heard a report via the BBC's Dari Service concerning the plight of seventeen thousand of those refugees. Nearly all were women and children, and reports had them arriving in Kabul with their feet cut to shreds from the long march to escape the fighting. The Taliban had nowhere to house those desperate refugees but the vast, burned-out skeleton of the former embassy of the Soviet Union. I knew that building well, and I sensed that here was my opportunity. Here was a tragedy in the heart of Kabul crying out for humanitarian assistance. Here was a way to redeem my previous failure.

Though I knew little about the Taliban, I knew that they were students of Islam and that they were warriors. Certainly they were no aid workers. HTAC was far from flush with money, but once again people gave generously when they heard what I was planning. I begged, cajoled, and managed to raise $45,000 from our supporters—funds enough for the coming mission.

And so I set out to slay my ghosts in the city of Kabul.

PART II

Under the Iron Fist of the Taliban

1996–2001

NINE

The Tree of Amputations

I N SPITE OF THEIR MINDLESS RULES AND DICTATES, THE TALIBAN were the first to bring an end to the fighting in Afghanistan, which had lasted for almost two decades, from 1978 to 1996. I had been waiting for the moment when peace would come, so it might at last be possible to start some schools. Yet in a devastating and frustrating twist it was the Taliban who decided to ban education in my country.

Under their rule, girls were forbidden outright from going to school. The Taliban chose to misinterpret the Koran, arguing that Islam doesn't allow women to go to school, despite the fact that the Koran doesn't say that.

And in Kabul, at least, education for boys was pretty much forbidden as well. The Taliban believed that Kabul had been the crucible of corrupt, Western-influenced liberalism and debauchery, and that was what the schools there had taught. Under the Taliban, if Kabuli boys were to get an education, it would be of the "purest" kind only—learning about Islam and memorizing the Koran.

It was in meeting American aid worker Mary McMaken and Sabera, the Afghan headmistress, that all of this became clear to me. Over cups of tea and homemade cookies in Mary's Kabul kitchen we planned HTAC's first underground girls' school. I'd come around to accepting the idea of using Sabera's basement as our secret classroom, but it was the type of school textbooks available that proved the next greatest challenge.

The more I looked into what kind of textbooks were available in Kabul, the more I realized they were all related to war. Everything was about jihad, the Mujahideen, and fighting to drive out the Soviet invaders. During my youth it was three apples and two pears make five. Now it was all about three machine guns and two tanks make five. But those textbooks were the only ones available. I was torn. If we went ahead with our school we'd be using textbooks that I found abhorrent. If we didn't, we'd be depriving the girls of the gift of learning.

Eventually I decided that some education was better than no education at all. In any case, most of what we were doing under the Taliban was fudge and compromise. Our driving inspiration was to do something—anything—to oppose their mindless dicta and intolerance. We could fix the awful curriculum later. The first step was to have some schools to stand against the Taliban's blind ignorance and their war against knowledge.

I knew Sekander didn't approve of what I was doing with our school, but I needed his help. He acted as our banker in the field, and I felt comfortable, knowing that the money was safe with him.

"It looks like the school's shaping up," I told him. "So we've got to buy some school supplies. Do we have the money to do that?"

"We need it for the health clinic, Suraya-*jan*."

"Sekander, just tell me what money we have left."

He shrugged. "A little. A few thousand rupees."

"Well, guess what we're going to be doing with those few thousand rupees?"

"I know." He sighed. "Buying school supplies."

I was at the clinic later that day wondering where Sekander had gone with the money when he turned up out of nowhere and he plunked a heavy bag in front of me. "Here. I think that's about everything."

"What do you mean?" I asked.

"The things you needed for the school."

I stared at him in amazement. "You got the school supplies? But how do you know what we need?"

"Well, you need pens, pencils, erasers, rulers, and exercise books, don't you? It's all in the bag."

I looked at Sekander with speechless admiration.

"What are you staring at me and grinning for?" he asked.

"I thought you didn't approve of my school."

Sekander snorted. "Yeah—I'm just like a Taliban, right?"

I knew why Sekander had done this. He was so loyal and dedicated that he didn't want me running the risk of buying those things myself. Under the Taliban's warped rules, any woman caught in the act of buying school supplies would be arrested, beaten, or worse. Instead Sekander just did it, voluntarily, taking all the risk upon himself.

Later that week I went to visit the school in Sabera's basement. Imagine a room so dark that you can barely see your own hand. Kerosene lanterns smolder in the center of the windowless cellar, casting a pool of light over a circle of faces—all girls, all bent over fraying textbooks. The room is utterly silent. As the teacher scribbles on a battered blackboard leaning against one wall, you can hear the *scratch-scratch* of the chalk marks. This was the scene that met my eyes in our secret classroom.

Twenty girls were getting the gift of education here, something that the Taliban had stolen from them. Sabera had even arranged for the girls to arrive and leave at staggered intervals, so that they wouldn't attract unwanted attention. As I watched those lamp-lit scenes, I realized that I had never seen anyone so happy as those girls in the simple act of learning. It was almost as if they were eating the words that Sabera whispered as the chalk scratched across the blackboard, their lips silently mouthing the letters.

I knew then that I had created hope where hope had died, and given these girls the promise of a future. Running this secret school would require me to find more funding, but the costs were a pittance, really. An Afghan teacher earned about seventy-five dollars a month. With a few supplies thrown in, our total monthly costs were going to be less than one hundred fifty dollars. After seeing that first lesson, I knew that I would not let one single school fail from want of funding. I'd sell my own apartment if I had to.

That evening we celebrated founding that first HTAC school with a delicious meal. After we'd finished eating, Sekander voiced what was foremost on his mind.

"Suraya-*jan*, something bad happened today when I was buying those school things. These Taliban are very bad. Very, very bad."

I was worried that he'd got into trouble and kept it from me. "What is it, Sekander? Tell me."

"They even control the price of food, and today they were checking all the butcher shops. They came to one and asked him his price. The Taliban leader didn't like the butcher man's answer, so he whipped out this razor blade. And you know what he did? He shaved off half that butcher's beard. Even his mustache. It was so cruel. Then the Taliban said to the butcher: 'Now people will know that you did something wrong.'"

I had this image in my mind of the butcher trying to serve the rest of the day's customers with only half a beard. It was just so bizarre. I couldn't hold it in anymore—I burst out laughing.

"Imagine it!" I gasped. "The guy gets home, his wife opens the door and she exclaims—*what the heck?*"

Sekander was not amused. Like all men, he'd been forced under the Taliban to grow this thick beard, and he hated it. The Talibs carried these razor-sharp blades, and a common punishment was to shave someone's head. If your beard wasn't long enough: head shave. If your hair wasn't short enough: head shave. I hadn't the slightest clue where they got such crazed ideas. There wasn't anything even remotely Islamic about it.

"Can we get a photo of the butcher?" I asked.

Sekander glared at me. "The Taliban have banned all photography, remember?"

"You're teasing poor Sekander too much," Dr. Abdullah interjected. "What do you want a photo for anyway?"

"I'll put it in our newsletter, and then we can all kill ourselves laughing at what total goddamn idiots these Talibs are."

Beneath my humor there was real anger. The Taliban had put these insane rules in place for *themselves* first and foremost. They led by example. For reasons I found impossible to comprehend, they craved the path of ignorance. While most Afghans were desperate for education, the Taliban wanted to ban it in all meaningful forms. A series of madrassas had sprung up in and around the refugee camps in Pakistan—the key recruiting ground for the Taliban. Those madrassas brainwashed Afghan refugee kids in four things: to obey; to spurn women; to hate "infidels"; and to memorize the Koran.

Running our secret girls' schools was hugely risky. If a school was discovered, the teacher would be whipped to within an inch of her life, the girls would be savagely beaten, and even the fathers of the girls would be set upon—all because the Taliban embraced ignorance. The Taliban's war on schools was driven by fear: the fear that a little learning would challenge their rules and their hold on power. Even a basic education might give the lie to their brainwashing, so they despised knowledge and learning.

Before leaving Kabul I went to say good-bye to Mary, and to thank her for all her help in setting up HTAC's first school. She suggested a walk, and we ended up in a part of the city where the green and leafy streets had mostly survived the war. Having Mary there marked us out as foreigners, but with the Taliban in power the streets were mostly safe, as long as we didn't transgress any of their rules.

A woman approached us. I guessed from her torn and soiled burka that she had to be one of the millions left widowed by the war. She held out a hand to me, as if in supplication. I reached into my pocket for some money, but she raised her hand until it was pointing at the tree above.

"Look up," she whispered.

There was agony in those words, as if her soul were screaming. I did as she asked, yet I saw nothing but the branches of the tree spreading below a mottled green sky.

"Don't you see?" she whispered. "Are you blind?"

"No," I replied, "I'm not blind."

"Then for God's sake look and see. I cannot beg, for it's forbidden for a woman. And now they've cut off my son's hands, so how will I survive?"

"They did what?"

The woman started to wail, emitting a keening animal sound that gathered deep under the folds of her burka. It sent a horrible chill up my spine.

"Look! *Look at the tree.* There are my son's hands."

I glanced upward, and finally my eyes could see. Scores of amputated human limbs were hanging from the branches like shriveled fruit. Some were fleshy claws, turning splotchy gray as they rotted. Other were chalky white, the bones picked clean by God only knows what.

I wanted to be sick. I felt dizzy and on the verge of collapse. For an instant I had a flashback to that nightmare day when I witnessed the pack of dogs feasting on Kabul's dead. I didn't know which was worse, that unspeakable horror or this one.

I grabbed Mary's arm to stop myself from falling. I guessed she hadn't understood all that was going on, what with her broken Dari. I flailed around in my pocket and came out with a bundle of cash. I thrust it into the woman's hands, and turned and fled.

Back at Mary's house, after several cups of tea, she finally got the full story out of me. The severed hands belonged to those caught stealing, or otherwise breaking the Taliban's rules, Mary explained. Apparently the Taliban liked to show off their vile, vicious laws by hanging amputated limbs in the most public of places, so that people would see the consequences of disobeying them. Their tree of amputations was the ultimate form of intimidation and control.

Mary went to fetch something. She returned with a basket full of strange-looking dolls. I guess she was trying to get my mind off that tree of severed human limbs. She plunked the basket down on the table, then gave me this pained, haunted look.

"I'm sorry, Suraya," she murmured. "I've seen those trees before. I should have warned you before we went out. . . ."

Mary went on to explain what the basket of dolls was for. She was getting the women in her handicraft cooperative to make them, so she could sell them to Americans to put beneath their Christmas trees. But all they ever seemed to make were these grim figures in shapeless black dresses. Some were even clad in full, doll-length burkas. Those dolls were rough. They were dour. They were even a bit frightening.

"Mary, your dolls are ugly," I teased her. "Yuck! If I was a Christian and I had a tree, that's about the last thing I'd ever put under it."

She laughed. "Will you quit complaining? You know, Suraya, if you could just lend me a little cash maybe I could get them making some nicer stuff."

"Mary, if you need to borrow money, just ask. But only as long as it's not for your ugly dolls."

"Oh, I'm so embarrassed to have to ask," she equivocated. "And you know one day I will pay you back, I promise."

"Mary, just tell me what you need."

"Well, maybe just a little money to repair the leaking roof of the weaving workshop. . . ."

I guessed that I'd never see the money again, but I loved Mary, and I knew already that she was a living saint. I handed her a big bundle of bills.

She stared at the money, then at me. "Thank you, Suraya. You know something? I've just realized what you are. You're my guardian angel, that's what!"

It's funny, but some of the women at the clinic had started to call me *freshta nejat*, which in Dari means "guardian angel." Maybe they'd gotten the idea from my name: Suraya means "the highest and brightest star in the sky." But I didn't see myself as any angel. As far as I was concerned, I got more out of doing this work than it ever cost me. That didn't make me an angel; it just made me lucky.

Before I left Mary's place, she made an enigmatic comment. "You know, Suraya, there are even worse things than the tree of amputations."

Of course I had to ask what she might be referring to.

"There's an orphanage," she said. "Or at least they call it an orphanage." She told me the name of it. "It's now under the Taliban. Maybe one day you should go there."

The name stirred a vague memory. I had read about it somewhere during the Mujahideen times. I wracked my brain to remember. A newspaper article had described the horrors of an institution for orphaned kids stuck in the midst of the warring city. It had sounded terrible, and I wondered how it could be worse under the Taliban.

Right after speaking to Mary, I suggested to Sekander and Dr. Abdullah that we pay the orphanage a visit. It was easy enough to delay our departure by a day. We didn't have a great deal of money left, so we couldn't provide much in the way of help. But maybe we could do a scoping mission and return with proper assistance. Sekander went out and bought the kids some crayons and coloring books, so at least we had something to take them.

Even as we approached the orphanage in our taxi, it exuded a dark and haunting menace—the walls were bullet scarred, the glass in the dark windows splintered and broken. Qari, the man who ran the orphanage, came out to greet us. I could tell right away that he was another "Ali" figure—the guy who had been in charge of that corrupt refugee camp in Peshawar. If anything, this guy looked even worse.

He had a skeletal frame, his cheeks sunken and gray above a sparse and straggling beard. But it was his eyes that really scared me. There was something of the devil himself about them. One look and I knew that he would never be able to feel the orphans' pain, or to empathize with them.

Qari called himself a "Talib," of course. Everyone did these days. With women banned from working, it had been left to men like him to oversee the orphanage. He seemed happy enough to see us, for in his mind we had to be rich foreigners bringing funds. He led us into a room where a group of boys squatted on the floor on a few stained mattresses. There wasn't a single toy or book in the entire place, and it was filthy.

As for the orphans, they were dressed in soiled rags. They began whispering excitedly about the strangers who had come to see them. But as soon as they did so, Qari started to hit them with a thick stick. He was lashing out and yelling for quiet, and I could see right away that those boys were terrified of him.

"Stop beating them," I told him. "Stop it!"

"These are my boys," he retorted. "This is the only way to make them sit properly and keep quiet."

"Well, please don't hit them in front of me, Qari-*saheb*. I can't take it."

He laughed. "Oh, such a soft heart you have."

"I suppose your heart is of stone?"

He shrugged, kind of proudly. "I guess. I've seen a lot—yeah."

I was repulsed and disgusted by him. I crouched down and tried to say a few words to the boys. But it was obvious they were scared stiff of speaking in front of Qari. I suggested he show Sekander and Dr. Abdullah around the rest of the orphanage, leaving me to have a few minutes alone with the kids.

"I come all the way from America," I told them. "That's a country far, far away. And I've come from America to see how you're doing and how we might help."

One of the boys unfroze a little. "Where is America?" he whispered.

"What color is the sky there?" another asked.

And then the question that really broke my heart. "Do all the children there have parents?"

I had a small camera with me and I desperately wanted to take some photos of the kids. Without images, it would be so much harder to raise any money to help. But I knew the Taliban had banned all photography. I was just getting ready to snap some shots when Qari returned with the others.

"No photos!" he cried. "Surely you know Taliban don't allow it."

"I know, Qari-*saheb*." I forced a smile. I was trying to be nice to a man I absolutely loathed. "I know the Taliban don't allow it. But they're not here, are they?"

"Well, I'm here, and I can't allow it." It was like trying to melt a heart of ice.

"Well, hey—how about I take your picture?"

He shook his head, but I could see his resolve was weakening. For some reason the idea of having his ugly, twisted mug on film seemed to please him.

"Come on, Qari-*saheb*," I cajoled. "Come stand in line with the kids."

He smiled, showing his dirty yellow teeth. "Well, okay, maybe just this one time. . . ."

I framed up the photo, making sure he was well and truly cut off the end of the line.

"Wait!" Qari declared.

He pulled out a dirty brown comb and started to run it through his straggly beard. Yuck! Then he stood at attention, and I pretended I was taking his picture when really I was snapping that of the boys all around him.

Upstairs were the rooms for the girls, and if anything their situation was even worse. One little girl had been struck dumb by what she had seen. Soldiers had rushed into her house, and she had hidden in a cupboard as they raped her mother, tortured her father, and then killed them both in front of her. She was a beautiful child, but she stared at me silently with huge, deadened eyes.

My efforts to reach her met with only blank stares. I gave her some crayons, but she didn't respond. She just stared at them, lying in her hands. I realized then that it was impossible to find a way into her world. I couldn't imagine what it was like to endure that pain alone, to be locked inside a place that was a silent, shadowed skein of gray.

Qari was getting increasingly bored, and he left me to potter around the orphanage on my own. I came across an old man with a broom who had to be the caretaker. His face was wrinkled like a prune, and he was bent double, as if he had the weight of the world on his shoulders. He'd worked at the orphanage for decades, he told me, outlasting first the Soviets, and then the Mujahideen. Now he was under his new masters—the Taliban.

"*Baba-jan*, how is everything here?" I asked him. "I mean, what's it really like here?"

Baba-jan means "dear father" in Dari. He shot me a quizzical look. "Why are you asking?"

"I'm just curious, that's all."

He sighed. "Well, maybe you shouldn't ask such questions."

"Yes, I should, *Baba-jan*."

I changed the subject. I asked him where he was from.

"I was born and raised in Kabul," he told me. "But my family, we have endured so much."

"I'm sure you have, *Baba-jan*. I was born and raised in Kabul myself, and it was once such a magical city."

"You were?" He smiled, uncertainly.

I nodded. "Yes, *Baba-jan*. I'm a Kabuli, just like you."

He made an effort to straighten himself a little. "Kabul was once the finest city in the world. You remember those times, eh?"

"I do, I do. But tell me something, *Baba-jan*, who takes care of the girls here?"

He shrugged. "God does, I suppose."

"Of course God does. He takes care of us all. But who actually comes on a daily basis?"

"Nobody," he muttered. "They're just there." A beat. "They're just there waiting to be taken."

"Sorry, *Baba-jan*? Taken? Taken by whom?"

He glanced around himself, then came a step closer. "Taken by these rich old men who come and give a little money. Taken to be their wives or whatever. You know, I've seen girls as young as four being taken. . . ."

His words petered out. His eyes were watery, and he was trying not to cry.

"Tell me, *Baba-jan*, what happens to the boys?"

"You think boys are any safer?"

"No, *Baba-jan*. I'm asking you."

"Girls are safer," he muttered. "Girls are much safer." He brought up a corner of his robes to dry his eyes. "At least the girls go to someone's home. At least they get fed, clothed, and housed."

"What happens to the boys?" I asked again. "I saw Qari-*saheb* has this long stick. Does he beat them?"

He gave a bitter laugh. "Beaten? *Beaten?* You think that's bad. . . ."

"So what is bad, *Baba-jan*?"

"They're being abused," he whispered. "Sexually abused."

A tide of nausea rose up within me, but I fought to keep it down. What I needed now was information.

"Abused by whom, *Baba-jan*? By Qari-*saheb*?"

He shook his head. "Not him. All he cares about is money. He sends the boys with the men who come in their cars. He sends them away for a day or two. They come back very sick and they cry all the time. I cannot bear to see their pain. I cannot bear it. So I don't go to the boys' rooms anymore."

"How come you don't report this, *Baba-jan?*" I asked him, as gently as I could.

He glanced at me. There was an empty, haunted look in his eyes. "Who will listen to me? Who will give me a chance to talk? The Taliban? Forget it." He paused. "The next thing I know they'll harm my family."

"Just give me a name, *Baba-jan*. A name of these people who take the boys."

He shook his head. "Why don't you just go away and forget it. You are here for one time only. I am here forever." He turned to walk away. "Forget everything I've told you. It is what it is."

None of us said so much as a word on the drive back to the house. Once we were there I locked myself in my room and I cried. I cried for that little girl, the silent one I couldn't reach. I cried for those small boys, who looked so tough but were so fragile inside. I cried for the caretaker, that broken old man. And I cried for the fate of my country.

If there was a God, why didn't he come to the orphans' rescue? What would happen to those boys when they grew up; what would they become? At the time there were no suicide bombers in Afghanistan, but I could easily see those boys becoming our first. Their life was worthless. Life on earth was hell. They would run toward any paradise they were promised.

That evening I shared with Sekander and Dr. Abdullah what the caretaker had told me. Sekander didn't seem overly surprised. He'd heard the rumors. But the more I talked, the more Dr. Abdullah just seemed to draw in on himself. I grew increasingly angry both at Dr. Abdullah's unreachable silence and Sekander's mute acceptance of it all.

"We have to do something about this!" I insisted. "We have to do something!"

"Like what?" Sekander asked. "What exactly did you have in mind, Suraya-*jan?*"

"Well, from what I've seen there are good Taliban and bad Taliban. There are simple men and believers trying to bring security and peace to our country. We need to go and report this to the good guys. Surely to God they'll do something."

"They won't believe us," said Sekander. "How can they, when it's about their brother Taliban? They'll just say we made it up. They'll ask for our evidence, and we have nothing but the word of an old caretaker, and we can't put him in trouble."

"Well, we have to get evidence. There has to be a way."

"We can't," Sekander replied. "It's all just words. They'll say that you came to spread Western propaganda and to accuse a good man. You do this and you will put everything else you're doing at risk: the clinic, the schools, the lot."

I turned to Dr. Abdullah. He'd barely said a word since our visit to the orphanage. "How come you don't have anything to say? How come you don't react?"

"What do you expect me to say?" he remarked, quietly. "What is there to say? It is what it is."

I liked and respected Dr. Abdullah enormously, and I trusted him whole-heartedly. But he remained an enigma to me. He was a good and honest friend, yet still I felt as if I didn't really know him. He was always so quiet and unruffled—almost unnaturally so—as he was now, following our visit to the orphanage. I wondered if anything ever touched him, if really he had his heart in the work that we were doing.

I didn't want to retire to my room, for I knew the tortured faces of those orphans would parade through my dreams. Instead I stayed up, talking to Dr. Abdullah. Eventually I asked him if there was something that had happened in his life to make him so seemingly untouched by others' pain.

"Well, I was in prison," he remarked, quietly.

"I'm sorry, I didn't know."

"That orphanage reminded me very much of my prison years."

"You were in prison in Kabul? Under the Soviets?"

He nodded. "The first day they took me in, I was in a dark room with no windows. They closed and locked the door and I could see nothing. I had no idea what was in that room. I kept hearing these noises, like rats or mice scrabbling on the floor. In the morning it was still pitch-dark, but then my interrogator came for me. He opened the door, and I saw the room for the first time. I was sitting on these rags on the floor, and they were covered in blood. The walls were covered in dried blood. And the room was crawling with vermin. It was a torture chamber with no windows and a soundproof door."

"My God, I'm so sorry. It was like you were back there—in that orphanage?"

"A little, yes. That chamber was one of several in which thousands of people were tortured. I thought I was in the worst place in the world. But then they moved me, and I realized there was worse. In the new place I could hear the screaming of all the people being tortured. It was like I was in hell. The Afghan Communists were the cruelest—far worse than the Soviets. They yelled these things, these unspeakable things about what they would do to the man's wife or sisters or mother. I stayed in there for three years."

"My God. Three years." I shook my head in disbelief. I could hardly believe that he had survived, and that he had come through all of that such a kind and benign human being. "Dr. Abdullah, can I ask you a question?"

He gave me a gentle smile. "Of course."

"If you saw one of those son of a bitches who tortured you, and if they were dying, would you help them?"

"Yes, I would. I am a doctor. I would have to."

Later I would learn that Dr. Abdullah had ended up saving the life of the wife of the man who had locked him away. But it wasn't Dr. Abdullah who told me. He was far too self-effacing for that.

TEN

⚬◇⚬

It Is What It Is

I N DR. ABDULLAH, SEKANDER, SABERA, AND ALL THE OTHERS, I HAD so many good people helping me in Afghanistan. But once back in America I felt as if it was just me again, in my tiny, windowless office trying to raise funds. And my responsibilities were growing month by month. To the Peshawar clinic could now be added the Kabul clinic, plus our secret girls' school.

Sabera was determined to get twelve such schools up and running by the end of the year. I sat myself down and did a back-of-an-envelope calculation: I would need $160,000 a year to cover HTAC's ongoing costs, plus we needed funds for emergency relief missions. And there was an added challenge with the girls' schools. When raising funds, if I publicized our determination to establish the girls' schools to the wrong crowd, word might filter back to the Taliban. And if it did, our tiny underground schools would be finished.

One evening I paid a visit to the Mustafa Mosque in Annandale, Virginia, not far from my home. People gathered to hear me speak about my recent Kabul trip. Those in the room were from varied backgrounds— businessmen, taxi drivers, government officer workers; a few were still on welfare.

As I began speaking, I realized how raw the emotions were for me still. "Today, in Kabul, another type of torture is going on. The fighting has stopped under the Taliban, but people are desperate for health care, child care, and education."

I talked first about HTAC's achievements—about the secret schools, the women's clinic, and the aid that we had taken to the refugees. I wanted to stress the good that we were doing. But as I began to talk about the orphanage, I found myself in tears.

I noticed there were grown men in the audience also crying. I had expected as much from the women, but to see such emotion from these tough Afghan men moved me beyond words. Once I'd finished speaking, people came forward, handing me envelopes containing a check, or a few dollars. But among those who were giving, there was a young man who appeared untouched by all that I had said. He rose to his feet.

"I have a question for you," he announced. "Would you rather see the Mujahideen back—those who raped and killed and destroyed the city?"

"I saw the terrible atrocities under the Mujahideen," I replied. "To this day I shed tears about it, and I have nightmares. I do not want to see them back. Honest to God, I do not. But isn't it sad that it is either-or? Why can't there be a middle way that works for all Afghans?"

"Surely the Taliban is better than all this rape and killing," he persisted.

An older man turned on him. "You're just saying these things because you don't want to give!"

"She is a woman and we are men," another elder announced. "Yet we sit here eating and drinking and having a good life. I dare you to go there, where she has gone, and do this work. Then you can come and criticize."

That seemed to silence the young man. At least the power of the Afghan elders still seemed strong here. Most of the donations were in now. I handed the envelopes to the mosque administrator.

"Open them and let's see how much we've raised," I suggested.

"No, no—we don't need to know," someone in the audience cried out.

"We trust you," said another. "We trust you."

Even so, I could tell that they were curious. After a few minutes the mosque administrator announced that the counting was done. "By the Grace of God we've raised thirty-eight thousand dollars!"

The room erupted into a deafening round of applause. I immediately thought: *We're okay! We've secured nine months of our Kabul project costs with that money. Wow!*

There were no more than fifty Afghans present, so the donations averaged out at over seven hundred dollars per person. One guy alone had given me a check for $5,000. It was mind-blowing.

B ACK IN THE AUTUMN OF 1996, THE TALIBAN CONTROLLED MOST of Afghanistan, save one small section of resistance. Under the leadership of Ahmad Shah Massoud, the Northern Alliance was then holding out in the Panjshir Valley and a couple of surrounding provinces. But it had been anyone's guess how much longer they could resist the Taliban's relentless onslaught. It was three years since Dastagir had passed away, a little less since I had founded HTAC, and how the country had changed.

At that time the American government appeared to have recently woken up to the Taliban's presence. The tough question the U.S. administration faced was whether it should recognize the Taliban as the new legitimate rulers of Afghanistan. They were no ordinary regime, that was for sure. But they had brought a degree of peace and stability to the country.

America was torn in terms of how it should respond to the rise of the Taliban. In that fall of 1996 the U.S. Senate held a series of hearings on South Asia. Being one of the few people to have traveled inside the country, I was asked to speak. But when I sat down to write my speech I began several times, only to tear up each sheet of paper. As I struggled to find the words, a memory of my father came into my mind.

During my high school and college years, my father was forever trying to talk to me about politics. Several times he explained to me how every foreign power seemed to want to experiment in Afghanistan, to try its own model of invasion or control.

In 1996, it had seemed to me that the same thing was happening again, only this time in the form of the Taliban. The Taliban was a creation of Pakistan, with funding from the wealthy Gulf States, so it was yet another foreign adventure. The speech that I drafted in the memory of my father pulled no punches: I went to the U.S. Senate to issue a fiery call to arms.

"Thank you for the opportunity to speak, Mr. Chairman," I began, glancing up at the panel of U.S. politicians behind their polished wooden desk. "Mr. Chairman, you spoke earlier of a smart Afghan boy who once asked you what political party you belong to. Well, all of that is gone. The new generation knows nothing about the U.S., nor do they care, because they are illiterate. That child born seventeen years ago is now living barefoot in a plastic tent and in scorching weather, grossly neglected by the world.

"And I tell you something: if we do not help him now, the only language he will be speaking is that of hatred and revenge, and you and I, Mr. Chairman, will be calling him a terrorist. Ten years from now he will be sitting opposite you, negotiating the future of Afghanistan and the region.

"As I understood it, yesterday Congressman Rohrabacher mentioned that the U.S. has no money to help Afghanistan. With an extraordinary sacrifice of almost two million lives, the people of Afghanistan played a decisive role in the dissolution of the Soviet Union. How much is an Afghan life worth? Two hundred dollars? Four hundred? Please multiply that figure by two million lives, and give it to the Afghan people now.

"Mr. Chairman, recently five hundred million dollars was allocated by the U.S. to fight terrorism. If we invest just a fraction of that amount to educate young Afghans today, they will be able to fight fundamentalism and terrorism tomorrow, thus securing peace in the world. Childhood should be about hope, idealism, and innocence. Let's work to restore the Afghan people's human rights. Let's give them a future, Mr. Chairman—it's the least you and I can do."

After that speech, Congressman Rohrabacher had come over to have a quiet word with me. I had asked him why the United States hadn't engaged with Afghanistan after the defeat of the Soviet Union, and he had told me frankly that Afghanistan had fallen off the U.S. radar screen. I had known that, but to hear it from him reinforced my fears. Afghanistan was now under the Taliban, and we could expect no help from America anytime soon.

FEBRUARY 5, 1998, WAS A CHILLY DAY IN VIRGINIA, WITH AN ICY wind blowing in from the north. I turned the heat up high in my apartment and fixed myself some breakfast. I had CNN blaring away in the background, and I caught a brief bulletin about Afghanistan: a powerful earthquake had hit the north of the country. It had measured 6.1 on the Richter scale, and five thousand people were thought to have died.

Almost without thinking I grabbed the phone and dialed 411, directory assistance, and asked for CNN's phone number. I told the CNN receptionist that I ran a charity working across Afghanistan, and I asked to speak to someone regarding their Afghan quake news report. A male voice came on the line, and I asked if he was the producer on that story.

"I was the producer on that item, yes," the voice replied. "I understand you work in Afghanistan?"

"I run a humanitarian charity called Help the Afghan Children. Do you have any more information about the quake?"

"No. Sorry. We don't have any presence in Afghanistan."

"But five thousand people have died," I pressed. "I'm after facts: how many injured; how many made homeless; numbers of orphans—that kind of thing."

"I'm sorry, we don't have a presence in Afghanistan. You could try Voice of America—they might have someone there."

I did try Voice of America, but they knew no more than CNN. I called our Peshawar clinic to see what they might have heard. I got through to Nawabi on an echoing phone line, but he had little hard information about the quake.

"Are you planning to do something?" Nawabi asked me.

"We have to," I replied.

So far HTAC had concentrated on humanitarian aid, clinics, and education. Disaster relief would be a new departure for us, but in the face of the quake I didn't see how we couldn't act.

"Well, let me know what we can do to help," Nawabi offered.

Fortunately the BBC World Service carried more details of the disaster. The quake had torn hillsides apart, causing massive landslides that swept away entire villages. Aftershocks and further tremors continued to hit the region, causing more death and destruction. The quake region was incredibly remote, and it was the depths of winter. There would be thick snow on the ground, and the survivors faced freezing conditions. I doubted if any relief organizations had made it through, which further fueled my desire to act.

Recently I had appointed a formal board of directors to HTAC. It was something I'd done so I wouldn't feel so alone in the work, and to help me carry the burden. I contacted the chairman, Abdullah Malikyar, a lovely and dignified man who had been the Afghan finance minister during my father's time. He agreed that we had to move swiftly and that the key priority was raising cash. Abdullah was well into his eighties, but that didn't stop him from organizing a gathering of wealthy Afghan-Americans—restaurant owners and small businessmen—for a fund-raising dinner.

I went on the Afghan-American radio stations, appealing for quake-relief funds. Within four days we had raised $100,000. It was unbelievable, and a record as far as HTAC was concerned. At the same time, worshipers at one of New York's main mosques had raised $80,000. The imam there, a man known to everyone as Mullah—which means "holy man"—Rahmatullah, had asked if he might join HTAC's mission. He was born and raised in the quake region, so having him along should be a great help.

The final team that HTAC assembled consisted of myself, the New York mullah, and his assistant, plus Dr. Abdullah, who suspended his work at the Peshawar clinic to oversee the medical side of the mission.

A WEEK AFTER FIRST HEARING OF THE QUAKE, I WAS ON A FLIGHT to Tajikistan, the closest entry point into the disaster region. I'd never entered Afghanistan via this route before, and for me, Tajikistan was a complete unknown. We set up base in the Tajikistan Hotel, in Dushanbe, the Tajik capital. The Tajikistan Hotel was a stark gray concrete slab, typical of the buildings of the Soviet era. Everything seemed to have been left exactly as it was the day that the Soviets left, including the rusting crane loaded with cement blocks standing outside my window.

I couldn't wait to get out of Dushanbe and cross the border into Afghanistan. But first we needed the stamps in our passports and the permits that would enable us to move on. Like many states recently liberated from the Soviet Union, Tajikistan seemed to have few set laws or regulations.

Everything was negotiable. I fell back on what I always did in such situations: I used my skills at giving *bakhsheesh*—bribes. A small amount here, a few dollars there, and slowly we gathered the consents that we needed. But it was horribly frustrating, for I knew that as we haggled, the quake victims were suffering terribly.

By the time the weekend came around, we'd still not gotten out of Dushanbe. I hadn't packed a book, never thinking I'd have time to read. I paid a visit to this tiny bookstore that I'd noticed near the hotel, where at best I thought I might find a few trashy novels in English. Instead I discovered an entire shelf of beautiful old books, many of which were in Dari, the form of Persian spoken in Afghanistan. Centuries ago Tajikistan formed a part of Ariana, the ancient Persian Empire that we'd named our Peshawar clinic after. It had been a Persian-speaking country, right up until the Soviet takeover.

One title I recognized instantly: *Tajer Venicei*—Shakespeare's *The Merchant of Venice*. I plucked it off the shelf, admiring its fine leather binding, ancient typeface, and thick tan pages. I put it aside to buy. I pulled out another, entitled *Step by Step until We Meet God*. It was a work of philosophical Sufism, and it too joined the books I was going to purchase.

Without asking, the shopkeeper brought over another stack of Dari volumes. I smiled my thanks, and he returned the gesture, revealing a mouth of flashing gold. He was an ancient-looking Tajik, wearing a cap of black velvet embroidered with trees and flowers in all the colors of the rainbow. Beneath the hat were these enormous bushy eyebrows, and the jolliest, chubbiest face that I had ever seen.

"You can read all these books?" he asked me. "In Persian?"

"Yes, I can."

He peered at me from under his eyebrows. "So, where are you from?"

"Well, I live in America, but I was born and raised in Afghanistan."

"Ah." He smiled. "That explains it."

I ended up with six books that I just had to have, *The Merchant of Venice* and the Sufi philosophy volume among them.

"Right, time to talk money," I told him. "If I'm buying all these I want a bulk discount!"

He flashed me that gold-toothed smile again. "Well, you come from the U.S.A., so you must have a lot of dollars."

"Not all Americans do," I objected.

"Yes, but you have more than me." He grinned. "And where else can you find such ancient, fine volumes?"

I laughed. "Okay, I'm convinced. I'm having them."

He invited me to sit while he served me green tea and candy. I asked if he had any works by Rudaki, the famous Persian poet who composed his verses one thousand years ago.

He fixed me with a look. "You know Rudaki?"

Instead of answering, I quoted some lines at him in Dari:

> There is the great scent of a water garden called Mulian,
> The fresh smell of those streams and that garden come to me
> Reminding me of my kind and beloved lover.

The bookseller was in rapture. "Say it again, will you?"

I repeated the lines.

He glanced at me, and there was a real sadness in his eyes. "Do you know how painful it is that I cannot talk to my sons and daughters in Persian? My generation was the end of it. With the coming of the Soviets it all came to an end. Our lives were turned upside down. We lost our language. Our literature. Our identity, even."

"I'm so sorry," I told him. "But I keep my language and my love of literature alive, even in America. You can do the same here, you know."

He smiled. "You're right. Each time someone speaks those verses the poet lives again. Say them one more time, will you?"

FORTY-EIGHT HOURS LATER I FOUND MYSELF AT THE TAJIK-AFGHAN border. I shifted my weight uncomfortably as I did my best to hide the bundle of cash that HTAC had raised. I had it strapped to my stomach. I loosened my black shawl so it did more to shroud my torso, brushing down my long black coat with nervous hands.

The Tajik official took one look at me and shook his head. "What's a pregnant woman doing traveling into Afghanistan? Don't you know there's a war on?"

I shrugged and tried to smile my most innocent of smiles. He shook his head again, stamped my American passport, and waved me through the checkpoint. As I took my first steps into the territory of the Northern Alliance, I could read the expression on his face. *Stupid woman.*

We had made a deliberate decision that I would carry the cash. That bundle of dollars was safest hidden on a woman. To the average Afghan male I was the "lesser sex," and it was inconceivable that I could possess that amount of money, let alone smuggle it across borders.

After a bone-shaking journey over terrible roads we finally reached Taloqan city. It was late afternoon, and all around us the rock-hewn mountains of the Hindu Kush towered into the harsh blue of the winter sky. The lower slopes were awash with a sea of emerald green—the young shoots of poppy plants. This was prime opium territory, the poppy being the key source of the cash that funded the Northern Alliance's armed resistance against the Taliban. In a small muddy house in the center of Taloqan the Northern Alliance had their headquarters for all of Afghanistan.

We were received by Commander Doud, a young Northern Alliance leader with a thick beard and piercing eagle eyes. He had received a telegram from the Afghan consulate in Tajikistan that we were on our way, bringing aid to the quake victims. There wasn't a single aid organization in the area, and Commander Doud seemed genuinely relieved that we had come. He was smart, courteous, and keen to help.

I told him I had a large amount of U.S. dollars that I needed to change into local currency. Commander Doud ordered his men to escort us to the marketplace. The Taloqan market was thronged with locals wearing baggy pants above worn leather Aladdin slippers. Each wore a *pakul*, a traditional woolen hat, plus layer upon layer of clothing to guard against the mountains' icy blast.

Amazingly, in a place that appeared to have nothing, there was money available in every currency imaginable: rubles, yen, French francs, Indian rupees, U.S. dollars, and what I needed—afghanis. I knew the approximate exchange rate: 50,000 afghanis to one U.S. dollar. In the mid-1970s one U.S. dollar had been worth 60 afghanis. The collapse of the Afghan currency showed what two decades of war had done to the country.

I launched into a round of haggling, my years cutting deals as a real estate broker standing me in good stead. It took fourteen huge burlap sacks to hold the equivalent in local currency of over $100,000. By now the day was almost done. We would have to overnight in Taloqan, along with our fourteen sacks of money.

Commander Doud found a room in a private house. Our sacks were heaped in one corner, and he placed guards outside the door. Still, it hardly felt very secure: there was little law or order in this place at the best of times. But there were few alternatives when taking money into the disaster zone. Access was going to be difficult enough with those fourteen sacks of cash to carry. If we tried taking food or other supplies, I just knew we'd never make it.

Sleep wouldn't come, so I fetched my Dari copy of *The Merchant of Venice* and whiled away the dead hours, reading by flickering lamplight.

As the first glimmer of dawn crept into the house there was a faint knock at the door. Commander Doud was there for breakfast. Over tea and fresh-baked Afghan bread we pondered the coming journey. We'd been offered mule trains or human porters to transport our sacks of cash into the mountains. But I felt certain that both would not only prove too slow to reach the quake victims but also carry a high risk of robbery along the way.

"I know you are busy fighting a war," I remarked to Commander Doud. "But I also know that you have helicopters. Do you think you could call your boss, Mr. Massoud, to see if he can find a way to help us deliver the aid?"

With scarcely a blink Commander Doud got on his radio, talked for a while, then turned to me. "How many helicopters do you need?"

I tried to envision how many helicopters fourteen sacks of cash required. "Just the one should do it, don't you think?"

The commander agreed, and an hour or so later a lone helicopter thundered overhead, its rumpled gray-green camouflage stark against the icy sky. It came to rest on the outskirts of town, crouching like some prehistoric bird of prey. As we approached it, I could barely believe that just a few minutes earlier it actually had been flying.

It was a Mil Mi-24 Hind—a Soviet-era helicopter designed to carry as many as eight soldiers. But the exterior was riddled with bullet holes like a sieve, and the engines were blackened by oily scorch marks. For a moment Dr. Abdullah and I stared at each other. I knew what he was thinking: *Are we really going to entrust our lives to that?*

"It *did* make it here," I remarked. "So no reason why it shouldn't make it out again, I guess."

Dr. Abdullah shrugged. "It is what it is."

I tried a laugh. "It is what it is," I echoed. That was becoming the catchphrase of our missions.

ELEVEN

Stoned and Flying Out Here

I FOLLOWED DR. ABDULLAH INTO THE BELLY OF THE BEAST, A BARE and echoing aluminum shell. Pencil-thin beams of sunlight streamed in through the bullet holes torn in the fuselage. There were five of us in the HTAC team, and the fourteen sacks of cash would make up the weight of the three others this aircraft was designed to hold. Barring the thing falling apart on takeoff, we should be good to go.

But once the sacks were loaded, our pilot, Saifullah, started bringing his entire extended family aboard. Everywhere I looked there were men with bristling beards and close-cropped hair perched atop our precious bags of money.

A yelling started up from the cockpit. Our copilot, Akbar, was screaming at Saifullah. "No more! We cannot take more people! We're too heavy. We're going to crash!"

Completely ignoring him, Saifullah kept beckoning others onboard. "One more; one more; always room for one more."

By the time he was done we had: sixteen people; fourteen sacks of cash; half a dozen chickens; and four large steel ladders that they had somehow manhandled into the hold. Perhaps the ladders were to help with quake relief, I reasoned, and it would be churlish of me to object to them forming part of our cargo.

"We're doing some building work at home," one of Saifullah's relatives explained, in answer to my query. "We're just about to start on the roof."

There were no seats in the hold. I was passed a length of rope and told to tie myself to the aircraft's sides, to prevent me getting hurled around as the Mil Mi-24 banked and powered its way through the mountains. The engines were boosted to full power in preparation for takeoff. The body of the aircraft seemed to twist and turn, as it strained to be free of the ground.

Even with the rope lashed tight around my torso, I felt myself rolling this way and that. Beneath me was a metal box that looked as if it might offer some kind of support. I let myself sag and came to rest, with my bottom on the top of the box. I stole a glance at the others. I was glad to have a seat of sorts. Wild-eyed kids and grown men who were clearly a mass of nerves settled farther in among our money bags, holding on as best they could.

Saifullah gave a yell from the pilot's seat: "Okay? Is everyone ready?"

"*Balay!*—yes!" came the nervous reply in Dari.

"Hold on to whatever you can!"

There was a deafening, screaming whine as the turbines revved higher, and with a shuddering groan the aircraft began to rise before settling back down again almost immediately. I heard Saifullah yelling above the noise of the engines.

"We're too heavy! We have to get rid of some of the moneybags!"

"Not on your life!" I yelled back. "Get rid of some of your relatives!"

"I can't do that," Saifullah cried. "I don't normally get a chance to fly them."

"You know—I really don't care! This helicopter was sent to get us and our money to the devastated villages!"

Saifullah cut the engines, and gradually the crazed beat of the rotors slowed to a gentle *thwoop-thwoop.*

"Well, then I'm sorry, but I can't do this," he announced. "I can't and won't fly."

If he was bluffing, he was doing a fine job of it. It seemed to me that I had only one weapon left. I'd brought with me a rented satellite phone, and I planned to do some on-the-spot reporting from the quake zone. Voice of America (VOA) had agreed to take all the news reports that I could file, and I'd let the Northern Alliance know what I was up to.

In fact Commander Doud had thought that every time he spoke to me, it was being broadcast live by VOA, which partly accounted for why he'd been so helpful. He was pleased to have a reporter publicizing the plight of the quake victims, but he knew the power of the media and how any mistakes might reflect badly on him.

I reached into my satchel. "Well, I'll just have to get on the sat phone and report that our entire mission is being canceled because our pilot's refusing to fly."

Unfortunately Saifullah seemed all but immune to such threats. I was starting to realize why. As I assembled my sat phone, he sparked up a joint of hashish in a billowing cloud of smoke. Plus he kept popping snuff—*naswar*—up his nose, and pills into his mouth. In addition to the natural control-freakery of the average Afghan male, Saifullah was stoned out of his mind and totally incapable of logical thought or argument.

I stared out of the dirty, porthole-like windows, trying to decide what to do. The horizon was a slash of gray-brown mountains, the nearer, craggy hills melting into the snowcapped peaks beyond. Somewhere out there were tens of thousands of people in desperate need of help. The means to provide that help sat right here in this aircraft, but due to a hopelessly stoned pilot I couldn't get it to them. I felt my frustration and anger rising.

"So what now?" I heard a defiant Saifullah snort.

I pointed to my sat phone. "You get us airborne, or I'm gonna make the call."

"Do what you like. I will not relinquish command of my aircraft."

Aware of how every eye was upon me, I dialed the one number that I thought might make a difference—that of Ahmad Shah Massoud, the leader of the Northern Alliance. I didn't manage to reach him, but I did get his number two, Muhammad Qasim Faheem.

"Thanks so much for sending the helicopter," I told him. "But you know, there's a problem. You sent me a crazy guy for a pilot. We're trying to deliver emergency aid, and he's telling us to leave the bags of money behind so he can take his relatives for a ride."

Even across the echoing connection I could sense Faheem bristle. "There must be some kind of mistake. No pilot of the Northern Alliance would behave so unprofessionally."

Well, I could be bristly too. "Look, Mr. Faheem, it's really very simple. If we can't get this helicopter going today, that's one more day people in the quake-hit region will suffer. So I'm going to call VOA and do a live interview, which will not make you guys look good, will it?"

"Just wait. Wait a couple of minutes."

"Wait for what?" I objected. "This is a satellite phone. Each minute costs me twenty-five dollars. You need to call your man here in Taloqan, and tell him we've got to get this helicopter in the air."

"Okay, I'll call him."

"And while you're at it, can you send us another pilot?"

Mr. Faheem hesitated for a second. "I'm afraid I can't do that."

"Why not?"

"Because Saifullah is all we have."

At that point there seemed little sense in continuing the conversation. Clearly we weren't going anywhere without Saifullah. And there he was in his cockpit, puffing away and growling under his stoned breath.

A few minutes later Commander Doud turned up. I was unsure about what happened next. Perhaps money changed hands, or maybe our pilot's level of intoxication had lessened a little. Either way he was suddenly kicking people—not our moneybags—off the aircraft.

"Hey, boy!" Saifullah commanded. "You! Off the helicopter! And take those chickens with you!"

A thin boy in a ragged vest jumped down from the hold, dragging a basket after him. Inside, two scrawny chickens flapped about with their legs tied together.

Saifullah smiled. "Right, that should do it."

This was crazy, but it also made perfect sense in the way that only an Afghan would understand. Saifullah had no desire to actually crash the aircraft, of that I was certain. But at the same time, he didn't want to be seen to be following orders from a "foreigner," especially a woman.

And so it was that minus two scrawny chickens and one adolescent boy, our helicopter clawed its way into the thin Afghan air. We were hours behind schedule, but at least we were finally under way.

We banked at a crazy angle and turned away from the town. I glanced through the open hatchway into the cockpit and noticed Saifullah lighting up another joint. His lungs seemed to vacuum up the smoke in one long blast. Moments later he absentmindedly flicked the butt end over his shoulder. Pungent and glowing, it landed at my feet. Smoke curved upward, dancing in the sunbeams cast by the bullet holes.

Gazing out of the porthole I noticed the thin brown snake of a trail slithering between razor-sharp ridges below us. For a moment I wondered what it would be like to be down there, on foot or donkey, struggling to carry our sacks of cash into the mountains. Perhaps we didn't have things so bad after all.

At first Saifullah seemed to follow the turbulent, rust-colored waters of the Monjan River, climbing, always climbing, the aircraft's rotors striving to gain traction on the thinning mountain air. As we left the plain of Taloqan behind us, the aircraft weaved and writhed, searching for the elusive pass that gave access to the next hidden valley.

The horribly cramped hold was battered by the deafening beat of the rotor blades and thick with the stench of hashish. I closed my eyes, feeling a wave of claustrophobia wash over me. I opened them to the shock of blinding white peaks towering above and to either side of us, seemingly close enough for me to touch the solid ice blue of the glaciers.

I searched ahead with my eyes, but there appeared to be no way through the wall of rock and ice. I brushed my hand across my face, my palm sticky with the sweat of fear. I felt nausea rising in my throat as we peaked over a ridge, and Saifullah sent the aircraft plunging down the far side. We skimmed across the soft, disorientating whiteness of a vast snowfield. As far as the eye could see peak after peak rolled before us like a frozen sea—the Hindu Kush and Pamir Mountains leading unbroken into Pakistan, Tajikistan, and China beyond.

Dr. Abdullah tapped me on the arm. He had an odd expression on his face, the closest I'd ever seen him to looking afraid. He pointed at my feet. I glanced downward and noticed a thin trickle of liquid coming out of the metal box upon which I was sitting. At that moment Saifullah discarded yet another glowing butt end, and it landed at my feet.

Dr. Abdullah shook his head in dismay. I reached forward and ground the butt under my foot. As I did so, I noticed something written on the side of my metal box-seat: AVGAS. RESERVE FUEL TANK. And then I understood: I was perched on a tank of aviation fuel; it was leaking, and our pilot was flicking lighted joints at it.

I waved, frantically trying to catch Saifullah's attention. For whatever reason—my direct line to Commander Faheem, perhaps—he appeared a little more receptive now. He turned his red-rimmed saucer eyes toward me, giving me a thumbs-up.

"Everything all right, ma'am?" he yelled. "Now, as soon as we get there we'll fix up a nice place for you. We'll give you yogurt and tea, and nuts and fruit, and—"

He was coming to the end of another smoke and was poised to flick it over his shoulder.

"Hey, you know what?" I cut in. "I'm allergic to cigarette smoke. So the one thing I'd really appreciate is if you could stop smoking. What do you say?"

Saifullah looked crestfallen. A little hurt even. "Sorry? What are you talking about, ma'am? I can't see straight if I stop. I can't fly unless I'm smoking."

I guessed there wasn't a lot more to be said. *He can't fly unless he's stoned.* Well, at least now he'd *told* me. And, who knows, if I had to fly that bullet-riddled crate over those jagged, unforgiving peaks day in and day out, most of the time getting shot at by the Taliban, perhaps I might need drugs to keep me airborne.

Akbar, the copilot, had started shouting at Saifullah again. "You have to go straight! Straight ahead! If you carry on like this we'll hit the mountain."

"No I won't!" Saifullah countered. "You telling me I don't know how to fly?"

"Straighten up!" Akbar yelled. "You're going to hit the mountain!"

Saifullah laughed wildly. "We can pass it! We can pass! I bet we can!"

"You're too low! We can't pass! Pull up! Pull up! *Pull up!*"

"I can do it!" Saifullah screamed. *"Just watch me!"*

He hunched forward over the controls. He was like a child being dared to jump off a cliff into shallow water, and nothing was about to stop him. *This just isn't right,* I found myself thinking. *I haven't even gotten to distribute the money yet, and all because of a stoned pilot.* It's odd, the thoughts that cross your mind when you think you're about to die.

The helicopter plummeted earthward. Beneath the snarl of the engines a terrible silence filled the aircraft's hold. I brought my shawl over my face, to hide my stomach-knotting fear. I could feel my heart pounding, as every second I expected to feel jagged rocks tearing through the floor, rotor blades slashing and shearing into the icy rock face.

For a second the light flashed frozen blue all around us. My eyes darted forward. I expected to see sheer ice barely yards from the windshield, but there was only sky. Moments later we shot past the glaciated peak, our wheels practically kissing the ice, and we powered into clear air.

Saifullah's fist punched the air. "You see! *You see!* I told you we could make it!"

I felt the helicopter right itself. *It is good,* I told myself, *to be alive.* We started to descend, the bleak ice fields giving way to copses of raggedy poplars clutching at the mountainside. A slash of rust red flashed below us as the valley widened into a muddy river swollen with the first meltwaters of spring.

To either side, slabs the color of fierce amber showed where terraces had been hewn out of the hillsides. Each was fringed with the skeletal gray of orchards in winter, and dun-colored clusters of houses. We leveled out over the glistening golden brown of a high meadow tinged with ice. We were ready to land. Thank God, we were ready to land.

I dismounted from that helicopter with shaking knees, boots crunching into frozen grass. I felt almost as if I could kiss the ground. The journey had taken an age, and evening was almost upon us, but at least we had made it here in one piece.

As I gazed around me, I realized that the field upon which we'd landed was surrounded by the humped silhouettes of crushed and broken homes, each covered in a dusting of fresh snow. On the slopes above great ragged rents had been torn in the earth, spewing forth torrents of rock and soil in an angry, bloodred wave. In places, whole hillsides had completely fallen away, their stony edges left upstanding like the hungry teeth of some giant's comb.

This was the village of Rostaq—the epicenter of the earthquake. I had little doubt now that had we tried to make it here over land, we would have failed completely. A group of heavily armed, bearded men approached. The leader, a local Northern Alliance commander, had his *pakul* sloped rakishly over one eye and bandoliers of bullets wrapped around his torso.

"I am Commander Hakimullah," he announced, arms held wide in greeting. "Welcome to Rostaq." He turned to his men and ordered them to unload the sacks of money. "Hey! We've got fourteen sacks of cash from the CIA of America!"

After what we'd just been through, and because I needed the commander's help and protection, I was tempted to let it go. But I'd spent long enough doing this kind of work to know what's what in Afghanistan. To show timidity is fatal. It has always been so in my country. I turned to face the commander, getting eye to eye with him.

"What did you just say? This is *not* CIA money. This money was collected from Afghan-Americans who worked hard to earn it, because dollars don't grow on trees in the U.S., you know. This money comes from Afghans in America, not the CIA!"

The commander shrugged. "If the CIA hadn't let you bring this money, you wouldn't be here, would you."

I could feel Mullah Rahmatullah, the New York imam, scrutinizing me. I'd sensed already that he was uncomfortable with a woman leading the mission. Now he'd heard me labeled a CIA agent. Well, I couldn't be bothered to argue anymore. In any case, with the Taliban breathing down their necks the Northern Alliance was courting American support. Being labeled a CIA agent would probably do me no great harm, I figured.

I motioned to the fourteen sacks of money. "Commander, what I need most right now is a room. It needs to be secure, and with a lockable door."

"Yes, yes—of course." The commander pointed to a building a little up the hillside. "We have this place for our visitors. We call it Mehman Khana—The Guesthouse. And I will post guards to make sure that you and your things are safe."

The guesthouse was a traditional stone-and-mud structure, with rough whitewashed walls. The rooms inside were simple, clean, and tidy. I had the money piled into one of them, and then, having not slept for forty-eight hours, I curled up among the sacks of cash and the dusk shadows, and fell into an exhausted sleep.

Some four or five hours later I was shaken awake. A sumptuous feast was laid out on a rug in the biggest of the rooms. A sheep had been slaughtered and roasted over an open fire. There were juicy mutton kababs, piles of spiced rice, plus bowls of dried fruits and nuts—the kind of foods one could find in a mountainous Afghan village in winter. The room filled quickly, and soon there were some twenty-five men, with myself being the only woman.

"So much fine food," I remarked. "Who can I thank for all this?"

"The village chief," Commander Hakimullah replied. "He'll be with us shortly."

"Well, let's take some photos. Will the chief want to take a photo with me?"

Commander Hakimullah smiled. "Of course! Why not?"

If the village chief was willing to have such a photo taken, then he was clearly no hard-line Taliban type. The door to the room opened. I was expecting to see a tall guy with a huge stomach and an enormous beard walk in. That's what the village chief would have to look like to outdo Commander Hakimullah. Instead a tiny, pasty-faced, sick-looking guy came wandering into the room.

All around me people were getting to their feet. Maybe the little guy had come to announce the village chief's arrival, I reasoned. It was only when everyone started shaking hands with him and bowing that I realized: *Oh my God, he is the chief!*

He approached me. "*Salam alaikum*—peace be unto you."

"*Salam alaikum*," I replied.

He said: "I am Piram Qul. How are you, *khwahar*—sister? Thank you for coming."

"No, no—thank you. We are in a very comfortable place, and frankly you didn't have to cook all this food."

He looked at me. "You are our guest. What did you expect?"

"Well, everyone here is suffering so much. . . . Tea and bread would have been just fine."

He shook his head. "No, no, no—we don't treat our guests like that. God is great and he will provide." He glanced around the room. "Please, get started, or it will go cold."

After we'd eaten, Dr. Abdullah, Mullah Rahmatullah, Piram Qul, and I gathered with the village elders. The chief had called them together so we could discuss how best to utilize the quake relief funds. I asked the elders to explain just what had happened when the earthquake struck. I needed to get a sense of how bad things were, and where our cash would do the most good.

The quake had torn apart Rostaq, the elders told me. Centuries-old orchards had been ripped up by their roots; whole streets had been buried under mudslides; entire families had perished as the walls of their homes crumpled in on them. But the damage was worse in the highland areas. There, nine villages had been completely destroyed. Houses, mosques, grain stores—nothing had been spared on the "day the earth turned angry."

There were no exact figures for the number of dead, but thousands had perished, and many more were injured. In such a tight-knit community, everyone had lost someone. Each had been a much-loved father, son, newborn baby, mother, sister, teacher, farmer, herder, grandmother, wife, or husband. And more were dying in the quake's aftermath due to the intense cold.

After we'd finished talking, Piram Qul and I went to check on the sacks of cash. He issued some orders to his men in Uzbeki, a language that I don't understand. They started carrying the sacks out of the room, and I felt a stab of panic.

"Piram Qul-*khan*, what did you tell your men to do with the money?" I asked.

He laughed. "You don't trust us?"

"It's not that. It's just, it's a lot of money and I need to make sure it gets to the right people."

"You're right. And that is why I told my men to put the bags into the back room, where they can lock it and stand guard. I know and trust those men completely."

"Thank you, Piram Qul. I'm sorry for doubting you."

"*Khwahar*, as long as you are here in my territory nothing will harm you."

"Even the earthquake?" I asked.

He laughed again. "Well, I have no control over that."

Just then this horrible rumbling issued forth from below our feet, and I felt the earth shudder with an aftershock.

"You are scared when the ground does that?" Piram Qul asked me.

"Yes I am, Piram Qul-*khan*."

He smiled. "You know, God will keep you safe, because you are here to help. You can sleep soundly, knowing your money is safe, and the earthquakes won't harm you."

I did sleep soundly, and I awoke feeling mightily refreshed. Over breakfast I quizzed the village elders on which villages to prioritize. They came up with sixteen names, each of which was a good day's walk apart. Our ability to travel and our time was limited, so there was no way we could get to all sixteen of those villages. But we had to find a way to help them all.

I hit upon an idea. I asked the commander to fetch Rostaq's mullah, a man whom I had spoken to briefly during the previous night's feasting. The village mullah had to be in his seventies, and he was old enough for everyone to address him with the universal term of respect—*Mullah-saheb*, "Mullah-sir." He appeared to be very devout and deep thinking and was forever fingering his *Tasbih*—his prayer beads—a simple string of sandalwood beads that had a beautiful smell like spiced rose petals. Everyone seemed to know and respect him, and it was those qualities that I intended to tap in to for our relief work.

"You know how many people live in Rostaq, *Mullah-saheb?*" I asked him. "And you know how many have lost family to the earthquake?"

He nodded, sagely. "Yes, I do."

He was keeping his eyes on my male colleagues as we talked, but I didn't mind. He was a venerated elder and a religious leader, and he wasn't in any way disrespecting me. In any case, I liked this guy from the get-go. I sensed a deep wisdom and holiness within him, and I felt comfortable in his presence.

"So can you take us to those families who have lost people?" I asked. "The women and children who have been left alone, and those who have been badly injured?"

"I can, yes."

I then pushed the plan that was forming in my head a little further. "It would be wonderful if you could get all the mullahs from the quake-hit villages to do the same. Do you think that's possible?"

He nodded. "I think so, yes."

With the mullah's help, we decided to break the sixteen villages down into groups of four. We would take our aid to the central-most village of each, using the local mullahs to identify those families who were most in need, and getting them to come to us. In order to cover more ground, we would divide forces, with the New York imam forming his own party.

The villagers of Rostaq volunteered several dozen mules. Our sacks of cash were loaded aboard, and Dr. Abdullah strapped on his boxes of medical supplies. I laced up my winter boots, and we set off walking into the hills. The mullah of Rostaq led the way, with the train of heavily laden donkeys strung out behind us.

TWELVE

The Day the Earth Turned Angry

FOR HOURS WE TOILED UPWARD ON STEEP TRAILS THAT SWITCH-backed between jagged ridges and plunging ravines. As we climbed, it struck me that here we were, a handful of aid workers, village elders, and mullahs, plus a mule train loaded with a fortune in cash, trekking through a war zone. And we didn't have a single armed guard to protect us.

We crested a jagged knife-edge where an entire plateau had sheared off, rock and soil plummeting into the valley below. And there ahead of us stretched the scattered ruins of Ganj village. Here and there among the humped anthills of rubble were tiny splashes of color—survivors camping out among the ruins. Now and then a tiny figure could be seen moving as a lone child searched for lost family among the snow-enshrouded devastation.

As we moved into this ghost village, what struck me most were the haunted looks on the faces of the survivors. When the quake had hit, one in four people had perished. Countless more had been left injured and dying.

Eyes stared at us in a numbed silence as we shuffled past. An aged, bent woman, her clothes and hair wreathed in dust, turned to me in desperation. Her eyes were red, her face a mass of deep, careworn lines. She gestured helplessly at the ruins of a house, her eyes like empty pits of pain.

"What should I do?" she whispered to me. "What can I do?"

I paused to talk, to share a little human kindness. Eight of her family had been buried by the quake, and now she was alone, her future gaping and uncertain. As we spoke I realized how terribly young the children were that she had lost. I had presumed she was in her seventies, a grandmother already, but she had to be something like half that age.

Life here had aged her well beyond her years—her brief youth subsumed under pregnancy after pregnancy, and day after day spent searching for water, baking bread, digging vegetables, in a country wracked by a never-ending war. The whole epic struggle of her life was etched into that face. And now this unspeakable tragedy had come to her village and stolen away her family—that to which she had sacrificed her youth.

Another woman who looked to be sixty clutched desperately at her nine-month-old daughter. She had lost six of her family, including her brother and husband, to the quake. A blind man wandered distractedly, pounding the broken, upturned earth with a rough cane, searching for the lost. Groups of survivors huddled, bent in despair beside the rows of freshly dug graves. I remembered Dr. Abdullah's words: where there is life, there is hope. I was beginning to doubt them now.

We set up our aid distribution point at the center of the devastation. The women and children gathered, their cheeks flushed from the cold. The young girls had faces framed in bright red, green, and yellow Uzbek and Turkmen fabrics, but they moved slowly, if at all, as if unwilling to trust the very ground beneath their feet. As the mothers wept, their children stared with blank expressions and stunned, bewildered eyes.

The mullah of Rostaq explained that we would give two million afghanis to every family in need—the equivalent of twenty U.S. dollars. Although a tiny amount by Western standards, this should serve to stave off starvation until food could reach this area in substantial amounts—presuming that the international aid community did make it in here.

Each time I, or the mullah, called out the name of a surviving villager, he or she came forward to receive their bundled wad of cash. In spite of their suffering, these people who had lost everything—homes, livestock, fields, food, their families, and their livelihoods—waited patiently for the little we had to give. And not one of them ever came to beg. Their pride and their dignity remained intact. Their gratitude and their stoicism were humbling.

Perched high in the mountains, Ganj village had been engulfed in a crushing avalanche of mud and boulders. Whole families had disappeared in an instant as the tidal wave had driven all before it. In the center of the village was a scene that I had never imagined possible—a cracked and scabbed sea of ochre-brown, dotted here and there with the detritus of human existence. Everywhere I looked I could see people digging to unearth their dead from under the frozen wasteland of mud.

One woman was perched atop a pile of rubble, unmoving. I was drawn to her.

"*Salam alaikum,*" I greeted her.

She turned her head, but there was no reply. Her eyes were glazed and unfocused, as if she were not on this earth.

"I'm so sorry about what happened to you and your home," I tried.

Still she didn't speak.

She was so beautiful—and all the more so in a place such as this. I guessed she had to be about the same age as my daughter, but there the similarity ended. She was dressed all in black, but she had this incredible straw blond hair, and these ice-blue eyes. Maybe that's what had drawn me to her—she was so unbelievably striking. She was a blond, blue-eyed angel in the midst of so much death and devastation.

I desperately wanted her to speak. I noticed that one of her hands was cradled in the other. She kept nursing it, and I guessed it had to be broken. Well, here was a practical way in which I could help. Dr. Abdullah had set up a makeshift clinic at the aid center. If I could just get the girl there he could take a look at her injuries.

"You're hurting," I remarked. "Let's get the doctor to see you."

"No."

It was the first word that she had spoken. But at least she'd broken her silence. I tried to examine her hand.

"No," she repeated.

I couldn't understand why she didn't want me to help. A few of the women were watching us curiously from their ruined houses. I waved, and beckoned them over. One was a very old grandma, and there were a couple of mothers with their surviving daughters.

"What happened?" I asked. "What happened to this girl and her family?"

Before they had even started talking the tears began to flow. "This poor girl," the grandma sobbed. "This poor, poor girl."

I felt the tears streaming down my own face now. It was as if all the trauma and emotion of this day had finally broken over me.

"Tell me, what happened to her?" I asked again.

"It was her wedding night," the grandma began. "The earthquake came at seven in the evening. They were all in the mosque. You see the mosque, over there."

She pointed out the jagged, broken stump of a wall, which was all that remained of Ganj's mosque.

"Seventeen brides and seventeen grooms," the grandma continued, "in a communal wedding. She was the only survivor. That's why she's like this. She's been like it ever since."

I reached out for the girl's hand. "Let me see," I told her, gently. "Let me see."

She didn't look at me, but she did let me take her hand. I teased apart the fingers. The fist opened to reveal a palm that was painted in beautiful, earth-red whorls. On her wedding night an Afghan bride has her hands painted with beautiful henna designs—and to this girl, those blood red patterns were more painful than any injury could ever be.

I hugged her close and I cried into her shoulder. Grandma and the other women enfolded us in their embraces and bathed us in their tears. Eventually the girl looked at me with her incredible eyes. She opened her mouth to speak. I was dying to hear some words, any words.

"It is very painful," she whispered.

"Yes it is," I replied.

"Her name is Najiba," Grandma told me.

"It is very painful," Najiba repeated.

Those were the only words that she had for me. What more was there to say?

I returned to our makeshift aid center. The bodies of the dead had to be interred as quickly as possible so they could be granted the honor of a proper funeral. At the same time tradition dictated that burying the dead should be a man's job. The women were sitting by, feeling sad and helpless and weeping and praying. I made an effort to join in the grave digging, hoping to encourage the women by my example.

I called out to those around me. "See, I can do it! So can you! Take whatever tools come to hand and help."

For hours we worked digging these mass graves, laying out fifty bodies per pit. In the beginning I couldn't bear the sight of so many cold and lifeless corpses. The pinched and ghostly faces of the children will stay with me for as long as I live. The smell of decaying flesh turned my stomach, and the grim task all but broke my spirit.

The mullah of Rostaq must have noticed me breaking. "I see you are very tired, *saheb*." Just for a moment his gentle glance touched my eyes. "There's a small place we have prepared for you. There you can rest for a while. Come, let me show you."

I told Dr. Abdullah that I needed a little space, and I allowed the mullah to lead me away. A raggedy old tent had been pitched in a place of quiet on the outskirts of the ruined village. I crawled inside that tent, and alone within its canvas walls, I cried.

I was lying on some rugs spread on the floor, one ear to the ground. Beneath me I could hear this terrible groaning, as if the earth itself was in pain. Up here in the mountains the aftershocks were more or less continuous, but I didn't have the space or the energy anymore to feel fear.

That evening we returned to the guesthouse in Rostaq. I was so utterly exhausted that I had no appetite for the lovely food that Piram Qul had prepared. I couldn't face the meal or the company. All I wanted was to sleep and to forget.

Day two and three of our relief operations were similarly exhausting. Each evening we returned to the guesthouse in Rostaq, whereupon I hid in my bedroom and slept the sleep of the dead. On day four we set out early for our final destination, Kohe-zar, a village on the very roof of the Hindu Kush.

By now our sacks of cash were much reduced, and we made good progress. By midmorning we were approaching the village. The eerie groans of aftershocks echoed around the distant peaks, like the angry voices of some ancient army of the dead. As we pressed ahead there was a deafening rumble that sounded as if it came from the very heart of the earth beneath our feet. An instant later there was a terrifying tearing noise, and the ground heaved upward and split open. Our mule-train was cut in two by a jagged crevasse big enough to swallow a vehicle, one that spewed out clouds of a burning, sulfurous steam.

I was face-to-face with the earth-shattering power of the quake. I felt like I was in a movie. Thick white smoke billowed upward, and there was a horrifying, alien, gurgling burping sound, as if the earth itself had an upset stomach. I inhaled a lungful of gas that reeked of rotten eggs and worse and felt myself heave. To either side of me the locals were covering their faces with rags, and they yelled at me to do likewise.

I grabbed at my *chadar* and covered my mouth and nose, as those ahead of the chasm started motioning urgently for those of us behind to jump across. With my heart racing I followed the others and made the leap through the curtain of foul-smelling smoke, fearing that I was about to plummet into the open maw of the earth. On the far side we paused to catch our breath and say a short prayer of thanks. I glanced back at the jagged crevasse. It was three or four feet across where we had jumped it; in other places, far wider. I thanked God that I had made it across safely.

An hour later we reached the shattered center of Kohe-zar village. By now we had a comet tail of women and children following us. They formed a line to receive the money we were handing out, and my eye came to rest on a striking individual. With his snow-white hair and his silver beard, this village elder looked as ancient as the hills. And like Najiba, the young woman whose wedding day the earthquake had shattered, he had the bluest eyes that I had ever seen.

As he waited in line he kept laughing and smiling, showing a mouthful of missing teeth. His cheeks puffed out in ruddy good humor, and I felt the urge to squeeze those chubby cheeks. I was drawn to the kindness and the love that shone out of him.

"Look at that guy," I whispered to Dr. Abdullah. "What a cute guy."

Dr. Abdullah laughed. "He's cute?"

"Sure. He reminds me of Santa Claus."

The old man reached the front of the line, and I handed him a wad of afghanis.

"Thank you," he whispered. "God be with you."

He turned to leave, but I couldn't resist calling after him. "*Baba-jan! Baba-jan!*"

He half-turned. "Yes?"

I had this urge to talk to him. I just knew he had to be full of stories and wisdom and light. I tried to think of something to say.

"Tell me, *Baba-jan*, how old are you?"

He cocked his head on one side, thinking. "Maybe two hundred."

"Two hundred?"

"You see, I am very old," *Baba-jan* mused. "For as long as I can remember, I've been alive."

I laughed and laughed. "*Baba-jan*, you can't be two hundred. No one reaches two hundred."

He was smiling now, his cheeks puffing out and his mouth a happy, toothless grin.

"Oh, well, maybe I'm one hundred?" he suggested. "Really, you know, it feels as if I have lived for a very long time." He paused. "Thank you for bringing what you brought to the village."

He fished inside his robes and pulled out a necklace. It was almond and pistachio nuts threaded onto a string. He handed it to me.

"Well, this is for you," he told me.

I smiled. "You brought it just for me?"

"No. I didn't know you were here," *Baba-jan* replied, honestly. "I didn't think for one moment that a woman would come. I presumed it would be men."

"Are you surprised, *Baba-jan*?" I asked.

He looked at me. "Yes, I am a bit surprised. But take this, as a gift from me." I hung the string of nuts around my neck. "It is a bit like a necklace, but it isn't really, you know," *Baba-jan* explained. "It's made from nuts and you can eat it."

I feigned ignorance. "Really? Oh. Okay."

He got to his feet. "I have to go," he announced. "I have to get ready for evening prayers. You know, when you are this old it takes a long time to get ready for prayers."

We said our good-byes, and I watched as *Baba-jan* picked his way across the broken landscape of what once had been his village. A few days back, his home, his family, his land, his cattle, and his crops had been engulfed by the landslide that had come roaring and snorting down the mountainside. He had nothing left but the mud-stained cloak draped over his shoulders, one set of worn and patched clothes, and his battered shoes. He had worked hard his whole life only to have everything destroyed in an instant. Yet here he was with this amazing energy and this love that shined out of him, for everyone. It was hugely humbling and uplifting.

On the trek out, I showed the mullah of Rostaq the lovely necklace that *Baba-jan* had given me. "It's almost as beautiful as your sandalwood prayer beads," I joked.

He chuckled. "Thank you."

"But, *Mullah-saheb*, soon I will eat this necklace. So you should give me your prayer beads as a necklace to keep."

"I will not give it to you as a necklace simply to make you look good." He smiled. "But I will give it to you if you promise to pray with it."

"Give it to me and then I can decide," I teased.

He laughed. "I can't. But if you promise me you will pray with it, then it is yours to keep."

Sharing the dangers and the driving sense of purpose of our mission had brought us all closer together. Any qualms the mullah may have had about talking to a woman had dissipated somewhere in those ravaged, quake-hit villages. In any case, the Northern Alliance was nowhere near as rule bound as the Taliban. It was a liberal movement in comparison.

That evening, back in Rostaq, there was a palpable sense of relief among us that the quake-relief mission was over. Over dinner I showed off the pistachio necklace that *Baba-jan* had given me.

"Look," I remarked to Piram Qul, the village chief. "Don't you think it's beautiful?"

He examined the necklace. "Yes, it is."

"I was given it by this lovely *baba*, in Kohe-zar village. He'd lost everything, but he insisted I have it, as his way of saying thanks."

I asked Piram Qul to tell me a little of his life story. He had been born and raised in Rostaq and had lived there all his life.

"How many children do you have?" I asked him.

"Fifty-four," he replied.

"Excuse me?" I exclaimed. "*Fifty-four?*"

"Yes, fifty-four."

"How the hell? Are you sure?"

He laughed. "Yes, I'm sure. Fifty-four."

"Well, how many wives do you have?" I asked.

"I have fourteen wives."

"*Fourteen wives?* The Koran says four wives maximum, so how did you come up with fourteen? You added the number one in front of the four or something?"

The entire room was watching us, and people were struggling to keep a straight face.

Even Piram Qul was finding it difficult not to laugh. "You know, our holy prophet—peace be upon him—had nine wives."

"He did," I agreed. "But you have fourteen. I mean, first off, you're not the prophet; second, you beat the prophet by five! How old is your eldest child?"

"Twenty-two."

I did a quick bit of mental arithmetic. "So that means you've had on average 2.5 kids per year for the last twenty-two years?"

"Well, it didn't really work that way. Lately I've had more kids than before."

By now our audience had given up any attempt at keeping decorum.

People were rolling about with laughter—both at the impertinence of my questions, and the extraordinarily sanguine nature of Piram Qul's replies.

"Now, Piram Qul-*khan*, do you ever worry about how you'll feed all these kids?"

He shrugged. "Oh, you know, God is great."

"Yeah, I know God is great. But fifty-four kids! I mean, phew! How many houses do you have? I mean, you have to house them all, right?"

He laughed. "I have two big compounds."

"Seven wives in one and seven in another, plus all the kids?"

"Well, no—it's a bit different than that. It's three in one and eleven in another." He gave me a cheeky look. "You see, I have lived with those eleven for such a long time . . ."

His last words were lost in howls of delight. I was practically crying with laughter myself now.

Dear God—fifty-four kids! No wonder Piram Qul looked so worn out. All that energy was enough to finish anyone, and yet he was still having more children. The fact that I had interrogated the village chief and that he was okay with it had everyone in good spirits—all apart from the New York imam, that is. It hadn't escaped my notice that he had remained stony faced throughout our exchange. I guessed he thought that I wasn't behaving "properly." It might have been fine in New York, but it wasn't fine in Rostaq.

The New York mullah and I had hardly hit it off. In contrast to the mullah of Rostaq, with whom I had built up a lovely friendship, I felt as if Mullah Rahmatullah resented having a woman running the show, especially one as "ill-behaved" as I. Well, he could resent me all he liked. I wasn't about to stop being my outspoken self for anybody anytime soon.

Before leaving Rostaq, Dr. Abdullah and I talked about how we might best help these wonderful people long-term. The answer was pretty obvious, really. We'd managed to get aid to some five thousand quake-hit families, which hopefully would get them through the worst. And Dr. Abdullah had treated hundreds of injured. But there was little or no long-term medical care, so HTAC's priority had to be to establish a clinic. It would mean another ongoing financial commitment, but I was getting fairly used to that by now. Somehow the money always seemed to come.

"We will return, Piram Qul-*khan*," Dr. Abdullah and I promised. "We'll come back to Rostaq, and we'll build a health clinic."

Once we'd made the announcement, people came forward complaining of all sorts of ailments. Some of the men were asking for fertility treatment, for they weren't able to conceive any more children. *Heaven forbid if Piram Qul asked for any of that*, I told myself.

THIRTEEN

Life and Love

MY RETURN FLIGHT FROM TAJIKISTAN TO THE UNITED STATES WAS routed via Paris. I had a twenty-four-hour stopover, so I decided to visit my brother and go shopping for some French perfumes. My oldest brother, Hamid, and I are close. He's a gentle and caring man, and after my father's death he had become something of a father figure to me.

Hamid had fled to France to escape the Soviet invasion of Afghanistan. Now he was as French as I was American. In his Paris home, he would have five bottles of wine open and nine types of cheeses, some of which smelled distinctively revolting.

Hamid was always teasing his little sister, but deep down he really supported the kind of work I was doing. My flying stopover was a perfect excuse for him to take me out for some fine French cuisine. We went to his favorite restaurant, and the food was divine. Over coffee—tiny cups like thimbles, full of an exquisite French brew—Hamid finally got around to what he had on his mind.

"What do you want to do with your life?" he asked me.

It was an odd question. He'd always told me he admired my work in Afghanistan.

"You can see what I'm doing, and I've just been telling you all about it."

"No, not that. Not your *work* life. What do you want to do with your personal life?"

"Well, I just don't have the desire for a partner right now," I replied, a little defensively.

It was actually true. It was approaching five years since Dastagir's death, but still I didn't feel the need for anyone in my life. Maybe I had blocked it, but I just wasn't interested.

My brother gave a Gallic kind of shrug. "You know, Suraya, you cannot live forever just with someone's memory."

"My husband was a unique man. I really, really loved him. I'm not sure I can ever find anyone that I can love like that again. If I can't, I don't want to marry someone for the sake of it."

Hamid gave that gentle smile of his. "I can understand that. Fine. I agree."

My family had been dead set against Dastagir when I first met him. And in truth, I had started off despising the man that I ended up falling madly in love with. I had noticed this guy at college who looked kind of rough but cool. I had a lot of boys after me, and I couldn't understand how this one guy seemed to look right through me.

He drove a motorbike, dressed all in leather, and had long dark hair and a goatee, which was all the rage at the time. One day I took a closer look at his motorbike. It had the words LIFE and LOVE sprayed on the tank, which was pretty hip, I reckoned.

He kept coming up to talk to Reshmo, my best friend at college, but he didn't ever acknowledge me. I decided that he was deliberately ignoring me. Well, I was quite able to reciprocate. Whenever he came to say "hi" to Reshmo, I'd turn my back and find another boy to talk to. One day I asked Reshmo who he was exactly, and what was his problem?

Reshmo laughed. "His name's Dastagir. And you know what he keeps talking about? *You!* He keeps telling me he wants to talk to you, and how do I think you'd react?"

"He wants to *talk* to me? Hell, he can't even say 'hi,' he's so arrogant!"

I noticed that this Dastagir guy shared our English lectures. He would sit in the front row, busily scribbling notes, while I'd be at the back. One day the lecturer was talking about Shah Shuja, the Afghan king during British colonial times. I noticed that the lecturer kept putting his hand in his trouser pocket and shifting his crotch around, as if he needed to pee or something.

"Oh my God!" I exclaimed. "You just crushed the Shah Shuja down there! You just killed the king!"

Everyone must have noticed what the lecturer was doing, for the entire hall erupted with laughter.

"Poor king!" someone cried. "Poor king!"

"The king is dead!" another shouted. "Long live the king!"

"Maybe he was martyred!" someone else cried.

"You are really such a bad girl!" the lecturer scolded. "This isn't high school, you know! Just behave yourself, for God's sake!"

"What did I say?" I objected. "I was just talking about the king. . . ."

"We cannot tolerate this kind of behavior in class," a voice cut in. It was that Dastagir guy, and he was on his feet and glaring at me. "Either she goes, or we go."

"Dastagir is right!" the lecturer agreed. "You're disturbing the whole class!"

"You son of a bitch!" I tore into Dastagir. "Who the hell do you think you are? This isn't your class alone, Mr. Perfect!"

"Well, this isn't a kindergarten, either," he replied, stiffly.

"Okay, stop this! Stop this!" the lecturer interjected. "Suraya, maybe you should leave."

I stomped out and banged the door behind me.

I didn't just ignore Dastagir for the next month—I made it clear that I despised him. He might dress like a wild rebel, but at heart he was an overly studious Mr. Perfect. Weeks passed, and one day I was sitting alone in the corridor when I glanced up, and there he was, standing right in front of me.

"Reshmo's not here," I told him, bluntly.

"I know," he said. "Can I talk to you for a moment? Can we go for a cup of tea or something?"

"I know where the cafeteria is."

"All right, well, here goes." He sighed. "You know what it is? I want you to be my wife."

I stared at him. "You're kind of sick, you know that? You're a sick man. You need to go see a doctor."

He shook his head. "No I'm not. I know what I want. I want to marry you."

I laughed. "God! Are you on drugs? What have you been smoking?"

After that he started making these declarations in front of my friends. He'd announce that I was going to be his wife. We'd all laugh, and I'd take the rise out of him.

"Okay. Enough. The truth," he finally declared. "I love you. I just love you, okay?"

"Well, tough, 'cause I don't love you."

I was still playing hard to get, but in reality I was intrigued. There was a certain charm to his simple, open declarations of love. He had revealed his heart to me and made himself hugely vulnerable, and that alone was immensely brave. Maybe that was what finally melted my heart. We started to go out together, and that was the start of a romance made in heaven.

Dastagir came from a relatively impoverished background, but he made some money writing magazine stories, and with that he managed to run his motorbike and help support his family. Everyone knew that my life was very different from his, and they presumed that I'd tire of him eventually and break his heart. We were opposites in so many ways, yet I fell head over heels in love with him.

I saw something incredibly special in Dastagir. He had this honesty and decency, and this thirst to be someone. Plus I had never seen anyone who loved me as much as he did. He taught me how to ride his motorbike, and the very idea of an Afghan woman driving a motorcycle—nothing like it had ever happened at Kabul University.

Dastagir and I became a sort of symbol of freedom and the good times. We did what we wanted and we followed our hearts, and ours was like a fairy-tale love story. Over time, my family learned to love and cherish Dastagir almost as much as I did. And perhaps it wasn't so surprising that when I lost Dastagir, everything in my life changed so dramatically.

A FTER ROSTAQ, I RETURNED TO THE UNITED STATES WITH A RE-
newed sense of mission. So many children had been orphaned by the
quake, and the last thing I could handle was any of them ending up in a place
like Tahia Maskan, the Kabul orphanage. I was determined to set up some
kind of alternative, and the more I spoke to people about the earthquake orphans, the more offers came in from Afghan-American families wanting to
adopt. I began raising money for a return trip to Rostaq, so we could set up
the promised clinic, plus scope out the possibilities for an adoption program.

I'd been home no more than a week when I got a worried phone call
from my mother. "Have you been watching the TV?"

"No," I replied. "I'm tired and I'm busy. Why?"

"Well, maybe you should see what's being said."

"What the heck is going on? Not another earthquake?"

"No, nothing like that. Suraya, in spite of all the efforts you have made,
there are people who are bad-mouthing you."

"Mum, if you are successful there are always people who will criticize.
So maybe it's just a sign of our success."

"No, silly, this is a bit more serious than that. This is about you stealing
the money."

"*Stealing the money?* Stealing whose money?"

"Look, just turn on the TV, 'cause they're going to repeat the interview."

I switched on the TV in my apartment, and there was the New York
mullah. He spoke for a while about the quake relief trip, and all the good
work he had done there. Then he started to speak about how ineffective
HTAC had been.

"What do you mean?" the interviewer queried. "HTAC got a lot of
money from Afghan-Americans. How many people did they help?"

"I think they helped only the one village," the mullah replied.

"So what happened to all the money they raised?" the interviewer pressed.

"In all honesty, the situation there was so bad that if I had had that
much money, I would have spent it all."

"You're saying the money was lost somewhere? You're saying that it's not been accounted for?"

"I guess so," the mullah agreed.

Upon hearing the mullah's accusations, I felt a mixture of emotions. I was disappointed and sad, but I was also angry. I hadn't supposed that he'd liked me much, but I *had* presumed we were all working for the same cause—the relief of the quake victims. I called Dr. Abdullah and asked him if he'd seen what was being said. He hadn't, but he didn't seem particularly worried.

"Maybe this is just because you're so successful," he told me calmly. "We'll go back and establish the health clinic, and our actions will speak louder than any words."

Dr. Abdullah's calmness reassured me. Still, I did contact the Afghan-American radio stations and newspapers, doing a series of interviews outlining what we'd achieved. Mostly I received wonderful support from the listeners, but there were one or two attacks. A couple of people phoned in to complain about "those supposedly helping, who are actually taking advantage and using up the money."

Those attacks were anonymous, but the comments still hurt. In spite of knowing the truth—that every penny we raised we spent on the mission—those words stung me. My mother surprised me with how supportive she was at this time. She was my rock. She raged about how ungrateful Afghans could be. She fumed about how her daughter, a woman, was risking her life, while cursing these "cowardly men in America" attacking me.

There were other, equally stupid rumors. The best had me painted as a CIA agent working undercover in Afghanistan. I had to laugh at that one. If I *had* been working for the CIA, at least I might have been earning a decent salary. For the first few years of HTAC's operations I'd paid myself nothing at all. In fact, HTAC had drained my savings dry.

Three months after our first quake relief mission, a second tremor hit northern Afghanistan. This time it was in Badakhshan, a neighboring region that was equally remote and inaccessible. In spite of the way the criticism of our Rostaq mission had stung me, I hadn't lost my commitment or my empathy for the victims. I sensed here a chance to make good on our promises to the people of Rostaq, while at the same time taking relief into the new quake zone. HTAC went into fund-raising overdrive.

Within days we'd pulled in $100,000, and with the money we'd put aside for the Rostaq clinic we were good to go. In a way, I felt as if this was God telling me the time had come to clear my name. But this time, I stuck to my old faithfuls to form my team. Dr. Abdullah would treat the quake victims; Nawabi would organize the Rostaq clinic; Sekander would do security; and I would be the money mule.

We traveled in via Pakistan on commercial flights, then by bus to Kabul. There we caught an International Committee of the Red Cross (ICRC) light aircraft to Badakhshan—the only way in at the time. From there the way onward was on horseback. We threaded our way along narrow river valleys, the area dominated by gray-brown escarpments, plunging from a series of remote and angry peaks. It was as if a giant pair of hands had taken the earth and squeezed it together, leaving it rumpled into a series of impossibly chaotic folds.

The quake that hit this area had been as powerful as that at Rostaq. The difference here was that the level of death and injury was far lower. It was a hot and humid June when the quake hit, and most people were out working in their fields. It had left countless homes in ruins but caused far fewer casualties. And without the winter snows to hamper relief efforts, other, bigger aid agencies—the UN, the ICRC—were moving in, bringing food, tents, and medical aid.

We headed for the remotest villages, to which very little aid had reached. Sekander was acting even more protective of me than normal. His greatest fear was that I'd never ridden a horse before. My short legs couldn't reach the stirrups, and the only option was to bind my legs to the saddle. Sekander kept going on about how bad this was, for if the horse fell then I would fall with it.

"The minute you hear a dog barking, get ready to jump," he ordered. "Dogs are the first to know if there's an aftershock coming. Aftershocks will send the horse crazy, and it'll throw you."

Sekander's constant vigilance was a lifesaver. He refused to ride himself, so he could walk at my side, leading my horse by the bridle. He wasn't sleeping much, either. Each evening we'd camp up wherever we found ourselves, and he seemed genuinely worried for our security.

"It's so tiring looking after a woman," he grumbled. "I wish you hadn't come. This place is really not for a woman."

"Well, what about the women who live here? Or don't they count?"

"But you are not one of them. You're a city girl." He paused. "Well, you're not even a city girl, actually."

"What do you mean by that?"

"Well, you live in America," he remarked, adjusting the line of march of my horse with a gentle tug on the reins. "Women there do not do what you are doing."

"Maybe," I conceded. "But I drive. I work. I cook and clean. And I do it all by myself."

"It's not the same," said Sekander. "At least you are safe over there. And from what I hear everything is a switch-on-and-switch-off life."

Every now and then Sekander would put his fingers in his mouth, and make a call a bit like a whistle. Each time Sekander "whistled," the horse would stop or change direction, or slow or quicken its pace.

"Did your family ever have horses?" I asked him. "Is that how you learned to talk to them?"

He feigned ignorance. "Who says I can talk to them?"

"Sekander, I can see you talking to my horse."

"Well, okay, maybe I can," he conceded. "But it's not something for women to know. You can do a lot of things, but you can't talk to horses. Not here in Afghanistan, anyway."

At the end of the third day we stopped in a village that was surrounded by fields of opium poppies. We set up camp among them, and so I finally got to sleep among the Devil's Flowers—the thing that I had wished for during my first aid mission to Afghanistan. But by now they had lost all their allure for me.

Around the village there were signs and slogans denouncing the drug trade. ISLAM IS TOTALLY AGAINST DRUGS read one. STRIVE TO ERADICATE THE OPIUM POPPY read another. The UN had sponsored some kind of drugs-eradication program, and the signs were about as near as anyone got to doing anything concrete about the poppy harvest.

Once the women of the village discovered that I was an Afghan, they gathered around excitedly. They showed incredible generosity: one brought creamy goat's yogurt; another, fresh-baked bread; a third, a basket of dried fruit. Eventually I managed to work the conversation around to the drug trade.

"Why don't you grow wheat or something you can eat?" I asked them. "The only crop I see is the opium poppy."

"You're right, we know we should," one of the women told me.

"So why don't you? If you grew food crops, at least then you could feed yourselves if there's another earthquake."

The women gave a resigned shrug. "This earthquake is our punishment from God for growing the poppy. This drug is against Islam, so God has punished us. And he will keep punishing us until we stop."

I didn't contradict her. Who knows, perhaps it was.

We took a day to cover each of the quake-stricken villages, and once we'd achieved what we had set out to do we caught a flight out of there to Rostaq. The helicopter was loaded with medical supplies, plus a team of doctors and nurses that we'd recruited in Badakhshan. The reception we received when we touched down in Rostaq was incredible. The mullah welcomed us almost as if we were family, and Piram Qul lost no time in serving up a sumptuous feast.

After dinner Dr. Abdullah announced the obvious—that we'd come to establish the clinic—and there were cheers all-round. Piram Qul had prepared a building already. It was small but striking in the midst of a village where everything had been smashed to pieces by the recent quake. The entire community had come together to rebuild, clean, and paint the place. It boasted freshly whitewashed walls, plus blue windows and doors, and you could see it from afar, like a beacon of hope.

It had five rooms, enough for a storeroom, some consulting rooms, and a couple of sick bays. With Sekander, Nawabi, and Dr. Abdullah on hand, plus the team of doctors and nurses that we'd flown in, we got the clinic up and running within twenty-four hours. That evening I was having supper with the mullah, and I broached the question that was foremost on my mind.

"*Mullah-saheb*, last time I was here I witnessed such suffering," I began. "And we met so many children who were orphaned by the earthquake. Those orphans—they stayed with me in my mind, back in America."

"I'm sorry, *Saheb*," he replied. "You must not let it trouble you."

"But it also gave me an idea." I pressed on. "You know, we can take those orphaned kids to the United States, so they can find new parents and families."

The mullah shook his head. "This isn't possible."

"Not possible, *Mullah-saheb*? But why?" I presumed he meant not possible financially. "We'll take care of the finances, and in the United States they will be placed with loving families—Afghan-American couples who can't have kids themselves."

"*Saheb*, this is not possible." The mullah seemed almost angry now, which was so out of character.

"Why do you say it's not possible?" I had to know, especially if somehow I had angered him.

"No matter what happens here, we would never let our children be cared for by others. This would be a huge insult. We would never let our children go to another village, much less another country."

"But the quake victims are in desperate need. How can they be expected to care for children who aren't their own?"

He glanced at me, and the softness was back in his eyes. "*Saheb*, even if we have nothing, still we can give them so much love. We don't have a lot of material possessions, but still we will treat those children as if they are our own. We may have very little, but we will freely give them our love."

"Are you sure of that?" I asked him. I had to be certain.

"Yes, I am. I was born and raised here. I know how people feel about children."

"Is it like this only in your province?" I asked.

He shook his head. "Not at all. You will find people everywhere share the same values. No matter how poor they are, they take care of the orphans. It would be a huge insult to let someone else take care of them."

"Thank you so much for telling me this, *Mullah-saheb*," I told him. "It's the first time I've heard it, and those are the most wonderful, special values."

The mullah of Rostaq had opened my eyes. And I was so proud of the fact that in spite of the years of war and suffering, these principles had endured. It was such a noble way. War can change people's values and beliefs, but here at least this hadn't happened.

On our last day in Rostaq a crowd descended from the mountain villages to see us off. I gazed out of the helicopter's portholes and saw a mass of people, waving and cheering as the rotors beat the meadow grass like a wind-whipped sea. Among them were the mullah of Rostaq, Piram Qul, and the staff from Rostaq's new clinic. But mostly these were the ordinary mountain folks who we had helped survive the quake.

As the helicopter lifted off, I felt so uplifted, so full of joy. And then I saw him. Somehow, standing in and among and over that crowd was Dastagir—*the person who is always helping others*. As I gazed in disbelief at the scene before me, and the helicopter pulled farther away, I heard his voice as clear and as close as if he were sitting beside me.

"You see, my love, if I were still alive, do you think you would be here? Do you think you would be helping these people? Maybe that's your answer, my love. Maybe that's why I had to go."

Hearing those words made me realize what I had gained in losing the man that I loved. Sure, I had paid a price. I had felt abandoned by my soul mate, while his dying had been so quick and so easy. I had even envied Dastagir that he wasn't the one left alone to suffer. But in losing my love, I had found my true self and my mission. And without his dying I might never have done so.

I had learned something else too. I had gained a respect for death. Death does not discriminate. Money, wealth, fame, power—all things are equal before death. And while we may think we are the masters of our universe, there will always come a time when our lives will fall apart and we need to be lifted up again. The wisdom of Dastagir's words had truly lifted me up. All things happen for a reason, even the harshest and most traumatic events in our lives. Even our loved one's dying.

We flew from Rostaq to Peshawar, and the entire staff of our clinic turned up at the airport to welcome us. Badakhshan was known to be a wild area of warlords, drug traffickers, and bandits, and everyone was relieved to see us back safe and sound. Among the crowd was Aziz Qarghah, a fellow Afghan-American with clinics in Afghanistan and an office in Peshawar. Aziz ran Afghan Health & Development Services, a medical aid charity, and we'd run into each other several times in Peshawar over the past few years. It was always good to renew an old and special friendship.

Aziz and I had known each other growing up in Kabul, for his father and mine had been close friends. He was a handsome and smart boy, if a little shy, and his family had the "right" background as far as my family was concerned. Back then it was a match that all would have endorsed wholeheartedly. Of course, I'd gone ahead and got engaged to Dastagir, and some years later Aziz had married an American woman. Recently Aziz's wife had passed away, leaving him with four sons to care for.

He came over to greet me. His dark hair was graying now, but he had aged gracefully. "It's so good to see you back safe and well. Why don't you come and eat with us this evening? All I can offer is some soup, but—"

"I'd love to," I told him. "What time do you want me?"

"Let's meet early. I want to hear all about your trip. Everything!"

I headed for the hotel and showered and freshened up. Aziz came and collected me, but a short drive away he pulled over in a smart area of downtown Peshawar.

"What're we doing? I asked. "I thought we were heading to your place?"

"Well, I . . . um . . ." Aziz faltered. He had his eyes rigidly to the front, staring through the windshield. "You know, I was really worried about you in Badakhshan. *Really worried.*"

"Well, thanks, but I'm back now," I replied, breezily.

"You know, there were nights you were away when I couldn't sleep, I was so worried what might happen."

"Hey, I'm used to going to dangerous places. It's okay."

"But I was really, really, really worried."

"Well, don't worry. I can look after myself."

Aziz turned to face me. "Look, you're either dumb or you're playing with me!"

"What the heck does that mean?" I burst out laughing.

"Well, I'm not very good at these things. . . ."

"You're not making much sense," I teased. "What aren't you very good at?"

He'd gone back to staring out of the windshield again. I studied his profile. He was a handsome man, but I hadn't really thought of any man like that since losing Dastagir. I didn't think I was ready to start doing so now.

"Well, you know, it is very difficult to say that I love you—"

"Well, you just did say it, didn't you?" I interrupted. "You just said it."

For a few seconds there was an uncomfortable silence. I knew that Aziz was waiting for me to reciprocate. No doubt about it, he was a lovely guy. But twenty-four hours earlier Dastagir had appeared to me in a magical vision over Rostaq. After asking God countless times why he'd taken Dastagir from me, I'd finally found my answer. I wasn't about to go declaring my love for another guy the day after all of that.

For the rest of the evening, I tried to act as if nothing unusual had happened. I did my best to enjoy the fine food that Aziz had prepared, which was far more than just some soup. I told him all about my travels, except for the part where Dastagir had appeared to me in the vision. I thought it would be too cruel to tell Aziz about that.

In any case, a part of me didn't want his hopes to be dashed completely. A part of me felt as if I might just get to like Aziz Qarghah.

FOURTEEN

Young Enough to Wed

B Y AUTUMN OF 1999 THE TALIBAN HAD HELD KABUL FOR THREE
years, and they looked to be unassailable. As they tightened their vise
on the country, news kept filtering out regarding their suppression of the
Afghan people, and especially the women, who were becoming prisoners in
their own homes. In America in particular this drew people's anger. As one
of the few women going into and out of Afghanistan, I was invited to a
conference in Los Angeles on women's rights under the Taliban.

The Feminist Majority, a U.S. women's rights organization, planned the
conference, and Mavis Leno, Jay Leno's wife, had gotten a host of stars involved. Everyone was wearing a tiny piece of light blue cloth pinned to
their clothing—a scrap of burka material—as a sign of their solidarity with
the women of Afghanistan. One of the conference delegates came to speak
with me. She was a modern, intelligent, highly educated woman, but the
first words out of her mouth practically bowled me over.

"Can you imagine how those poor women get vitamin D wearing a
burka? I mean, draped in that tent the whole time, their skin never getting
a ray of sunshine. . . ."

If you'd said this to an Afghan woman she'd have died laughing. The
burka isn't worn within the home, and in the summer months most of Afghanistan is baking hot. A few minutes hanging washing in the backyard
was enough to top up any woman's tan.

"You know, in Afghanistan it's not about vitamin D or the lack of it—
it's about basic survival," I told her. "If you've never been in survival mode,
you won't get it. But try imagining waiting in a camp for two days under the

baking sun for a UN tanker to bring drinking water. Unless you've done that kind of thing you won't understand how precious water is. Or seen your kids starving. Or seen your husband and brothers killed before your eyes. If you had, why would you ever give a damn about vitamin D?"

The woman was a little taken aback. "Well, wouldn't you agree that you're here enjoying the freedoms of a Western women, and don't you want Afghan women to enjoy the same?"

"Of course, but that's an entirely different issue. It has nothing to do with vitamin D."

To be fair, the people behind that conference had achieved many great things. In part it was the Feminist Majority's lobbying that had pressured the American government into not recognizing the Taliban. Once the United States had refused to recognize them as a legitimate government, the rest of the world had pretty much fallen into line. The Taliban wasn't a government: it was the seizure of a country by those whose only law flowed from the barrel of a gun.

But this drive for women's liberation and to throw off the burka—it wasn't an Afghan reality. If you asked Afghan women what their needs were, few would say: *we need to be liberated from the burka*. In fact, quite the reverse. Many chose to wear the burka, for it offered a refuge from the predations of uneducated, ignorant men.

In the West our basic needs—water, food, shelter, clothing—are met. Most Westerners can barely conceive of an alternative reality like that which exists in Afghanistan. We Westerners assume it is the same the world over, and so we presume that other cultures and peoples have the same priorities as we do. In trying to break down such assumptions I'd taken to asking Americans the following question: *would you choose food for your children to fill their empty bellies, or equal rights as a woman?* The answer was so obvious: women's rights were irrelevant to a mother with a starving child.

We tend to impose our "universal" view of human rights, women's rights, and democracy on others, but in doing so Afghans see us as insulting their ancient culture, their traditions, and their beliefs. If the mass of rural Afghans don't hear us, it's because they are on a different frequency. They welcome the things from the West that make life easier—cell phones, computers, vehicles. But then they say: *Why do we have to be like the rest of the world? Why can't we do things our way, as we always have?*

Not long after that L.A. conference my daughter announced that she was engaged. Mariam was in her early twenties, she'd been going out with this guy called Christopher for five years, and they seemed very much in love. Christopher hailed from a white, middle-class, all-American family that had been in the United States for generations. He was charming and kind, but most importantly he loved my daughter deeply, and I'd seen him develop a genuine interest in Afghan culture and ways.

Mariam was the first in our extended family to consider marrying a non-Afghan, and she was a little worried about how the family would react. She came and asked me if she would be ostracized by anyone. I told her that I was all for the match, and as for the wider family, the buck stopped with me. I just wanted her to be happy.

Once we'd announced the engagement, one or two family members did try to raise objections. "She's a lovely-looking girl, so she could easily find a nice Afghan-American boy," they argued. "Then there'll be none of these cultural barriers."

"You know, she loves this man very much" was my answer. "And anyway, I married Dastagir against everyone's wishes, and we had a great life together, so how could I ever tell my daughter to do otherwise? Mariam's got my blessings."

None of my family could argue with that.

I cried a little at the wedding, mostly tears of happiness. We ate fine Afghan and American food, danced, and had a wonderful time. But afterward I did feel awfully lonely. My daughter had truly flown the nest, and now there was only me rattling around in my apartment. But I told myself Mariam's happiness was what mattered, not how lonely her leaving home made me feel.

As a foil to my loneliness, I buried myself in my work. God knows, there was more than enough to do. Our Kabul clinic was running at beyond full capacity, yet still we couldn't cope with the demand. The poor doctors were forever running short of critical medical supplies and life-saving drugs. It was next to impossible to raise the kind of money we needed for all the costly medicines, but I saw no reason why some of the American pharmaceutical companies shouldn't help, by donating drugs.

I set myself the target of securing a million dollars' worth of medicines— enough to keep the clinic running for an entire year. I managed to make contact with a wonderful California-based charity that specializes in securing donations of medical aid. Afghanistan was one of their priority areas, and they promised to do the unthinkable, and get me the million bucks' worth of medicines.

Within a matter of weeks they had done just that. There were half a million Tylenol capsules alone—a powerful painkiller and fever-reducing drug. They offered to ship the entire consignment of medicines to the port of Karachi, on the Pakistani coast, at no charge. All we had to do was hire some trucks to drive the stuff to Kabul. Nawabi got on the case, and I booked a flight to Pakistan so I could join the mission.

I'd asked Dr. Abdullah to let Nasreen, my college friend, know that I was coming, in case she needed me. Not that she ever seemed to: rather, it was always me trying to see her. But when I reached Peshawar Dr. Abdullah had some sad news: Nasreen had passed away. She'd had cancer, and there was nothing he could have done to save her. Nasreen—the "beautiful flower"—was gone. I told myself that perhaps it was better this way. Her life had been so full of pain, and at last she'd found the peace of the grave.

In the company of Nawabi and Dr. Abdullah, I set out on the mission to bring the million dollars' worth of donated medicines to Kabul. Once we reached the city, we linked up with Sekander, who was there buying supplies for our underground girls' schools. We reached Laghman Province without mishap, and with dusk approaching we pulled over by the roadside. The Taliban had imposed a nationwide curfew in an effort to maintain law and order, and no vehicles were allowed on the roads after dark.

The truck drivers wandered off to a nearby mosque for prayers. Dr. Abdullah, Nawabi, and I shared some dried fruit and nuts, after which I lay down across the rear seat to sleep. Soon it was pitch-dark, with just the barest glimmer of moonlight. I awoke to find this enormous guy with a huge black turban rapping on the front passenger's window. Dr. Abdullah wound it down.

"Who are you and what are you doing here?" the guy asked. He wasn't particularly hostile, and I guessed he had to be a Talib commander.

"I am a medical doctor, and the lady behind me is a nurse," Dr. Abdullah replied. "We've got three truckloads of medical supplies that we're delivering to hospitals and clinics in Kabul city."

"God bless you for doing such work," the man replied. "While you are here, you are guests in our area."

"Thank you. God is most kind to us."

The Talib studied Dr. Abdullah for a moment. "But tell me, brother, why are you doing this? Are you a friend of the Taliban?"

"We're friends of all the Afghan people."

The Talib peered into the back of the truck. "And this is the nurse?"

"That lady is our nurse, and she is also my sister," Dr. Abdullah replied.

He knew the rules, and we would never have attempted this journey without someone posing as my obligatory "male relative" escort.

"Okay." The Talib smiled. "You take care of your sister. It's your obligation to do that. And rest assured that here you are in a safe place." He turned to leave, then added, "I'm sorry, but I don't have much to welcome you. We are soldiers. We have little to give."

An hour or so later the Talib returned. He passed through the window some local Afghan bread, a huge and soot-stained kettle of tea, and a bowl of sugar.

"You and your sister should stay in the truck, for I have nowhere that a woman can sleep," he remarked. "But the other men can stay in the mosque with me. By the grace of God, eat well and sleep well," the Talib added, and then he was gone.

The encounter left me with a strong impression. No one liked to admit it, but the Taliban were often welcoming and fair. They didn't take anything for themselves, and they kept an iron grip on security. If they wanted to rule like this and slowly open up the country to positive influences, surely that was better than what had gone before. If we could just open a dialogue with the Taliban, perhaps we could work with them to bring about positive change.

After all, peace was the one thing that the Afghan people had craved for so long, and only the Taliban seemed able to deliver it. Admittedly, it was a very "Taliban" kind of peace, but it was infinitely preferable to the anarchy and bloodshed that had gone before. A few years back, traveling this road with a million dollars' worth of medicines would have been suicide. Under the Taliban, it was fine, as long as you kept to their rules.

The following morning we pushed onward and reached Kabul without mishap. There was no way in which we could distribute our three truckloads of medicines without the Taliban's blessing, so our first port of call was the Taliban's Ministry of Public Health.

Dr. Abdullah and I were shown in to meet Mr. Stanikzai, the deputy minister of public health. Mr. Stanikzai had lived for years in New York, and we were vaguely acquainted from his time there. He was almost as American as I, and I wondered what on earth an educated Afghan-American was doing here, serving in the Taliban administration. I was dressed in my standard uniform for such missions—black *chadar* and black trench coat. I had my head scarf pulled tightly around my face, and I wondered if the guy would recognize me.

Right away, he broke into a warm smile. "Ms. Sadeed, welcome! I think we know each other?"

I returned the smile. "Yes, I think we do—from New York."

After an exchange of pleasantries I explained the nature of our mission, and Mr. Stanikzai made it clear how welcome our medicines were.

"I'll send a couple of my people with you, so you are free to move around and distribute your medicines as you see fit. What is the name of your clinic, so I can tell my people to be ready?"

"It's the Kabul Aria Clinic, based over in Shari-naw."

Mr. Stanikzai faltered. He checked something on his desk. "I'm afraid there may be a slight problem."

"What problem?" I asked.

"Well, it seems that clinic has been closed down."

"Closed? When? Why? And who closed it?"

This was the kind of senseless stupidity I'd come to expect from these people. I was so angry and frustrated. After all the work getting the clinic up and running and securing the million dollars' worth of medicines, they'd finally found an excuse to shut us down.

"It was the Ministry of Planning who closed it," said Mr. Stanikzai. He read some more from the note on his desk. "It seems you gave some interview somewhere. I guess you said something in the media."

A few hours later Dr. Abdullah and I were sitting in a waiting room at the Taliban's Ministry of Planning. Dr. Abdullah had changed into a spotless Afghan robe for the meeting, while I had opted for the all-enveloping burka. But inside it I was fuming. How could they shut down our clinic, especially when we'd trucked in a million dollars' worth of medical supplies? People were desperate for health care—especially the women—and this was how they treated those trying to provide it.

I presumed that the Taliban's minister of planning, one Qari Deen Mohammad, had to be a real hard-line Talib to have done what he had done. But my real fear was that they'd discovered that we were secretly treating women there. If so, we were in deep trouble.

Qari Deen Mohammad turned out to be a youngish guy, dressed in the obligatory Talib uniform of gray robes under a massive black turban. He invited us to sit down and ordered his assistant to bring tea and sweets. Once we had been served, he turned to Dr. Abdullah.

"So, Doctor, how can I help?"

"Mr. Minister, we have a clinic here—the Kabul Aria Clinic—and we believe it's been closed down."

The minister glanced at me, then back to Dr. Abdullah. "Ah, so this is the sister who did the interview?"

"Mr. Minister, the sister is here, so why not talk to her directly?" Dr. Abdullah suggested.

"Well, of course, we Taliban know we aren't perfect," the minister continued. "But we are trying. We are bringing law and order and we are trying to improve things. We don't need people doing bad interviews about us."

"What interview?" I blurted out. "I didn't do any interview!"

The minister turned to me. "Sister, you talked about the refugees coming such a long way with bloodied feet. You said they had come one hundred kilometers with bloodied feet, to take refuge in the embassy here in Kabul. This was wrong."

My mind was in turmoil. What on earth was he talking about? He could only be referring to my relief mission to the Soviet Embassy refugees. But that was three years ago now. I might have given some interviews, but I couldn't for the life of me remember.

"Well, they did walk all that way and they did have bloodied feet," I countered.

"No. They did not walk one hundred kilometers," he corrected. "It was actually eighty-five."

I felt like saying: *Eighty-five kilometers, one hundred; what's the goddamn difference? They still got their feet cut to shreds.* But I didn't think that would get me very far. The minister wasn't being particularly aggressive or unpleasant, it was just that I had broken the rules. I'd broken the rules by getting the distance wrong, as a result of which they'd shut down our clinic. In the mind-set of a Talib there was a simple logic to what he had done.

He tried a smile. "Well, sister, now that we've aired this issue, you can remove your burka."

"But you're not my *mahram*," I objected. A *mahram* is a woman's immediate male relative and escort. Under Taliban rules, no one else was supposed to lay eyes on a woman's face.

The minister shrugged. "Well, you're sitting here in my office, so I don't think it matters much."

Rather than cross him further I shrugged off my burka. He stared at me for a long moment.

"Oh, I am surprised," he remarked.

"Surprised about what?"

"Well, hearing about you I had always presumed you were an old lady who had nothing better to do in America. I assumed that was why you had remembered your country and its plight. But you could actually still get married if you wanted. In fact, I—"

"No thank you," I cut in. "I'm quite happy—"

"You know," he interrupted, "according to Islam it is really not good for a woman to be alone. I feel certain that you could find a husband."

"No, thank you," I repeated.

I was trying to sound stern, but I was actually on the verge of laughter. Here we were, trying to get our clinic reopened, and instead I was fending off marriage proposals from a senior Talib. I'd always told myself to expect the unexpected when dealing with these people. But I'd never envisioned this, not in my wildest imaginings.

Qari Deen Mohammad turned out to be a fairly decent guy, once the matter of the fifteen kilometers had been properly aired, and the marriage proposal fully but politely rejected. We explained what we were doing in Kabul, and how frustrating it was to arrive with our medicines only to find our clinic shut.

"Normally, we don't accept unsolicited donations," he explained. "But, since you brought them yourself, in person, you can go ahead and distribute your medicines. And as for your clinic, now that we have spoken, it can reopen."

The truckloads of drugs we delivered to our newly reopened clinic were enough to keep it going well into the following year. Those barrels of Tylenol alone were a lifesaver. With few if any countries recognizing the Taliban, Afghanistan had fallen off the radar in terms of international aid. Dr. Abdullah calculated that the drugs we had brought would help some sixty-five thousand desperate Afghans.

Any woman trying to get to our clinic could only do so accompanied by a *mahram*. But with 60 percent of Afghan women widowed by the war, where exactly were they supposed to find a suitable male escort? Women had started to defy this rule out of sheer desperation. Many were caught by the Taliban's roving patrols and savagely beaten. But so frequently was this happening that the Taliban couldn't stop everyone. As with so many of their crazed rules, the Taliban were being forced to turn a blind eye.

While in Kabul I went to visit Mary. She didn't look a day older than when last I'd seen her.

"Suraya—my guardian angel!" she exclaimed. "You're back! And you know, that money you gave us to repair the weaving workshop roof—boy, was that a godsend!"

It didn't escape my notice that what originally had been a "loan" had become a "donation," but I didn't mind. Mary was a saint, and I'd help her any way I could. The more I learned about her life, the more I understood why she was here. She'd first come to Afghanistan in her youth, as a volunteer aid worker. Fast-forward several decades hence and she was divorced, her kids had left home, and Mary was bored and lonely. She'd had an easy life in the United States, but she wasn't *living*, and so she'd decided to return to Afghanistan.

Mary gave me an update on our secret girls' schools. By now we had twelve of them, and they were thriving. We'd just graduated our fourth batch of students, and still the Taliban hadn't caused even a hint of trouble. Mary figured they maybe knew about the schools, but as with so many things, unless it was thrust under their very noses, the Taliban were choosing to ignore our rule breaking.

The Taliban's attitude seemed to be growing more laissez-faire and forgiving, or at least so I thought. It would take my next trip into Afghanistan to prove otherwise.

❁❁❁❁❁❁❁❁❁❁❁❁❁❁❁❁❁❁❁❁❁❁❁❁❁❁❁❁❁❁

FIFTEEN

New York Comes to Kabul

I RETURNED TO THE UNITED STATES TO AN APARTMENT STUFFED FULL of fresh flowers. I opened the fridge to find it stacked with my favorite foods. On the coffee table was a note: *Welcome home, Mom.* After getting married and leaving home, Mariam seemed to be making an extra special effort to show her support for the kind of work that I was doing. I was so touched.

Dastagir and I had only had the one child, and there were times when I regretted it. After all, my mother had eleven children, and big families were something of an Afghan tradition. The reason why we'd only ever had Mariam was rooted in Lebanon. We'd moved from Kabul to Beirut so Dastagir could study for a further degree at Beirut's American University. Mariam was just a toddler, and I found myself working two jobs to make ends meet.

The Lebanon civil war was at its height, and there was a curfew in the city. One evening I popped out to buy some milk just before the curfew. Mariam was sleeping soundly, and I told myself I would only be a few minutes. I locked the door to our apartment and scurried down the bullet-scarred street. I was just paying for the milk when there was this almighty explosion. I left the milk on the counter and went flying back to our apartment block, finding it wreathed in dust and smoke.

I raced up the stairs, feeling sick with fear and cursing myself for locking the door. My hands fumbled with the key and still it wasn't opening, and I could hear myself screaming in frustration. Finally I wrenched it open, and there was Mariam, standing stock-still and wide-eyed with terror. The explosion had woken her, and she'd run to find her mommy only to discover a locked door.

As I folded her in my arms I realized that she was soaked in the sweat of fear. I felt so guilty, and I cursed myself for being so irresponsible. And I cursed my husband for bringing us to live in this war zone. When Dastagir got home I told him that I was never going to have another child, not until we were somewhere totally safe and secure—which certainly wasn't Beirut.

As the months went by I found myself longing for some literature in my own language. I went with Dastagir to the Beirut University library and asked if they had anything in Dari. By pure chance they had a newspaper that an Afghan student had left behind. I glanced at the front page, and there was a photo of a man who looked like my father. He had been ill for some time, and I hadn't been expecting to see him in the news.

"Look, isn't that my father?" I remarked to Dastagir.

I went to grab the paper, but Dastagir got there before me. "I'll take it," he remarked. "You can read it when we get home."

"No. I want to look at it now."

"But it's getting late and we can read it at home."

"No," I insisted. "I want to read it now."

Eventually Dastagir relented. That front-page article *was* about my father, and in reading it I learned that he had died. The obituary listed his achievements and the names of the eminent people who had attended his funeral. Dastagir had tried to hide the newspaper from me so as to protect me, for my family hadn't yet been able to telephone us with the news.

At first I was consumed by sadness and a burning anger. I felt cheated of my father's dying and the opportunity to grieve. But a few weeks after reading that obituary, the Afghan Communists seized power in my country, with the backing of the then Soviet Union. That was the start of the arrests, the torture, and the executions. All the prominent figures were taken, and I was glad then that my father was gone. I couldn't have lived with that happening to him. It would have destroyed me.

In losing my father, and learning of the horrors that followed, I knew that we couldn't risk returning to Afghanistan. Somehow we had to find a place of peace and security where we could raise a family. Beirut wasn't it, and once Dastagir's scholarship was finished we would have to move on. The only option open to us was Germany—for by an accident of history, Afghans didn't require a visa to visit Germany at that time.

During World War II the Allies had demanded that the Afghan government hand over all German nationals resident in the country. The Afghan government had refused. Foreign residents in Afghanistan were considered the guests of the Afghan people, and none that had come to our country in peace would be refused the Afghan traditions of welcome and sanctuary. After the war the German government had rewarded the Afghan people with a reciprocal—and visa-free—welcome.

Once his studies were done, Dastagir, Mariam, and I traveled to Germany, where we spent two years in limbo. We were refugees in transit to the United States, and it was certainly no time to be thinking of having children. And by the time we felt secure enough and were well established in America, the idea of having more kids seemed to have passed us by. By then I was working as a Realtor and deep in the money trench, living and breathing the American dream.

Making money had taken priority over everything, even having children. I wasn't about to take a pause and gaze at my navel and ask—as Dastagir seemed so inclined to do—the big question: *how much is ever enough?* There was never enough, and I was about as far away as I could be from the person who would one day start running aid and hope into war-ravaged Afghanistan. I was about as far away from me as it was possible to go.

U NTIL NOW, THE MAJORITY OF HTAC'S FUNDS HAD BEEN RAISED from Afghan-Americans. The rest came from a handful of other Americans plus a couple of small trust funds. I had to raise some $200,000 annually just to cover our ongoing costs, with the emergency appeals raising the total to some $300,000 or more. Furthermore I was forever pushing the envelope and committing to things for which we didn't have the funds. In the face of need, I just didn't seem able to say no.

One day in April of 2001 I was at the office, and the phone rang.

"Hi," a voice announced. "My name is Randall Scerbo, from New York, and I'm a freelance TV journalist. I'm interested in doing something on Afghanistan. I've done some homework, and the State Department told me that you are the only person who is really going inside Afghanistan. I'd love to talk with you some more. Is there any way we can meet?"

"Yep, if you make it to my office here in Virginia."

By now HTAC had moved out of The Bunker and into more salubrious premises. The new office was in Vienna, a smart suburb of Virginia, and it even had windows and space enough for three desks. I'd hired an assistant, a young Afghan-American man called Omar. Plus Aziz Qarghah, my friend running Afghan Health & Development Services, used the third desk whenever he was in the United States. Of course, I hadn't forgotten Aziz's pledge of love, but I didn't imagine it would get in the way of our working lives.

It was to our Vienna office that Randall Scerbo paid a visit. She was petite, with sandy hair and hazel eyes, and looked to be in her early thirties. She was a typical New Yorker, speaking superfast and with a restless energy. At the same time she seemed to be very health conscious, refusing coffee or tea and biscuits, and drinking only water. She explained to me that she had a burning desire to make a film about Afghanistan under the Taliban.

"Tell me, Randall, why do you really want to go to Afghanistan?" I asked her. "Are you just after taking some pictures of life under the Taliban to sneak them back here? If so, the media's full of those images of women in burkas. That's nothing new."

"You know, that's why I came to you," Randall confessed. "I don't want to go for a couple days, interview some women, and come back with any old report. I want to go and see the people and country for myself, and see how a woman under the Taliban can do what you do."

"Who was it at State that sent you?" I probed.

Randall checked in her notebook. "I got to speak to a Ms. Lois Schakenhawer. She praised your work and said you're the only one who goes deep inside and gets stuff done. She said you don't make a fuss about the women's situation—you just do what you have to do. Go talk to Suraya Sadeed, she told me. See if she can get you in."

My instinct told me that Randall was genuine, but what she was proposing was hugely risky.

"Randall, if I take you in to film there's one thing you must understand," I warned her. "I will never forgive you if you do anything to threaten the safety of our staff, our clinics, or our schools. You go there, you are mine. You are under orders. You do what I tell you. And remember that taking pictures is banned under the Taliban. You can be put in jail for it. This really is not for the faint-hearted."

Randall nodded, enthusiastically. "I totally understand. When are you going next?"

"Probably June."

"June. That's two months away. Perfect. I'm going to go with you in June, if you'll let me. I'm trying to get funding, but it's tough. But either way, I'm going."

After she left, I thought long and hard about whether I could do this. Randall would need to bring a camerawoman with her, and she had in mind an American friend of hers. Taking two American women into Afghanistan to make a movie under the Taliban—the risks were legion. Everyone in the United States was bashing the Taliban, and it would be enormously dangerous: for them, for me, and for all of HTAC's work.

But at the same time, the film could gain widespread exposure, which would translate into more funding. In the final analysis, it was Randall's burning desire to do the story that won me over. I made up my mind that if she got the funds together, then I'd take her.

Randall went ahead and hired a well-experienced camerawoman named Christine Burrill. Christine had filmed all over the world, but the first time I laid eyes on her my only thoughts were: *Oh my God—disaster!* She was this tall, leggy, blue-eyed blonde, and she just screamed out: *I'm an American!* Yet there was a calmness and stillness to Christine that I hoped would act as a foil to Randall's ceaseless New York frenzy.

I told Randall and Christine to take everything that they might need, for you couldn't guarantee to find anything in Afghanistan. In early June the three of us caught a flight to Pakistan, and from there we made our way to Peshawar.

The aim of this mission was threefold: I needed to pay a visit to our Kabul clinic and our secret schools; I wanted to scope out a new clinic that we were hoping to start in a rural part of Afghanistan; and the girls needed to shoot their film. I hadn't told my Peshawar team that I was bringing the filmmakers, for I knew they'd try to stop me. But I needed Sekander on this mission. His common sense and his nose for security would be invaluable.

As soon as we got to the Peshawar clinic, Sekander started eyeing Randall and Christine suspiciously. "I presume these two are just going to the refugee camps around here?" he asked, in Dari.

"No," I replied. "They're going with us to Afghanistan."

"What!" he exploded. "*Inside. Saheb*—ma'am—have you thought of the dangers this could pose?"

"Sekander, are you worried about yourself?" I teased.

"Me? No! It's not myself—it's them! And I'm worried about you also." He shook his head in despair. "This really is a bad idea. This is the worst yet. What are their reasons for going?"

"They're going to take pictures," I replied.

"*Take pictures?* Don't they know the Taliban won't allow it?"

"Of course they know. I told them. They know all about that. They'll be very discreet."

"Discreet!" Sekander snorted. "What's discreet about *them?*"

Sekander was worried sick. He started to lobby everyone he could think of to try to stop us. He got the entire clinic staff to gang up on me, in an effort to prevent me from taking the "two American women" into Afghanistan. And he had to make a superhuman effort just to be polite and courteous to Randall and Christine.

"Say, you guys seem to be getting on swell," I announced when Sekander next met the two girls. "From now on whatever you girls need, you just ask Sekander."

Sekander gave me a look, as if to say: *I cannot believe what you just did. This really is the last straw.*

"Whatever you need *in Peshawar*, please feel free to ask," Sekander told the women, somewhat stiffly. "You are staying in Peshawar, aren't you?"

"Oh no," Randall replied. "We're going with you guys to Kabul."

Over the years I'd learned that the best way to deal with Sekander's "Western-women-worries" was to gently make light of them. Generally he'd crumple under my teasing. Sekander was getting the message by now: we three women were going, and resistance was useless.

By now there was a regular taxi service plying the route between Peshawar and Kabul. We pulled up at the Pakistan-Afghan border, and I told Randall and Christine to stay in the car as Sekander and I went to speak to the Taliban border guards. The story that I gave them was that Randall and Christine were medical doctors helping us with our work. The chief guard stared at the two American women, wrapped in the black shawls and robes that I'd made them wear.

He fixed me with a doubtful look. "Are you a Muslim?"

"Yes, I am," I replied.

He glanced at Randall and Christine. "And *them*? Are they Muslims?"

"No, they are not. But I'm working on it. Taking them to Afghanistan is a big help, don't you think?"

The Taliban border guard nodded. "It's good work that you're doing, bringing these people to Islam."

With that he stamped our passports and waved us through. An hour later we were driving through the valley where I had first seen the Devil's Flowers some seven years before.

"My God, it's beautiful here," Christine remarked. "You think we could stop by the river? Maybe have a picnic and cool our feet. I'm boiling!"

We did as Christine suggested, and the water was wonderfully cool and refreshing. But Sekander wasn't joining us.

"See," I remarked, once I'd rejoined Sekander in the car, "a lovely spot for a picnic. Lovely Taliban border guards, and what a lovely time we're having with these lovely American ladies."

"Well, we're not in Kabul yet, are we?" Sekander retorted.

The remainder of the drive went without a hitch. Every now and then we stopped to do a little filming, but only when there was no one around. Randall and Christine were being very careful, and before we reached Kabul they hid their cameras. We checked into The Intercontinental, the only hotel at which the Taliban permitted "foreigners" to stay.

The Intercontinental was stuck in a time warp. It was as if it had been frozen in time sometime back in the 1970s. To make matters worse, the walls and roof were riddled with bullet holes, and every now and then you had to step over a bucket catching the drips from busted plumbing. Few rooms were undamaged, but with the place practically deserted we got ones that actually still had glass in the windows.

We went onto the balcony, and I talked Randall and Christine around the blasted city. Very little had been rebuilt, and they were in a stunned silence. Huge high-rises had been reduced to a series of floors and supporting pillars, with walls and windows blown away in the fighting. Entire neighborhoods were little more than a series of splintered stumps of brickwork. But what struck the two of them the most was the silence that hung over the city like a shroud.

In a way, I had gotten used to the unearthly quiet. This was Kabul under the Taliban. But to Randall and Christine, the silence was unnerving. Few people had vehicles, and Kabul was a city of bicycles with little if any traffic noise. There was no music, no TV, and little chat or laughter. The quiet was like a silent scream, one that couldn't be ignored, and the only sound that punctuated it was the call to prayer.

The hotel's one restaurant, the Bamiyan Room, was off-limits to women. We stayed in our room and snacked on the food we'd brought with us, while I gave the girls a refresher on the rules. None of us were allowed out of the hotel without a *mahram*. To that end Sekander was posing as our "brother," although how the three of us could ever be sisters—me, five-foot nothing with jet-black hair; Randall, several inches taller and sandy-haired; and Christine, a six-foot blue-eyed blonde—escaped me. Yet there was one set of Taliban rules we were going to have to break, and very deliberately so.

"Okay, this is how we play it with the cameras," I told the girls. "Around Kabul you can film only when I say so. Don't ever let your guard down. When you don't think you're being watched is when you will be. Taking pictures here is no joke. The Taliban will come after you and kick you out at best, and our people can be put in real jeopardy."

We were exhausted from the journey and retired to our beds early.

The next morning, in an effort to ease our tensions, Sekander invited us all over to his place for lunch. On the drive he pointed out the mosques in various stages of construction. They were the only new buildings in the entire city. He gave us a running commentary on what had stood on the land before the glistening new domes had been built there.

He gestured to one side of the street: "That was a soccer field. And there it was open parkland." We turned a corner, and he glanced around the shattered neighborhood. "You know what's missing around here—we need another mosque!"

Sekander's lovely wife—Surat Begum, "the beautiful-faced lady"—rustled up a fantastic feast. The last time I had eaten at Sekander's place was during the time of the Mujahideen infighting. There was no doubt about it, things were better under the Taliban. At least his wife could go to the shops—*mahram* permitting—without getting raped or shot, which was an enormous weight off of Sekander's mind.

Before leaving Pakistan I had contacted the Taliban's deputy minister of foreign affairs, Mr. Zahid. He had a reputation for being a reasonably moderate Talib, and he was from Logar Province, which was where I wanted to build our new clinic. He had told me there was a clinic of sorts in Logar, but that it had no medical supplies and few staff. He was keen to meet with us to see how HTAC could help.

Over lunch I gave Randall and Christine some instruction about the forthcoming meeting. They weren't to thrust themselves forward or try to shake hands, for Mr. Zahid might not wish to do so with a foreign woman.

We were to dress all in black and remain with our heads covered at all times.

I'd warned Mr. Zahid that I was bringing two American "doctors" with me. What he didn't know was that I was going to ask if they might film an interview with him. I had no idea how he would react to such a brazen request.

SIXTEEN

Singing with the Taliban

THE MINISTRY OF FOREIGN AFFAIRS WAS ONE OF THE FEW BUILD-
ings in Kabul that hadn't been destroyed in the fighting. Somehow
the cool stone floors and pillared galleries had survived. We were led into a
quiet room of polished marble where rich rugs were scattered over the floor.

Mr. Zahid ushered us to some chairs. He was wearing a spotless Afghan
robe, and the Taliban's more "stylish" kind of turban, one with an enormous
length of grayish cloth wrapped around a central skullcap. Bowls of dried
fruits and nuts, plus freshly brewed green tea, were laid out on a low table.

"You are welcome," he announced, gesturing toward the refreshments.
"It isn't much, but the best we Taliban can offer. I must thank you all for
coming, and for helping the country. We hope more like you will come, for
we are in great need of outside assistance."

Mr. Zahid spoke almost faultless English, and I didn't doubt his sincerity. He turned and gestured to a younger man who was standing behind
him. "I must introduce my assistant, Qari-Basir."

As Qari-Basir sat down I noticed the pistol he had thrust into his belt.
Randall and Christine had also seen the gun, and their eyes were out on
stalks. The significance of the younger man's name didn't escape me. *Qari*
signifies someone who has memorized the Koran, and I was half expecting
some kind of hard-line zealot. He glanced at the three of us, greeted us in
excellent English, then started to laugh.

"I'm sorry," he chuckled. "I don't mean to be rude. But tell me, please,
why are you dressed identically, and all in black?"

Randall gave a sheepish grin. "Suraya told us to, so we don't attract attention."

"But that is exactly what you will do." He smiled. "How many other women have you seen dressed like this? Afghan women don't wear such clothes."

"What, you'd rather have us all in burkas, would you?" I demanded.

I knew he was only teasing us, but it was best to give as good as we got. As with all Afghan men, the Taliban respected strength. To show weakness was to lose.

He threw up his hands in surrender. "I didn't tell you to wear a burka. There are alternatives. But like this you look like you're off to a funeral."

The banter about clothing done, I talked a bit about HTAC and our mission in Afghanistan. I told them we had three clinics running already, one in Kabul, one in Peshawar, and one in Rostaq. Neither man appeared particularly concerned that we were operating in Rostaq, the territory of the Northern Alliance—their enemies.

"God be with you in everything you do in Afghanistan," Mr. Zahid remarked. "In Logar I hope we can achieve something similar, and we will help you in any way we can. Either my deputy or I will take you on a visit, so you can gather all the information you need."

"Thank you, that's very kind," I told him.

Mr. Zahid sighed. "You know, the Western media often portrays all Taliban as bad. But we are trying to help the people. We're trying to do better."

I sensed an opening here to push for Randall's interview. "If you're not that bad, why don't you let Westerners come here and take photos or film?"

He grimaced. "Well, that's a different issue. It's not permitted."

"Not permitted by whom? Islam says nothing about photography being bad. There's nothing about it in the Koran. You guys just banned it for no reason."

"You know, I am not the one who makes the rules," Mr. Zahid remarked, enigmatically.

"Okay, so this rule against photography, does it extend to you guys? I mean, if my American colleagues want to film this conversation, is that okay with you?"

Mr. Zahid glanced at his deputy. Both men gave a slight shrug. "I don't think it is a problem if your friends want to film," he said. "But it might be if you were, for example, trying to film an Afghan woman inappropriately."

"So it's okay for us to film?" I pressed.

"I see no reason why not. We are having a fine conversation, and these issues need to be aired."

I nodded at Christine to get the camera going. We'd been speaking in English, so they had followed pretty much all of what had been said. Mr. Zahid and I continued talking in a kind of informal interview as the camera rolled.

"One thing I don't understand," I ventured. "You say people are happier under the Taliban, so why are these masses of people leaving the country as refugees?"

"Look, we brought security," Mr. Zahid replied. "That was the first priority. Now, we are trying to work for the people. Just give us time."

"I'm the first to recognize that you brought security, and what an incredible achievement that was. But it's still a fact that there's a net outflow of refugees into Pakistan and Iran. Why are so many leaving under the Taliban?"

"The answer is simple: they are leaving because we can't provide them with food and sometimes jobs, and this is not helped by the international community cutting off all aid. But it is still our responsibility, for we are the people in control of the country."

I nodded. "I do understand that. The fact that there's no aid doesn't help."

"Let me tell you a story," Mr. Zahid continued. "A little boy fell off his bicycle. He was left bleeding on the streets. His father came and found him and asked why he had been riding his bicycle out on the street. Not satisfied with the boy's answers, the father interrogated him on and on. Finally the boy said to his father, 'First get me to the hospital to stop the bleeding, and then I'll tell you what happened.'"

Mr. Zahid paused and took a sip of his tea. "Afghanistan is in a similar situation. The country is bleeding. We are in such dire straits because of earthquakes and the refugee situation, and we must be given help to keep the people alive. But the world community will not recognize us, and because of that they say we cannot receive any aid. Yet it is us who brought about an end to the fighting, without which aid wouldn't be possible."

"You know why they won't send aid, don't you?"

"Well, they make a lot of noise about women."

"Exactly. Girls' schools are closed. Women are not allowed to go out alone and—"

"This is the way of our lives," Mr. Zahid cut in. "This is the way we brought peace to the country."

"But the international community doesn't have to accept that. In fact, it's the other way around. You should accept their rules if you want their aid."

"Sister, know this," Mr. Zahid declared. "There are good Taliban. There are Taliban who want to bring change. It will take time for us to put our thoughts together on this. But if you think all Taliban are evil, that is not the case."

"I believe you. I believe there are Taliban who the world community can work with. I know that."

"Where are you and your guests staying?" Mr. Zahid asked, signaling that our informal interview was over.

"The Intercontinental."

"You know, I would have invited you to be my guests, but I hope you understand that I can't have foreign visitors staying. But while you are here in Afghanistan, you will be the guests of the Ministry of Foreign Affairs."

We agreed on a date to travel to Logar Province to inspect the clinic. In the meantime, I had a busy schedule ahead of me. My first priority was to check on our girls' schools. Sabera and I had been talking on the phone, a means of communication that we reckoned the Taliban couldn't interpret. Recently she'd alerted me to a pressing need at the school. Leaving Randall and Christine in the Intercontinental, Sekander and I drove to Sabera's place to investigate.

This picture from a wedding in Virginia in spring 1993 is the last picture of my husband Dastagir, my daughter Mariam, and me together. A few months later, we lost Dastagir, whose name means "the one who is always helping others." (*Abdullah Nasim*)

This is the camp where I carried out my first aid mission in 1994 and where I met Fatima, a young woman who reminded me of my daughter. (*Suraya Sadeed*)

In 1997, the Taliban ruled Afghanistan, and we were not allowed to take pictures, but American aid worker Mary McMaken and I smuggled in a small automatic camera. Mary was integral in setting up our Kabul girls' schools. *(Suraya Sadeed)*

After a heart-stopping flight in an ancient helicopter, we landed in Takhar Province in February 1998 with money for over 10,000 earthquake victims. *(Mohamad Zahir)*

In February 1998 in Takhar Province, two local commanders and a heavily armed bodyguard walk along with me to protect the money we're bringing for aid. *(Mohamad Zahir)*

In March 1998 a village chief in Takhar Province prepared a feast to thank us for helping the region's earthquake victims. (*Mohamad Zahir*)

Opium poppies, called "the devil's flowers," thrive in Afghanistan's remote Badakhshan Province, Summer 1998. (*Suraya Sadeed*)

In July 1998, to bring money to families devastated by natural disasters, I smuggled tens of thousands of dollars disguised as a pregnant belly. (*Dr. Abdullah*)

As fighting escalated in Afghanistan in June 2001, hundreds of thousands of people fled across the border to Pakistan seeking shelter in camps such as this one. *(Christine Burrill)*

Because I am an American woman running a charity that helps Afghan people, many Afghan men consider me an "honorary man," which means they are free to speak to me directly. Here, in June 2001, I'm in the midst of tough negotiations with a refugee camp administrator about distributing food and tents. *(Christine Burrill)*

In June 2001, Help the Afghan Children (HTAC) delivered several "family size" tents to young mothers in Peshawar, Pakistan. *(Christine Burrill)*

Families displaced into camps in June 2001 often fell sick because of cramped living quarters and lack of clean water, food, and health care. *(Christine Burrill)*

In July 2001, an Afghan woman complains about the unbearable heat and the lack of drinking water at a Pakistani camp. *(Christine Burrill)*

A few weeks after the September 11 attacks, I posed with displaced children who had just received aid in the Takhar Province. *(Doug Hostetter)*

After the U.S. bombing campaign began in October 2001, I traveled with humanitarian Doug Hostetter, filmmaker Randall Scerbo, and journalist Michael Lerner to deliver food to 45,000 Afghans. Here, we stand at the border between Afghanistan and Tajikistan. (*Chris Anderson*)

In October 2001, our convoy of trucks carried food and blankets into northern Afghanistan for Afghan civilians caught between the U.S.-backed Northern Alliance forces and the Taliban. (*Doug Hostetter*)

Girls in the Paghman District near Kabul eagerly wait for the first HTAC school to be built in 2002. (*HTAC staff*)

After an earthquake in 2003, I helped HTAC distribute local currency to over 3,000 families in the Nahrin District.
(*HTAC staff*)

In March 2003, I had the honor of cutting the ribbon to reopen the Karte Parwan School, which HTAC renovated after it was bombed during the civil war. An estimated 5,000 students now attend the school.
(*HTAC staff*)

In 2006, President George Bush and First Lady Laura Bush invited me, along with other NGO leaders, to a meeting at the White House to discuss U.S. humanitarian and educational programs in Afghanistan. (*White House photographer*)

This is the Kabul guesthouse where we founded our first secret school for girls in 1997. The Taliban had banned girls from getting an education, so we hid them in the basement, where lessons were conducted by candlelight. The students' burkas hang from the windows. (*Suraya Sadeed*)

When this photo ran in *Reader's Digest*, the article was titled "Everyday Heroes." To me, the everyday heroes in my story are the long-suffering and dignified people of Afghanistan. (*Photo first ran in* Reader's Digest, *May 2002; Michael O'Neill*)

We'd been working with Sabera for four years, and she'd managed to get some three hundred girls into our secret schools. But some of them were in sixth grade by now, after which we had nothing more to offer them. We had neither books, staff, nor premises to take their studies further, regardless of how well they were doing.

I greeted Sabera and Mary, who had come to talk things through with us. "So, how many girls do we have graduating?" I asked. "And what are we going to do with them?"

"Suraya-*jan*, there are thirty-five," Sabera replied. "But as to what do we do with them after they graduate, I don't know. But we have to give them hope. They are so eager to learn!"

"Let me think awhile," I told her. "There's got to be something we can do. In the meantime, can't we give them something special, like maybe a graduation ceremony?"

"But how?" Sabera asked. "These are girls educated in secret in the semidarkness of my basement."

"So we'll use your basement to do it," I said. "We'll buy cookies and cakes and fruit, and we'll hold the ceremony down there."

"*Buy cookies?* Not on my . . . I'll make them!" Mary volunteered. "Mary McMaken makes the best home-baked cookies in all Kabul."

"You know . . . it's a lovely idea." Sabera smiled. "The girls will be so happy. But, Suraya-*jan*, they don't even have any proper outfits."

"So buy some nice material and get their mothers to sew some smart new clothes. Sekander will pay for whatever you need, and I can be there on the day to oversee their graduation."

Sabera and Mary looked at each other and grinned. "We'd better get moving," Mary announced. "We've got a whole lot of baking and sewing to do!"

And so it was decided: under the very noses of the Taliban, we would hold our first ever graduation ceremony for our secret girls' schools. I knew that Randall and Christine were dying to be there to film it, and I knew the kind of support HTAC would attract if those images were broadcast across America. But it couldn't be done. We didn't even talk about the schools in

our newsletters, for if we did, the pro-Taliban Afghan-Americans would report it back to Kabul, and everything would be finished.

Randall and Christine were chomping at the bit to get some filming
done. They suggested starting with my childhood family home. I agreed, as
long as we remained in the car, filming through a partially opened window.
I warned them to keep alert for Taliban patrols, for the hated Ministry of
Vice and Virtue guys were everywhere in their white pickup trucks.

We did some drive-by filming at my old home. There were families living like squatters in the shattered ruins, but I was glad to see that someone was making use of the place. We did the same at my old school, Rabia
Balkhi, Sekander slowing the car to a crawl as I did a running commentary.

Randall and Christine couldn't seem to get enough of filming the
ghostly devastation of downtown Kabul, and all of a sudden the inevitable
happened. From out of nowhere three Toyota pickups came screeching to a
halt, blocking us in from all sides. The Vice and Virtue guys vaulted down
from their pickups and swarmed around the car. Each was dressed in an
identical black outfit, sporting a gigantic turban totally out of proportion to
their heads. What was more distressing, however, was that each man carried a Kalashnikov assault rifle, and they had these leather whips hanging
from their belts.

Their leader had this horrible mop of oily black hair sticking out from
under the biggest turban ever. He dragged Sekander out of the car and
started beating him around the head.

"Tell them to give us the camera!" he yelled. "We followed you for
hours! We know all about your dirty filming!"

Sekander didn't so much as flinch as they beat him. He just stared back
at the guy saying absolutely nothing.

I turned to the girls. "Get the film out of the goddamn camera! Quick!
They're gonna take it off us!"

The girls looked terrified, but if anything, Randall seemed less fazed by
this than Christine. It was almost as if she had been willing the Taliban to
pounce, and now that they had, this was the angle she needed for her film.

"Tell them to give us the camera. NOW!" the Taliban leader screamed.

I heard the faint mechanical whirr of the tape ejecting. "Right, hide the goddamn tape and give me the camera," I hissed.

Christine's eyes met mine. "Where . . ."

"Somewhere where these goddamn idiots won't dare look for it!"

I held the camera out the window, thrusting it toward Sekander. He handed it to Mr. Monster Turban.

"Ask them what they have been filming," Monster Turban demanded of Sekander.

"Nothing much," I replied, not waiting for Sekander to relay the question. "No people. Just the ruined buildings."

"We'll see," Monster Turban snapped. "Follow us."

With one pickup in front of us and two behind, we were escorted through the streets of Kabul. I had a good idea where they were taking us. It would be the headquarters of the Vice and Virtue Ministry, which was located in a government building in which my father once had worked.

"Sekander, I'm going to call Mr. Zahid at the Ministry of Foreign Affairs," I suggested. "I'm gonna tell him we're in trouble."

"Not yet," he replied. "Wait. I hope I can sort this out myself."

"What else do they want? They have the camera."

"They want to talk to me," Sekander replied, quietly.

"Tell them we're guests of the Ministry of Foreign Affairs. Tell them the ministry knows we are here, and that the two foreign women are medical doctors. Tell them about the Logar mission, and the clinic we'll be starting there. Just keep repeating that we are the guests of the Ministry of Foreign Affairs."

We reached the Vice and Virtue offices, and Sekander was frog-marched inside. We women had to remain in the car. I glanced at Christine and Randall. Christine was white faced, and she'd gone horribly quiet, but Randall seemed kind of excited that there was some action at last.

I was scared for Sekander. The guys who had picked us up were eighteen- and nineteen-year-old thugs, and they answered directly to whoever their controllers were, across the border in Pakistan. There were distant, shadowy forces pulling the strings of the Taliban, and each seemingly had a conflicting agenda. That in part accounted for why there were "good" Taliban and the really, really bad ones.

"Can I smoke?" Christine ventured, nervously. "Are women allowed to smoke? I could really go for a cigarette right now."

"What? With a burka on?" I joked.

All three of us started to laugh. None of us were actually wearing a burka, but the black headscarves covering our faces were almost as constricting. I spotted one of the guys who had arrested us coming out of the building.

"*Salam alaikum*—peace be upon you," I greeted him out the window.

He glared at me. "*Salam*," he muttered. He tried walking on, but I was determined to find out what was happening to Sekander.

"You know we are your guests," I called to him. "Don't you even offer tea here? And what's happening to our brother inside?"

"I am not allowed to talk to you!" the guy snapped, before marching onward.

It was getting dark by the time Sekander emerged. He didn't seem to have been beaten, although I knew the Taliban had ways of hurting people that left few outward signs. The young Taliban thugs were with him, plus an older guy who I guessed had to be in charge.

"You know we are the guests of the Ministry of Foreign Affairs," I announced, just as soon as the big guy was in earshot. "We have special permission to be here, and you have no right to take our camera. You are to return it immediately."

The guy bristled. "We are going to keep your camera until we decide otherwise." He peered at me through the car window. "Are you an American or an Afghan?"

"Are you an Afghan?" I countered.

"Of course!" he replied.

"Well, we've heard all the stories about the famed hospitality of Afghans, so where is yours? You've kept us sitting here in this car for hours on end, and not even offered us tea. If you cannot even welcome us properly, the least you can do is return my friend's camera."

The guy stared at me. He was searching for a fitting response, but he knew how rude and unwelcoming they had been. There was a hurried discussion among him and his minions about whether they should send a car to the Foreign Ministry, so that Mr. Zahid could vouch for us. There was little point showing these guys any paperwork, for they were most likely illiterate. Any vouchsafing would have to be done verbally and in person. Eventually they decided to check in the morning. In the meantime they were keeping our camera.

It was such a blessed relief to pull away from that building onto the darkened streets of Kabul.

"What did they do?" I asked Sekander, just as soon as we were under way. "Did they beat you? Are you okay?"

"I'm fine," Sekander replied. "They didn't do anything much. Nothing really."

"They didn't even hit you?"

"Just let it go. They just kept asking who we were and what we were doing."

"What did you tell them?"

"Well, the big guy kept asking about you. *Who is she?* he kept asking. And about HTAC. He kept asking, *What is this organization?*" Sekander laughed. "It was like we were the CIA or something."

As soon as we reached the Intercontinental I called the Ministry of Foreign Affairs. Luckily, Mr. Zahid's assistant, Qari-Basir, was still there. I told him all that had happened and asked for the camera to be returned. Qari-Basir apologized for the behavior of his Taliban colleagues and promised to do all he could to get it back.

It had been a horribly stressful day, and the three of us were dog tired. Before retiring to bed, Randall tried to put my mind at rest about the missing camera.

"Don't worry. We have two others. We can afford to lose one."

"That isn't the point," I explained. "I don't want those thugs feeling like they have power over us. If we allow them to keep the camera, it puts them in the right. That's why we have to try to get it back."

"Well, okay, I guess you know how best to deal with these people." She yawned. "Is it lights-out time yet? What a day! I'm pooped."

With that, Randall, Christine, and I wished each other good night.

I was woken sometime in the early hours by a harsh banging on my door.

"What the hell . . . ," I muttered, sleepily. Then, more loudly. "Who is it? What do you want?

"Where are the pictures!" a voice yelled through the door. He didn't need to identify himself. It was Monster Turban, the leader of the Vice and Virtue thugs. "All of the film that you took—we want it now!"

I was out of bed before he'd finished and unlocking the door that connected my room to Randall and Christine's.

"Get in here, now," I hissed at them. "And bring your cameras and the film."

I turned to my door and yelled out a reply. "You know we cannot let you in! You are not permitted, for we are three women with no *mahram* to safeguard us. Don't you know the Islamic rules?"

There was a moment's silence outside. I guessed Monster Turban was trying to get his head around that one. Under the Taliban's own laws what I had said was true. There were a few halfhearted bangs on the door, then a hawking and a spitting, before feet stomped off down the corridor. I didn't doubt for one moment that he'd be back, and I guessed he'd retreated no farther than the hotel lobby.

Randall, Christine, and I set to work. We decided to create three different sets of tapes—the originals, and two copies. That way, Randall and Christine could each keep a set of the tapes secreted on their person, and we could hand over the third set to Monster Turban. Around four in the morning, the time of the first call to prayer, the Virtue and Vice guys were back. There was a series of thumps on the door before Monster Turban started his yelling.

"Open up! We've given you time to sleep! Open up and leave the room, so we can get what we came for!"

I checked one last time. We'd left one set of tapes lying on the bed next to one of the cameras. It all looked very convincing—or at least it should do to these brain-dead Vice and Virtue thugs.

"You ready?" I whispered to the girls.

They were ashen-faced and exhausted, but they nodded bravely. I didn't know where they had the tapes hidden, but I could guess. I hoped it wasn't too uncomfortable.

"Open up! NOW!" came a growl from behind the door.

I went and unlocked it.

"Over there," Monster Turban ordered. "Wait on the balcony until we're done."

With the three of us standing outside, Monster Turban and his thugs proceeded to turn over the room. They pounced on the tapes and the camera and made a real show of checking that nothing had been hidden. Still, I felt sure they wouldn't dare search us. For them to lay their hands on a woman would have been a grave crime. It was the kind of thing that would result in them getting their hands lopped off and added to the Tree of Amputations.

Finally, they were done. "We have what we wanted," Monster Turban declared, waving his gun in my face. "You, come outside. The other two stay here."

We stepped through the door, and he turned on me. "We are here! We are here! We run this country! We make sure the Islamic rules are implemented! Who do you think you are, challenging me?"

As he ranted and raved, he had this burning, fanatical glare in his eyes. Fanatics. How I despise them. It doesn't matter what brand of fanaticism they espouse—communism, Islamism, fascism, racism—I just can't abide their blind prejudice and hatred. Monster Turban epitomized all that was wrong with our country. I was sickened by him.

"Go ahead and take whatever you want," I retorted, my fury boiling over. "But one thing is certain. I was raised here. Much of this city was built by my father. You think I would ever desert this place because of people like you? I have seen so many of you come and go. I was here before you, and I will be here after you and all your kind are gone!"

He glared at me, his eyes bulging as he prodded me with his gun barrel. "You are crazy. *Crazy!* You better watch your words—"

"No! You watch your words!" I cut him off. "You and all your kind. I was here before you and I will be here after you. And don't you ever damn well forget it!"

"If you were a man I would kill you." The words were grated out, full of a menacing evil.

I eyed him for a second, challenging him to fire. "You never spare your weapon on anyone, whether women or children or the old, so why start now?"

"You lie!" he yelled. "We never kill women, because they are defenseless. We only ever beat them!"

"Listen, you got what you came for, so just go. Go!" I turned back into the room and slammed the door. "Just get the hell out of here!" I yelled through it, in English. "And take all those dumb, mindless, fanatical sons of bitches with you!"

I was pissed as hell. But I was also scared to death, and trying my best to hide it. They could take us prisoner at any moment, and the good guys in the Taliban seemed to have no power to do anything about it. I was scared for my life, but more so for that of Randall and Christine, those two American women who had trusted me enough to take them into Kabul under the Taliban.

Later that morning I headed to Sabera's house for the graduation. As soon as I got into her basement, my anger and fear dissolved. Within seconds I had tears in my eyes. The sense of joy and excitement and achievement here was palpable, and totally overpowering. I'd gone from being so burned up in anger to being able to see the beautiful light at the end of the tunnel, and all in a matter of hours.

We lit candles in the basement, and their dancing flames shed a warm glow that beat back the shadows. It was stiflingly hot and airless, but it wasn't as if we could open a window. That would risk the forbidden sound of girls' education filtering out onto the streets of Kabul, which in turn risked drawing the attention of Monster Turban and his ilk.

One by one the soon-to-be-graduates trickled in. They were cute fourteen- and fifteen-year-olds, and for a moment it struck me how incongruous they looked, crowding into Sabera's candlelit basement in their smart new outfits. But what affected me most was the amazing faith they had in the future, in spite of the risks they had run getting here and the uncertainty that lay ahead. They had an innocence and a trust that melted my heart. Whatever it took, we simply had to find a way to keep educating these girls.

I stood out front alongside Mary and Sabera. Sabera had handwritten these beautiful graduation certificates, each of which bore the individual child's name. One by one the girls were called. Sabera handed each their certificate, and Mary gave them a basket of sweets and cookies to take home. We couldn't even give a round of applause, for fear the noise would alert the Taliban. As I watched Sabera and Mary handing out those precious graduation gifts, I knew in my heart what truly wonderful women they were, and how much this meant to each and every one of those girls.

For me this was a bittersweet moment. On the one hand, I tried to share in the girls' pure and simple joy. On the other, I was worried about what we would do next. When we had started these schools I had just presumed the Taliban would never last. But now we were graduating our first students, and what we really needed was a proper high school. And how on earth were we going to start one under the eagle eyes of the Taliban?

The girls left in ones and twos to return to their homes. Mary readied herself to leave. She gave me a hug and a kiss.

"Suraya-*jan*, that was beautiful. And you know something, you did a wonderful job. I'm looking forward to the next one already!"

Sabera and I were left sitting at her kitchen table. She glanced at me. "Suraya-*jan*, I thought you would be happier. You look sad."

I tried to shrug off my mood. "You know, I'm worried about those girls.

They're soon going to be young women, and then it won't be so easy for them to sneak past the Taliban patrols."

Sabera nodded her head. "I know."

"We could get away with it when they were little. But now . . . They've got so much hope, Sabera, and so much faith in us. What the hell are we going to do?"

"God is great," Sabera replied, simply. "Something will turn up."

"Sabera-*jan*, where are you from?" I asked her

"I was born in Samangan Province. I stayed there until my father got a government job in Kabul. So I guess I am a Kabuli, but my heart is still in Samangan."

"Let's hope one day we can go there, to Samangan, and start a school."

Sabera gave me a look, as if she couldn't believe that it might be possible. "Do you promise, Suraya-*jan*? That if we can, we will start a school in Samangan?"

I smiled. "Of course."

Sabera reached out to me, and we sealed that promise with a handshake across her kitchen table. She sat back with a smile and a laugh, as if it was all so easy, as if that Samangan school was already a certainty.

Perhaps it was due to our run-in with the Virtue and Vice goons, but for whatever reason, both Mr. Zahid and his assistant, Qari-Basir, decided to accompany us on our journey to Logar to assess the clinic there. Shortly after we'd left Kabul for the long drive south, Qari-Basir pulled a music cassette out of his robes and handed it to our driver.

The driver stared at it for a second. "Sir, what do I do with this?" he asked, hesitantly.

"It's a tape cassette," Qari-Basir replied. "You have a tape player in the car. You put the cassette into the player, and press play."

None of us quite knew how to respond. Under the Taliban, all music was banned. If they caught you playing any music at all, it was big trouble. And after my experiences of the last twenty-four hours I didn't feel like taking any chances with these guys.

"So, shall we have some music, or not?" Mr. Zahid prompted.

"But I thought music was forbidden," I ventured.

Qari-Basir laughed. "Well, we are human, aren't we? We are all human in this vehicle. So let's have some music!"

The driver slotted the cassette into the tape player. It turned out to be a compilation of songs from the popular Afghan singer Nashenas. Soon Mr. Zahid, Qari-Basir, and I were singing along to the words.

What a crazy country Afghanistan had become under the Taliban. It was as if several parallel universes existed side by side, and you could never quite be sure which one you were living in.

SEVENTEEN

The Kindness of Strangers

I T WAS A SIX-HOUR DRIVE ON A TERRIBLE ROAD TO REACH THE LOGAR clinic, and even Qari-Basir's tape started to get a bit repetitive. The road wound ever higher into a series of dust-dry hills, which were humped into a barren, sun-baked landscape bereft of trees or shade. It was the burning heat of the afternoon by the time we reached the clinic, its whitewashed walls emerging from the furnace of the surrounding landscape, dancing and shimmering in the haze.

The building itself was smart but spartan. There were patients galore, but what was completely lacking were any medical supplies. A few dedicated staff were hanging on in the hope of a miracle—one that would deliver to them the drugs that they so needed. As I walked into the main treatment room, Christine and her camera were right behind me on my shoulder. The women hurriedly covered their faces. It was fine for them to be unveiled in the clinic, but not before foreigners bearing a film camera.

I spoke to one pregnant mother who had walked for six hours to get here. "How old are you, sister?" I asked her.

"Twenty-five," she replied.

By now I had grown accustomed to how life in rural Afghanistan aged people. But when I translated for Randall and Christine, I could see how shocked they were. The woman had a lined and careworn face, and most of her teeth were missing when she smiled. By "our" standards she could easily have been sixty-five years old.

"How many children do you have?" I asked.

"Six."

"Why do you have so many, sister?"

She shrugged. "I can't control it, and my husband believes God sends the children food, so we have no need to worry."

Hers was a common-enough story in rural Afghanistan. Christine paused to film a particularly striking image. There were health posters tacked to the walls, but those showing women had tiny cloth "veils" taped over their faces. It made me laugh, but at least they weren't enveloped in an all-encompassing burka. In fact the women in the clinic seemed remarkably free. Beneath their white coats, the female staff had skirts and stockings, and some were even wearing makeup.

"Tell me something, Mr. Zahid," I asked our Taliban host. "The women here seem relaxed in their dress. So why are the Taliban so harsh on Kabuli women?"

"Well, Kabul has been Sin City for years, and Kabuli women are very Westernized. That is not the way women should be. Women should always obey their fathers, brothers, and husbands. Those are the rules within Islam."

There was an inherent contradiction in what Mr. Zahid had said, for by anyone's reckoning the women's dress and makeup here was partly "Westernized." It was almost as if the Taliban were punishing the women of Kabul for their past by oppressing them. But I didn't ponder it too deeply: the Taliban's rules were plagued by inconsistencies and contradictions.

On the drive back to Kabul I did some rough, back-of-the-envelope calculations. The Logar clinic served some two thousand patients a month. If HTAC were to get involved, we'd keep most of the existing staff, hire more, and stock the clinic with medicines, after which we could easily double the number of patients. We'd be helping over twenty thousand Afghans a year who at present had precious little access to health care. Taliban or no Taliban, it was a no-brainer, really. Once I was back in the States I'd put it to the HTAC board. It would mean raising more funds, but I figured it was worth it to help that many people get access to health care.

It was late by the time we reached Kabul. Under the Taliban, the only flights going into and out of Afghanistan were run by these tiny charter airlines. We had booked one to fly us out of Kabul the following morning. The company that we were flying with was PACTEC, a U.S. operation and one of the more reputable ones. Still, I wasn't relishing the prospect.

We were all desperate to get some sleep prior to departure. I awoke early and went to reception to deal with the bill, but I was told that the Ministry of Foreign Affairs had covered it. Mr. Zahid was no saint, yet true to his word his ministry had paid for our stay. We loaded up a taxi and left for the airport. Randall, Christine, and I would be leaving, Sekander remaining in Kabul to spend some time with his family.

"Sekander, I'm really sorry the Taliban beat you when they grabbed our camera," Randall ventured. "I'm sorry that had to happen. I hope it wasn't just 'cause we were there filming."

"Don't worry," Sekander replied. "I am a soldier and an Afghan. They may beat the body, but they cannot kill the spirit."

Sekander detected that we had a tail. It was the thugs from the Vice and Virtue Ministry. Unsurprisingly, they followed us right to the airport. I joked about how nice it was for them to be seeing us off in person, but beneath the humor I was worried. Randall and Christine had dozens of tapes hidden in places I didn't even want to imagine. We all sensed how near we were to having pulled this off, but until we were on that flight, we had nothing.

The Virtue and Vice guys cornered us in the airport, threatening arrest and imprisonment if we didn't hand over all that we had filmed. Finally I cut a deal whereby Randall and Christine were allowed to board the tiny charter aircraft, but not me.

"Your friends have been taking pictures and it is forbidden!" the Vice and Virtue guy harangued me. "We know what these stupid foreigners do! They come here, take pictures of our women, and then you see those photographs on the front pages of their newspapers. It's like they're laughing at us. They can't tell us how to live our lives!"

It was on the tip of my tongue to say: *Don't flatter yourself, buddy! The world doesn't care. Afghanistan is a forgotten land.* But I knew that wouldn't get me onto that airplane.

"I will make sure those pictures show nothing that's disrespectful to Afghanistan," I told him.

"If there is, we will not allow you back into this country," he threatened. "We'll stop you running your clinics! We have the power to do that, you know."

"I promise nothing's going to be shown that's disrespectful," I repeated. "Now, you either let me get on that plane or I'll miss it."

"You know how the evil Western media distorts the truth about the great things the Taliban are doing in Afghanistan. Their agenda is anti-Taliban and . . ."

On and on he went. I could see the aircraft's propellers spinning up to speed, and every minute it sat there was another in which this idiot might decide to haul Randall and Christine—*and the tapes*—off the plane.

"Look, I promise the evil Western journalists will do nothing to bash the Taliban," I told him. "But I've got to go. My flight is leaving . . . *now*."

I turned and ran toward the plane. I placed my foot on the steps, and hands reached down to haul me inside. The door slammed shut, and I let out a sigh of relief.

"What happened?" Randall exclaimed. "What did they want?"

"I had to promise you evil Western Taliban-bashing journalists wouldn't show any nasty pictures. They said unless I promised, they'd never allow me back again."

"What?" asked Randall. She looked worried and confused.

"Look, it's been a rough few days. Don't worry about it. We're getting out of here!"

As the aircraft lifted off, Randall started cheering, and suddenly we all were. I turned to wave good-bye to Sekander. As we pulled away from Kabul toward the soaring mountains, Randall and Christine started fishing tapes out of their underwear.

"Thank God I don't have to sit on those anymore!" Randall exclaimed.

From my perspective, it was mission accomplished. I had gotten the women in and out of Afghanistan with their film. It was Randall who now had the mountain to climb. She had to raise the money to edit the film and find a broadcaster to show it. I didn't hold out any great hopes: media interest in Afghanistan was lukewarm at the best of times. But if it happened, the positive exposure for HTAC would be fantastic. It might even help us raise the money I needed for the Logar clinic, which was my next priority.

PART III

Battling for Hearts and Minds

SEPTEMBER 2001–PRESENT

EIGHTEEN

The Darkest Day

THERE WAS NEVER ENOUGH MONEY—OR AT LEAST, NEVER ENOUGH for the increasing range of commitments that HTAC was taking on. Each trip seemed to bequeath a new burden. I couldn't share my money worries with Omar, my assistant in Virginia; I was paying him a wage, and he needed to believe that HTAC was a reasonably reliable employer. Increasingly I'd found myself confiding in Aziz Qarghah. I knew I could trust him completely, plus he ran his own charity, Afghan Health & Dvelopment Services, so he knew about the challenges of raising funds.

Aziz was a fantastic listener, and I suppose I unburdened myself on him an awful lot. I hadn't forgotten his declaration of love, and a part of me knew that he was listening to my grumblings largely out of affection for me. He was an incredibly easygoing person: anyone who could put up with my ranting had to be!

One day shortly after our return from the Kabul filming mission, I was bending Aziz's ear. "We're at 250,000 dollars a year basic running costs, and most from individual donations. It's like walking a goddamn tightrope. And now we have this Logar clinic to find money for."

"You know," he said, smiling, "I think I know so much about your financial problems that I've actually memorized your bank account number."

I guessed that was his polite way of telling me that he'd had enough of my whining, and that he had his own problems too.

A couple of months after getting back from that filming trip, I put a call through to Randall in New York.

"Guess what's happened?" I asked her.

"No idea. What?"

"I've just gotten your camera back! The one the Vice and Virtue goons stole. It arrived today in the post, and it looks completely unharmed. All the way from Peshawar via the postal service. Amazing, huh?"

Randall just couldn't believe it. But I'd come to expect the wholly unexpected with Afghanistan. Randall had secured some interest in her film, but she figured she needed more footage to really hook someone.

"Do you know when you're next going?" she asked me.

"For sure, before the end of the year."

"Okay, I'd like to go with you."

I appreciated how tough it was for Randall to get any mainstream media interested in Afghanistan. Under the Taliban, the country had fallen off everyone's radar screen. But little did I know how that was about to change. Afghanistan was about to be thrust into the world headlines, and for the worst of all possible reasons.

I sat down to breakfast in my apartment one morning a few days after speaking with Randall. I'd become a total news junkie since starting HTAC, and I had the TV permanently tuned to CNN. I wasn't paying any great attention, but out of the corner of my eye I saw this image of an airliner plowing into one of the Twin Towers in New York. *Oh my God, what a tasteless ad,* I told myself. *What people will do to sell life insurance!*

I didn't think any more of it. On the drive into work I was running through the day's tasks in my mind. I was first into the office, but when I turned on my computer and logged onto the Internet, there was that ghostly image again. I clicked on the image and read the breaking news, and suddenly I realized that this was for real.

"Oh my God!" I exclaimed. "Oh my God, no!"

Moments later the story changed from New York to Washington—my hometown—as reports of a plane striking the Pentagon came in. I rushed down to the front desk of my office building. I was desperate for some human contact. To talk to someone. Anyone. The only person there was the receptionist, who was in floods of tears.

"Did you hear about the planes?" I blurted out.

"Which one?" she sobbed.

"They just hit the Pentagon!"

"Oh my God!" I could see the disbelief and fear in her face.

Back in our office news was coming in of a fourth hijacked plane crashing somewhere. Then Aziz arrived. He gave me a long hug, which was what I really needed, and then Omar was there. I shut the office door, and the three of us stared at one another in utter horror. I could tell what they were thinking: *What on earth are we going to do now?*

"That's it. It's all over," I blurted out. "There's nothing to do but to go home."

Omar shook his head in confusion. "What do you mean?"

I was tearful now. "Omar, I'm sorry. I know how much you love HTAC. But I really think we have to kiss this organization good-bye. We're finished."

"But . . ."

"Listen, guys, let's be realistic! Yes, we've got clinics and schools and so much to do there, but Osama bin Laden is in Afghanistan, and no one's pretending that he didn't do this. I know America will retaliate, and rightfully so. We've got so much to do there, but we're finished. It's over, guys. *It's over.*"

Anyone who'd worked for as long as I had in Afghanistan knew that the Taliban leadership was close to bin Laden. After leaving his native Saudi Arabia, bin Laden had made Afghanistan his base for the last seven years, and his enmity toward the West was renowned. Bin Laden had made it clear he planned to launch "spectacular" attacks on America, and I had no doubt at all that he was responsible.

I went out of our office and ripped down the HTAC sign. I gazed at it: HELP THE *AFGHAN* CHILDREN. The word *Afghan* screamed out at me. How on earth were we going to explain ourselves? It was from Afghanistan that bin Laden had masterminded the unfolding horror. And to most Americans,

Afghanistan would soon be known as the country that had attacked them.

I felt as hurt and angry as any American, but who would ever believe me if I tried to tell them? Why would anyone listen? A lot of Americans would react by saying let's nuke Afghanistan, and I couldn't say I blamed them. It was a horrible, sickening mess, and I just knew that HTAC was done for.

I shut the door and locked the office. I went home and popped a couple of sleeping pills. As I drifted into unconsciousness I said good-bye to all the people who we had helped: Fatima; Naqibullah; the Kabul girls' school pupils; the lovely people of Rostaq; Sabera; Mary and her ugly dolls; Sekander; Dr. Abdullah; and now the patients at the Logar Clinic. HTAC was finished. Bin Laden and his lunatics had slain the dream.

The following day I drove into the office to begin shutting things down. Everywhere I looked I could see the fear and anger on people's faces. For the first time ever in America, I was afraid. The American people had been hurt badly, and they didn't know who they could trust anymore. I wasn't afraid of being attacked physically, but I was afraid of what people might say. I was afraid that they would blame me for what had happened, because I was an Afghan and a Muslim.

But the worst thing of all was feeling separate and apart. I felt like an alien in my own country, dislocated from the land that I call home. I had lived in the United States for nineteen years, longer than I had in Afghanistan. I loved this country with a fierce passion, and I too was hurting because we had been attacked. Difference was, I didn't feel like I could talk to my fellow Americans about it, for I was feeling guilty and somehow responsible. It was as if a barrier had slammed shut between us.

For the average American, this was about the pain of losing three thousand innocents to an act of mass murder. It was the pain of witnessing an unprovoked attack on American soil. I knew the retaliation from the United States would be fast and furious and would hit my birth country hard. The conflicting emotions were tearing me apart. My pain was twofold. I had the pain of being an American in a country that had been attacked, and I had the pain of being from a country that I was certain would soon be at war. More lives would be lost in Afghanistan, and nothing would be achieved.

I was convinced from the word go that none of the suicide attackers could be Afghans. (So it would prove: none of the hijackers were from Afghanistan.) Suicide bombing was not something that Afghans would do, not unless they were brainwashed in those Pakistani madrassas. But to many Americans there was little difference: Afghans, Pakistanis, Arabs—we were all guilty. I wanted to yell and scream: *I am hurting as badly as you, only more!* In truth, I was scared. I feared that my American friends would be angry and accusatory. I was convinced that no one would believe me, or listen, or care.

So I sat in our office the day after 9/11 and contemplated the unthinkable: breaking the news to our people that it was all over. I checked our bank balance and did some rough calculations. With the funds HTAC had remaining I figured we could continue for three months, so that was the time when I would have to let everyone go. Sooner or later I had to pick up the phone and start delivering the bad news.

My thoughts were broken by a ringing of the office phone. It startled me. Since the horrific events of the day before, the office had fallen eerily silent. Maybe it was one of the guys—Dr. Abdullah or Nawabi, calling from Peshawar. Maybe they knew the game was up, the clinic was finished, and they were calling to make it easier on me. I reached over and answered.

"Suraya Sadeed."

"Hi, my name is Susan," a very American-sounding voice announced. "Susan Appleyard. You don't know me, but I've been supporting HTAC for years. I send one hundred dollars a month. I was a Peace Corps volunteer in Afghanistan, and I have such wonderful memories of your country. The Afghans are such wonderful people. . . ."

The line went quiet, and I realized that Susan was crying. I felt the tears rolling down my own cheeks.

"This must be such a difficult time for you," Susan struggled on. "So I just called to say I totally understand what you're going through, and you are in my heart."

I broke down and started sobbing. I didn't know what to say.

"As an American, I'm very angry," Susan continued, "but I can't get the images of the wonderful people of your country out of my mind. I know the U.S. will retaliate. But I also know that if I'm thinking of those wonderful Afghan people that I knew so long ago, then God only knows what you must be going through."

Susan and I spoke for forty-five tearful minutes. At the end of the call she made me a promise.

"We Peace Corps veterans are going to put a letter together to the White House," she said. "We're gonna write to President Bush, begging him to spare the Afghan people, for they are the victims of bin Laden and his lot. They've been suffering under him for so long, and the Taliban too. They don't need our bombs. They really do not. . . ."

"I really appreciate that," I told her. "Please, will you e-mail me a copy?"

"Of course, I'll keep you in the loop."

"And, Susan, I really, really appreciate your call. You have no idea how much this means to me."

I put the phone down and stared at the receiver. Maybe I had misjudged the American people. It was such an extraordinary thing to have happened. The day after 9/11 it was the last thing I had been expecting. A couple of minutes later the phone rang again. I picked it up with a trembling hand.

"Suraya, how're you doing?" I recognized the voice instantly. It was Christine, Randall's filmmaker friend. "I've been thinking a lot about you over the last twenty-four hours."

"You know, Christine, for me this is extra hard. This time is extra hard. . . . I want to . . . I wish there was a way to let everyone know that Afghans have been suffering for so long under these sons of bitches like bin Laden. And that this has nothing—*nothing*—to do with the poor Afghan people."

"Suraya—I know. I saw the people in the refugee camps. I saw their misery and how they were suffering under the Taliban."

"Thanks, Christine. Just hearing that from an American means so much."

"Why don't you write a letter to President Bush?" Christine suggested.

I laughed. "You think he would read my letter?"

"What do you have to lose? Tell you what—I'm gonna write the letter. You write me an e-mail talking about your fears about what will happen to the Afghan people. I'll draft it into the proper form and context for you to send to Bush, okay?"

I did as Christine had asked. I sat at my desk and typed an e-mail venting all my emotions. I talked about the pain and suffering of the Afghan people, and their fear of retaliation by the United States. I talked about how many Afghans had died fighting the Soviets, so we could win the cold war. I talked of how bin Laden was an unwanted guest in Afghanistan. I e-mailed it to Christine, and she sent me back a fantastic draft letter.

But I almost didn't have the time or space to mail it. My in-box was inundated. The phone just wouldn't stop ringing. And mostly the calls and e-mails showed me a side of America that was simply extraordinary. They were so full of sympathy and a breathtaking generosity of spirit. More and more people kept asking where they could mail their checks, to support the work that HTAC was doing in Afghanistan.

I was stunned. I had honestly believed that HTAC was finished. Instead, funds started flooding in. In a way I fell more in love with my adopted country than ever before, and at a time when it was poised to attack the country of my birth. Those days were the most agonizing of my life. I was in love with America but so fearful that this great and powerful nation would fail to differentiate between the terrorists and the Afghan people, who'd been victimized for so long.

Donations flooded in from across the country. I was humbled. America— it never ceased to amaze me. We got the odd hate mail, but by far the vast majority of the notes were wonderful. *How are you guys holding up? We know what you're going through. We just want to know where we can send a little support.* This was the American people at their best—compassionate, generous, openhearted, and caring—and Omar, Aziz, and I soon found ourselves having to work flat out to deal with it all.

When I got a moment I did mail that letter to President Bush, plus I circulated it to the thousands of e-mail addresses on our database. This is what I wrote:

Dear Mr. President,

I am crying behind the closed doors of my office, because I cannot cry outside. Why? Because I was born in Afghanistan.

The fear that I have had for years has been realized. I knew that Afghanistan would have to pay for having Osama bin Laden as its unwanted "guest." The fact that Osama bin Laden is in Afghanistan has nothing to do with the Afghan people themselves. He is not an Afghan and he is not supported by Afghans. He came by force and will only leave by force. Did the people invite him? No. Can they remove him? No.

Afghans are terrorized themselves. I have seen the unspeakable pain and agony of millions who are in constant fear, living a powerless, shackled existence where even learning, or showing a woman's face, is now outlawed. Afghans did not elect their government. They have no voice.

For too long Afghanistan has been a forgotten nation—one that paid a heavy price by fighting a war for freedom against the invading Soviet Union, which benefited the United States and the world—a war that helped bring about the end of the cold war.

Our small nation sacrificed over one million lives, had five million refugees, two million widows, over one million orphans, over half-a-million amputees. Afghanistan is a country in enormous pain and is drowning in her sorrows.

I ended the letter making a plea for America's response to be proportionate, and not to further punish the Afghan people. The response I got from circulating that letter was overwhelming. Within twenty-four hours I'd gotten over seventeen hundred e-mails. Mostly people said that it had opened their eyes to the plight of the Afghan people, caught between bin Laden's blind hatred and America's righteous rage.

A call came in from the *Christian Science Monitor* newspaper. Someone had forwarded a copy of my letter to them, and they asked to publish it. I said that I was fine with that, for it was good to get as much exposure for it as possible. There was a flood of reactions to that publication. Maybe 10 percent were negative, or even downright hostile.

One e-mail read: *If I was in the White House I'd nuke your Goddamn country.*

Another read: *Let them all burn in hell.*

But perhaps the worst was this: *For every American who died we want 500 to die in Afghanistan.*

Yet the remaining 90 percent were kind and supportive and full of redeeming hope. Every letter we received in the mail seemed to come with a check.

One American lady wrote me the following, which had me in tears:

> *I'm 88 years old and I'm a great-grandma. But I know about the sad history of Afghanistan, for I was a history teacher. My prayers would be with you and your people. I'm sorry that this is all I can give.*
>
> *Ruth, Oklahoma*

With the letter was a five-dollar bill. To me that five dollars was as valuable as any fifty-thousand-dollar donation. It was so uplifting. I took that five-dollar bill and put it beneath the sheet of glass I had covering my desk. Every time I looked at it I remembered Grandma Ruth from Oklahoma, and it lifted me up. Whatever was going to happen next, I told myself that I wouldn't want to live anywhere but the USA.

It was maybe a week after 9/11 when I turned to Omar and Aziz and said: "You know, maybe we're not finished. Maybe we're not finished after all."

Barely a week after that we had nearly $500,000 in the HTAC account. All I could think was: *God, what a country.*

"Can you imagine, we've never had this much money—*not ever*," I remarked to the guys. "Imagine, we can take some of it and build schools in Afghanistan. Proper schools. *Real schools.* We can afford to, you know. The Taliban will soon be gone, and then we can start building schools. God— that's my dream."

"You think this money is going to keep flooding in?" Aziz remarked. "Don't overreach yourself. Try not to run before you can walk."

"Well, that's just a typical man's comment," I teased. "Men! Always ready to criticize."

"Women!" Aziz shook his head. "You never know what they're thinking from one moment to the next. You were the one saying that we were done for!"

"What do you mean by that?" I countered.

"Fifteen days back you said we were all done."

"Well, who could ever have predicted this kind of reaction! I mean, all these letters and these donations—it's mind-blowing."

"Women! You never can tell what they're thinking!" Aziz kept on repeating that phrase until I started laughing.

"Great!" he exclaimed. "Now that's what I wanted to see. You haven't smiled for days, but that did it!"

Three weeks after 9/11 the media inquiries started coming. Exhausted from tracking the terrorist connections, the American press was searching for different angles. I took a call from *USA Today*.

"I want to know how you're bearing up," the reporter asked. "How are things, for a group like yours that works in Afghanistan?"

"It's simply amazing," I told him. "We're getting donations from the American people on a level we've never experienced before."

"Amazing! So how does that make you feel?"

"Well, it's fantastic. It's so uplifting. It's made me love this country and its people more than ever."

USA Today put HTAC and several other nonprofits on the front page. The story was all about the amazing way the U.S. public had reacted to the horrors of 9/11. The response to that story was huge, and among the many calls that I received was one from a guy called Doug Hostetter. Doug worked for two charities—the Mennonite Central Committee and the Quakers' American Friends Service Committee.

He quickly got to the purpose of his call. "Are you planning on going to Afghanistan in the near future? We have some emergency funds we'd like to give."

"Well, we'd like to," I told him. "But I'm not sure where we'd go. Things are difficult right now. We can't go to the Taliban areas. We could go to the north maybe."

"I've heard there's a lot of people stranded between the Taliban forces and the Northern Alliance?"

"Yeah, that's what I've heard too."

"Well, we have forty-five thousand dollars, and we'd like to donate it to HTAC, if it can go toward helping those people."

I did some research into Doug's two charities, the Mennonite and American Friends committees. Their goal was to help wherever there was suffering in the world, regardless of race, color, or creed. They had a strong Christian base and a long-lived tradition of peacemaking and nonviolence. Their $45,000 donation would be the single biggest that HTAC had ever received.

I started researching what exactly HTAC might do to help the refugees trapped between the Taliban and the Northern Alliance. I called Randall to tell her that was what our next trip was shaping up to be and to get her bags packed and her cameras ready.

But she sounded oddly subdued. "You know, Suraya, I've been speaking to the State Department, and they say it's not a good time to go."

I laughed. "Come on! When has State ever said it's a good time to go? They never say that."

"Yeah, but it's kind of different now. I mean, they know more than we know about what's gonna happen. And, you know, maybe you shouldn't go, Suraya. It could be very dangerous. Maybe they're planning to do something—"

"Of course they're planning to do something," I cut in. "But when's that ever stopped us from going?"

Randall said she'd think it over and get back to me. It was fair enough. Things had changed. Post 9/11 the world would never be the same again, for Afghans more than just about anyone.

I got a call from ABC News, asking if they could send a crew to film our forthcoming mission. I told them that I'd get back to them. I felt obligated to Randall, and I had to let her have first refusal. I called her again.

"Randall, I've got ABC saying they want to come," I told her. "They've promised they'll send Diane Sawyer with us and get us on prime time. I'm calling you first, but I need your response within twenty-four hours, okay?"

"Suraya, I'm definitely coming," Randall assured me. "I'm talking to people right now about a fantastic film deal, so I'm gonna put my worries to one side and come with you. Trust me, I'm definitely coming."

"Okay. That's fine. That's enough for me."

Randall came down to our Virginia office. She'd gotten herself a fantastic offer to make a film for Oxygen Media, a cable TV company founded by a group of media executives including Oprah Winfrey. I could tell that Randall was happy, but underneath the excitement there was something else.

"You're real angry, aren't you, Randall?" I asked her.

"Hell, I'm a New Yorker!" she replied. "The day this happened it changed my life."

The events of 9/11 had happened in Randall's backyard, and she'd witnessed it pretty much firsthand. The destruction of the Twin Towers and all the associated death and darkness had hit her hard. If anything, it reinforced the sense of loyalty I felt to Randall and the conviction that it was she we should take to Afghanistan.

I desperately wanted Sekander on this trip, for I knew security was going to be paramount. But try as I might, there was no way to get him—or Dr. Abdullah and Nawabi—out of Peshawar and into the territory of the Northern Alliance, which was our only route into the displaced persons area. All flights had been shut down, due to the coming air war. I was forced to assemble a team bereft of all my regulars. There was Randall, but no Christine, for Randall had hired a new cameraperson, Chris Andersen.

A tough and worldly journalist called Michael Lerner was also coming, plus Doug Hostetter.

I'd jumped at the chance of having Doug along. Even over the phone there was something about the guy that communicated this calm and principled honesty, and I just knew that he'd be invaluable support. It was going to be a tough mission, my toughest yet, I reckoned.

NINETEEN

The Wrong Side of the Border

I MET UP WITH DOUG AT THE AIRPORT. HE HAD TO BE IN HIS SIXTIES, tall and slender with curly white hair and a pepper-gray beard, and he had a wise, peaceable aura about him. Doug had first experienced war in Vietnam, and from there on he had dedicated his life to spreading peace. He had seen a lot in his life; I could read it in his eyes. I felt instinctively that I could trust him.

Upon reaching Dushanbe we began a process similar to that of our quake-relief mission to Rostaq. In addition to getting the usual permissions and paying the necessary bribes, we had to hire trucks to carry the food aid and blankets. Fortunately Doug was a veteran of war-zone relief operations, and he soon had all of that under control.

We were staying in the Hotel Tajikistan again, but this time it was crawling with foreigners. Every news organization on the planet had sent a crew, and they were fighting to be first across the border. We played the usual waiting game: waiting for visas; waiting for travel permits; waiting to get our supplies of aid, which I was sourcing locally. Randall went off to shoot some footage around Dushanbe, and I decided to pay a visit to the bookseller of Dushanbe—for here I was, again desperate for something to read.

It was four years since my last visit, but the minute the bookseller laid eyes on me he broke into that dazzling golden smile.

"Welcome back!" he declared. And then, sadly: "I'm so sorry about what happened in America. I know that bad things will happen in Afghanistan now, but at least we will be rid of bin Laden and the Taliban. We were so worried they were coming to Tajikistan."

I didn't want to talk about 9/11 and the coming U.S. response. I noticed that he was wearing a similar hat to last time, but not as pretty.

"Hey, what happened to your cap?" I asked. "The black velvet one with lovely flowers all over it."

He laughed. "You remember my cap?"

"Sure! It was beautiful."

He glanced down at his bulging tummy. "You know, I got very fat, and the cap no longer fit me. And my wife said that I looked silly with it perched on my head, so I gave it to my son. I have some new books in Persian," he added. "Last time, you chose *Step by Step until We Meet God*. Is that the kind of thing you're after?"

I smiled. "Yeah. It is."

In the pain of the aftermath of 9/11, I really hungered for some Sufi philosophy. I craved the words of those who preached enlightenment, love, and tolerance, not the totalitarian creed of hatred and blind prejudice espoused by bin Laden and his cronies. I chose four books, but the one that really interested me was called *Az koja aamada aim wa ba kaja merawaym?—Where Do We Come From and Where Are We Going?*

"I tell you what, will you keep these safe for me?" I asked, handing the bookseller the other three volumes. "I have to go to Afghanistan."

"Of course," he replied. He gave me a look, a mixture of curiosity and real concern. "But do you really have to go? We don't want to lose you. I'll be lost."

"Yes, I have to go," I told him. "So, any discount on the books?"

He shrugged. "Okay, whatever you can pay is fine."

"But once you say that, you know I can't pay less than what you ask."

He grinned mischievously. "I know—that's the idea." I handed him the money. "God be with you on your journey, my sister," he told me.

Forty-eight hours later, our convoy was crawling along the road to the border. Progress was painfully slow, mostly because of the flow of traffic against us. Everyone who could appeared to be leaving Afghanistan, in advance of what they knew was coming—the U.S. bombing campaign. I recognized the logos on most of the four-wheel-drives: they were the big aid organizations. Whenever we stopped to let a vehicle pass, this weird, distant droning filled the air.

"B52s," Doug remarked. "The same as they used in Vietnam."

We passed through a series of roadblocks manned by Russian soldiers. Tajikistan may have been an independent country, but the Tajik's fear of the Taliban was so great that they'd invited the old enemy—the Russians—back in. At the final checkpoint a Russian soldier stinking of vodka pointed a crooked, drunken finger at the sky.

"You see those planes," he said, leering. "American B52s. Remember what happened to our comrades here? So now the American fools are coming."

I glanced up, and all of a sudden the horizon erupted in a series of enormous detonations, followed seconds later by an ominous, earth-shaking rumble. For a moment I stood there rooted to the spot, gazing at the slash of explosions sprouting from the distant mountainside. A part of me was frightened. The very idea of driving into an area where such massive lethal force was being unleashed was terrifying. But at the same time I knew that one hundred thousand Afghan people were trapped in there, caught between a resurgent Northern Alliance and Taliban forces that had vowed to fight to the bitter end. And with all other aid agencies fleeing the area, they would be in desperate need.

I turned back to the Russian soldier. "Please, just stamp our passports and let us through," I implored. "We've got work to do over there."

In the no-man's-land after the border post, I found myself transfixed. The earth juddered and shook with a never-ending series of blasts. *What was it about Afghanistan?* I wondered. First the British Empire, then the Soviet Union, and now the United States of America came to focus their military might on our nation. What was it about this poor, blasted land that everyone seemed to want to fight their wars here?

Those were American bombs falling, ones paid for by my tax dollars. For the cost of one of those bombing runs, I doubtless could have fed and clothed and cared for those 100,000 displaced people. For the cost of another bombing run I likely could have educated their children. And that would have done so much more to defeat the blind prejudice and hatred spawned by the Taliban, and bin Laden.

A scene came into my mind as if it were only yesterday. At the time, it was one of the proudest days of my life. Five years after we had arrived in America, Dastagir and I had stood in line in an Alexandria courtroom to be sworn in as citizens of the United States. I had raised my right hand and sworn with all my heart to be faithful to America. I'd promised to bear arms and defend my country against all who might wish her ill.

But I had never imagined that one day America would attack Afghanistan. Had I been able to fast-forward fourteen years from that day and see what I was seeing now, would I still have sworn to be faithful to America, and bear arms on her behalf? I doubted it, for what I was seeing now was unendurable.

Another string of bombs fell, the powerful eruption of smoke and debris engulfing the mountain range before us. I felt a presence beside me. It was Doug Hostetter.

"You know, war is a terrible thing," he remarked. "I can understand how you're feeling, Suraya, but not to the depths you must be feeling it."

I turned to speak to him, but the words just wouldn't come. All I could feel were the tears of frustration and anger that were burning in my eyes.

A scene a few feet away caught my attention. Randall and her cameraman had set up their kit to film the bombing. They were joined by some other journalists. I could see them talking excitedly and gesturing across the water below us—the river that divides Tajikistan from the territory of the Northern Alliance—toward those almighty explosions.

"Jesus, this is picture-perfect!" one of them remarked.

"Awesome," another exclaimed, as his shutter clicked. "Awesome pictures!"

"The first scenes of the bombing!" a third exclaimed. "Got to be!"

"Goddamn it!" I yelled. "This isn't just a picture! Those are *real* bombs, and there are *real* people beneath them! People are getting blown to pieces over there right now. There's nothing goddamn *perfect* about it!"

Randall looked chastised. "I'm sorry, Suraya."

The rest of the media pack stared at me as if I were an alien. God, was I angry. This was a human tragedy of untold proportions, yet I was surrounded by people who saw it simply as a great photo. To make matters worse, Randall started sticking her camera in my face to record my reactions to the bombing.

"Get out of my face!" I yelled at her, tearfully. "I don't want to be filmed! This is not some goddamn show! This is a humanitarian mission. Go film the civilians who are under those bombs."

Doug took Randall to one side. "Listen, you've got to back off. You don't understand what she's going through right now. This is her country getting bombed here."

We managed to hustle ourselves some places on the rickety ferry that was the only way to cross the river-border. But there wasn't room for our aid trucks, not with the mass of news agencies that were heading into the war zone. I didn't like leaving them behind, but the drivers offered to sleep with the vehicles, which gave a little security.

We'd been advised to seek out the Agency for Technical Cooperation and Development (ACTED), a French NGO and one of the few humanitarian charities remaining in this part of Afghanistan. ACTED was based in the tiny border town of Khwaja Bahauddin, about ten miles short of the camps. There we were introduced to the local head of ACTED, Cyril Dupres de Saint-Maur, a pale-faced, hyperactive Frenchman. ACTED had no intention of leaving, despite the bombs. These guys were the real heroes. As soon as Cyril learned that we were fellow aid workers, he offered us accommodations in their compound and free use of their vehicles.

Cyril advised us to start our aid distributions at the most needy displaced persons camp, Kum Qeshlaq. We could base ourselves at ACTED and move back and forth between there and the camps, which were no more than half an hour's drive away. The problem was getting our truckloads of aid across the border. All the following day we waited, as the ferry kept arriving crammed full of these news agency satellite trucks, and without our vehicles. I was getting more and more angry, and even peaceable Doug was fuming.

He shook his head in despair. "They can afford to hire their own helicopters, yet they monopolize the ferry. They pay the operator over the odds, so our trucks stand idle. They see our trucks with HELP THE AFGHAN CHILDREN on the side in huge letters, yet they're happy to shoulder through to get their story."

I shared Doug's sense of outrage. I had naively expected the media to allow our trucks to go first, but everyone was fighting to get the first pictures of the bombs falling, and that was all that mattered. It was sheer bloody madness.

Two days running we returned to the river, only to find our aid trapped on the far side. At one point a guy from the BBC asked me to do a live interview about our mission. Because it was live, I agreed. I knew exactly what I was going to say.

"I'm here on the Afghan border with Suraya Sadeed, aid worker with Help the Afghan Children," he announced as the cameras zoomed in on us. "The U.S. bombing campaign is under way, and we can hear the bombs falling not far away. Suraya, what's your message to our viewers about what's happening in your country?"

"My message is that you reporters suck, because you're stopping our humanitarian aid from getting through. You give all this money to the ferry operator so your satellite trucks get through, while our food aid convoy remains trapped on the wrong side of the border."

I'd caught the reporter totally off guard. "Well, we'll need to look into that—"

"What do you want me to say?" I demanded. "We're supposed to be bringing food and blankets to distribute to hundreds of thousands of displaced people. We have no option but to come overland with all the weight we're carrying, while you news teams could have come by helicopter. But our aid's trapped on the wrong side of the border!"

The reporter did his best to recover. "I'm so sorry. What can we do to help?"

"Just announce to everyone in the media circus that when there are humanitarians coming through, they must take priority. And help us get our aid trucks across that ferry."

He turned away from me to face the camera. "So, if there's media organizations listening to this, Help the Afghan Children's food aid convoy is trapped. . . ."

I didn't hold out much hope that the broadcast would help, but I did feel a little better having done it. By the evening of the third day, and with our convoy still trapped, Randall was getting worried. There was only so much she could film of me getting angry at the failure of our trucks to get through. She suggested we go visit a girls' school, one that served the camps for displaced Afghans. In terms of her documentary it would knit nicely with the schools theme, and that the Taliban had banned them.

We took some crayons and asked the schoolgirls to draw us images of their lives. Just about every one sketched these scenes of their homes being bombed and burned down. It didn't matter to them who was doing the bombing—whether Northern Alliance, Taliban, or Americans. These kids didn't care. What mattered was that they were trapped inside this never-ending cycle of war.

One child, Nazifa, insisted I come visit her family. Nazifa's mother was illiterate, but that didn't dampen Nazifa's hunger to learn. She wanted to study science so she could be a doctor and help people. The girl's eyes lit up like burning jewels when she told me about it. If ever I needed it, it was a reminder to me of the precious value of education, and of my dream of building proper schools across Afghanistan. For Nazifa's sake, and the thousands like her, I couldn't let my anger and my frustration eclipse all that.

A crowd had gathered outside of Nazifa's temporary home. Barely three miles away the B52s were dropping their long strings of bombs, and the shock waves had shattered windows and deafened people. On the spur of the moment I asked the crowd if anyone knew why the Americans had come to bomb their country.

"They come to rid us of the Taliban!" someone cried.

"And is that a good thing?" I asked.

"We are happy about it," a woman remarked. "If there is peace, we can return to our homes. The kind of cruelty shown to us by the Taliban is like no other."

A young man approached me. He held something out in the palm of his hand. "Do you know what this is, sister? They keep falling from the sky. We do not know it, so we feed it to the donkeys."

I unwrapped the shiny plastic package. Inside there were two small sachets. I opened one and sniffed. It was peanut butter. The other contained jelly. This is what the U.S. military were dropping as "food aid." Peanut butter and jelly sandwiches were about as alien to your average Afghan as eating roasted goat's intestines would be to an American. And so the sachets were getting fed to the donkeys.

I pointed out to Doug the writing on the packet. It had PEANUT BUTTER & JELLY written on one side, in English, and the same in Spanish on the other. We couldn't help laughing. It was unbelievable, but it looked as if the rations had been designed for some other war, in some Spanish-speaking corner of the world.

"Ask if there have been leaflets dropped from the sky," Doug suggested. "You know—paper with writing."

I asked, and in no time several people had produced scraps of paper. I took one and inspected it. On the one side was a picture of an American soldier shaking hands with a guy with an enormous turban. On the other side, in both Pashto and Dari, was written: WE ARE FRIENDS. WE ARE HERE TO HELP. WE ARE HERE ON A PEACE MISSION.

I asked one of the guys when they had started falling from the sky.

He gestured at his ears and shook his head. "Speak up, sister. I can't hear you. Since they started the bombing, my ears hurt. There's blood in my ears."

On the morning of day four our trucks finally got through. We headed directly for the displaced persons camp, driving the twenty-odd kilometers across the dark, bleak plateau of the Khwaja Bahauddin plain. I wondered what I was going to say when we got there. Normally I'd start by announcing that I'd brought help from the United States, but today, with the B52s dropping bombs on the near horizon, I just didn't feel I could go there.

Instead I let people know that I was an Afghan, and that we had brought food and blankets, and we invited the most needy to form a line. After a while I left Doug to oversee things, for I wanted to get a feel for how people lived here. I walked among the shapeless hordes of the dispossessed, their tents and their makeshift hovels stretching as far as the eye could see. It was October, and the freezing Afghan winter had come early for the refugees. I crouched in the chill by spluttering fires and hugged the women and babies. I asked a young girl what they were cooking.

"We have nothing," she replied.

Another girl wouldn't stop crying. I asked her why. The Taliban had killed her parents and she was completely alone. She was such a bright, beautiful child, yet if there was a school here, and if I gave her crayons, I knew for sure what she would draw. She would draw pictures of the soldiers gunning down her folks and burning her home. And probably every child in this godforsaken, windswept place would do likewise.

Everywhere I went Randall seemed to follow me with her camera. I tried to be as accommodating as I could. With the trucks arriving so late, she'd been tearing her hair out over her filming schedule. We were almost two weeks in now: one week traveling in via Dushanbe; the best part of another week waiting for the trucks. Randall was itching to get back to the United States, and none of our party had planned for a trip lasting this long.

That evening Randall and her cameraman prepared to leave for the long journey to the United States. They had to get back and file their stories. The aid distribution was far from finished, and Doug offered to stay to help. But I knew he was keen to be on his way, and to report on how we'd spent the donors' money. I guessed I'd cope. After all, the ACTED people were on hand to help.

That evening we drove back to the ACTED compound. Everyone was trying to get some rest, although for some reason Doug and I couldn't sleep. Maybe there was a crucial difference between them and the two of us: the others were here to get their stories, but we were here to try to help the people trapped between the bombs and guns. We were awake, our only seat being the bedding on the floor of our room.

"Suraya, after all we've seen on this trip, how would you describe God?" Doug asked me.

"I think I would say that God is love," I answered.

In the face of all the horrors that we had witnessed, all I had left to hold on to was God's love.

Doug smiled. "That's my kind of God, Suraya."

TWENTY

The Boy Who Killed the American

THE FOLLOWING MORNING, RANDALL, DOUG, AND THE OTHERS left to return to America. I drove back to Kum Qeshlaq camp and went ahead with the aid distribution, providing food and blankets to thousands more cold and hungry people. In the process of doing so I heard about a fourteen-year-old Afghan boy named Yar Mohammad, meaning "the friend of Mohammad," Islam's foremost Prophet. Everyone kept talking about this young Afghan boy and his brave and heroic acts.

I was full of curiosity to meet him, and eventually I persuaded the camp elders to make an introduction. With his white embroidered skullcap and raggedy clothes, Yar Mohammad looked like any typical Afghan kid, but at the same time he had this extraordinary fire burning in his eyes.

"My father says I'm very brave," he told me, proudly. "He says I'll grow up to be a great leader."

"That's wonderful," I remarked. "So, what is it exactly that you've done to earn such respect?"

"I am the first in our area to kill an American soldier," he declared.

"Sorry? What did you say?"

"I am the first to kill an American soldier," he repeated.

I couldn't believe what I was hearing. This war was barely begun and it was being waged from the air, in conjunction with the forces of the Northern Alliance on the ground. There were only a handful of elite U.S. forces located with the Northern Alliance, so how on earth could this young Afghan boy have killed an American soldier?

"I made a bomb," Yar Mohammad explained. "All you do is take a little gunpowder, tamp it down tight, and add a fuse. I put it somewhere where we knew patrols were passing. I waited until I saw one, then blew it up. That's how I killed the American."

"But why did you kill him?" I asked. "And why is that a good thing?"

He shrugged. "He came to my country. He can come here as a guest, and I'll give him all we have. But if he comes here as an enemy and an invader, then I'll kill him."

"But he came here as a friend, to help drive out the Taliban."

"Well, he came here . . ." The bravado was fading now. "My father said if they come—especially those with blue eyes and blond hair—you don't wait: you kill them."

"Don't you think God made them like that because he wanted them to look like that?" I asked, gently.

"My father told me . . . I wanted to prove to him that I could do what he wanted. I did it to uphold our honor."

I felt anger, pity, and empathy for this kid, all at the same time. But most of all I was bowled over by the sheer awfulness of it all. History was repeating itself, and a new generation was coming up that was proud to kill foreigners. I didn't blame this boy for what he had done. I didn't think a fourteen-year-old kid in America would necessarily have done any different. If Afghan soldiers marched through America's streets, would he also kill the "invaders"? Quite possibly. That didn't make Yar Mohammad's actions right, but perhaps it made them more understandable.

The boy who had killed the American soldier took me to meet his father. He was very distinguished-looking Pashtun man, with a craggy face and bristling beard. At some stage he'd lost his two front teeth, leaving a big, gap-toothed smile. He was tall but bowed, his face lined and folded in extraordinary ways. To be forced to live without his own home was the ultimate humiliation and indignity for a proud Afghan man such as him. "I'm so ashamed," he kept telling me. "I'm so ashamed. I can't even provide for my own family."

He invited me into their aid-issued tent. We were joined by the camp elders, and hot, sweet tea was served. There was a very old musket propped in one corner of the tent, and it spoke of centuries of Afghan history. I asked Yar Mohammad's father about it, and he started telling me about the old times, and the wars against the British. His grandfather had carried that musket into battle and killed dozens of British soldiers.

One of the elders butted into the conversation: "Why are you wasting your time telling her who your grandfather killed?" he asked Yar Mohammad's father. "She's a woman, and she knows nothing."

"So what am I supposed to talk to her about?" Yar Mohammad's father countered. "She's a woman and she's not from around here. You think of something to say."

They were speaking Pashto, a language they had to presume I didn't understand. Well, if they wanted to see me as a dumb woman, so be it. I just wanted a chance to talk to Yar Mohammad some more. Eventually the father and the elders ran out of things to say to me, and they left.

I turned to Yar Mohammad. "Tell me, this American that you killed—do you regret it at all?"

"No," he replied, defiantly. "Everyone is proud of me. It was an honorable thing to do."

"Yeah, well, forget about all that pride and honor stuff, is there even a part of you that feels regret?"

He paused for a second, staring at the floor. "You know something—the scene is so vivid in my memory. It keeps coming back to me."

"Back to you like how? In a bad way?"

"I keep dreaming about it. I have these nightmares. In those nightmares I don't want to do what I'm doing."

"Have you told anyone about them?"

He shook his head. "I can't. If I tell my family, it will be seen as a sign of weakness." He glanced at me. "I didn't like what I did. That scene is so vivid in my mind. Every night it comes back to me."

Somehow this boy felt he could confide in me, this stranger who wasn't from his tribe. Beneath the facade of the fearless young man, he was tortured by what he had done, and he wanted to clear his conscience and confess. I felt like giving him a big, motherly hug, but that would have been completely unacceptable in their culture.

I had no doubt that he had killed a man, for the dreams and the trauma were too real. It may have been an American, or maybe it was a Northern Alliance soldier working with the U.S. forces. Who knows? But for me the real tragedy was this: that first killing had been difficult. But next time, would it be easier? I wondered whether he would feel any remorse the next time, or if he would join the ranks of killers bereft of any regret.

Among the mass of displaced people here, everyone was pretty much alike: they shared a harrowing past and an unknowable future. But what had happened to Yar Mohammad—the killing of "the American"—made him different. That's what had made him the focus of a community that had lost everything. And once he had become their talisman, the last thing Yar Mohammad could ever admit to was feeling any remorse.

Yar Mohammad reminded me so much of Naqibullah, the teenage gunman who I had met on the road to Hesar Shahee camp during my first aid mission. Yar Mohammad started visiting the ACTED compound, so he could sit with me in the quiet moments and talk. He had all the curiosity of young boys his age, and he saw me as someone from whom he might learn. I'd brought with me a sat phone, and Yar Mohammad was fascinated by it.

"Can you just talk to Peshawar or the U.S. or anywhere, *Madar-jan?*" he asked.

He'd started to use the same term for me—*madar-jan*; dear mother—as had Naqibullah.

"Yeah, I can," I told him. "Give me a phone number, and we can call them."

He laughed. "I don't have any numbers, *Madar-jan*, I'm just curious, that's all."

Every now and then I'd glance skyward as a new flight of B52s droned overhead, releasing their bombs. I kept having the same thought: for the price of those bombs, we could educate all the Yar Mohammads in that camp. We could feed and clothe the people in those camps. We could come as friends in peace, and win their hearts and minds. It made me so angry I could weep.

For an entire week I shuttled back and forth to the camps, doling out the aid. Yar Mohammad was my constant companion and my guide. One afternoon I sat with him, his father, and the camp elders, discussing their ongoing needs. As is so often the case in Afghanistan, the conversation morphed into something else entirely.

"I know why you are doing this work," Yar Mohammad's father remarked to me. "You are trying to prove yourself to your father. You are trying to prove that you are really a man now."

The elders nodded their heads in solemn agreement. As an "honorary man"—for they saw me as a monied foreigner doing man's work—I was worthy of some proper respect.

"Tell us something," one of the elders remarked. "We know America helped us during the war, giving money and weapons to the Mujahideen to help fight the Soviets. So why are they coming back again now, to bomb our country?"

"Well, you know about the 9/11 terror attacks on America," I began. I glanced around the faces, most of which were blank. "You *do* know about 9/11, don't you?"

"I did hear something on the BBC Dari Service," one of the elders remarked. "But the Taliban deny everything."

"What is this 9/11 thing?" another elder asked. "What has it to do with us?"

For years the Taliban had kept tight control of the Afghan media. Stuck in the camps, and crushed between the warring forces, these people had precious little access to news anyway. They had little idea why America was coming to their country, or who exactly it was fighting. In their eyes America was attacking Afghanistan, for they had no information to tell them otherwise.

I tried as best I could to explain. "A couple months ago airliners were hijacked by terrorists in America and flown into buildings. Over three thousand people died. Osama bin Laden set up the whole thing, from his base in Afghanistan. So U.S. forces have come here to capture bin Laden."

"Well, of course we are sorry that three thousand Americans died," one of the elders remarked. "But remember, during the worst of the fighting against the Soviets that number died here daily."

"Each week that number dies here in the camps," another elder added. "And anyway, what has three thousand Americans dying got to do with us?"

"Well, like I said, bin Laden was in Afghanistan when he organized 9/11," I tried explaining. "The Americans want to capture him and put him on trial."

"Well, bin Laden's not *here*," the first elder remarked. "He's not here with us, in this camp. We're suffering too because of him. He's our enemy too. But the American bombs are falling right nearby. Why are we the ones being punished?"

"Bin Laden's not even an *Afghan*," another added. "He's a foreigner, and he's not wanted in our country. Is America so dumb that it doesn't understand any of this?"

I didn't know what to say. I was sitting in that camp being berated by the elders as the bombs fell around us, yet I couldn't for the life of me explain why those bombs were being dropped. I was in a place where my sense of self was being shattered. This was one of the most difficult moments in my life: I loved America, and I loved Afghanistan, but right now those twin loves were tearing each other apart.

In my mind I could see the faces of the innocents who had died during 9/11, yet here I was faced with these Afghans who knew nothing about why yet another superpower was "attacking" them. And I knew in my heart what we should have spent those war dollars on: we should have cared for and educated these people, and countless others like them. Knowledge was the enemy of the Taliban, for theirs was a movement that thrived on ignorance and blind intolerance. Likewise, Osama bin Laden. The best way to fight them was with learning.

It was the end of October by the time I was preparing to leave. I'd been in the camps for two weeks or so. The ground war had begun by now, and I saw the displaced people moving camp in the tens of thousands. In all the confusion, I thought I'd seen the last of Yar Mohammad. But he and his father came and found me before we went our separate ways—me to America, them to God knows where.

"I hope things will be better for you," I told them. "I hope this war will rid you of the Taliban, and bring a better alternative, something that will work for all Afghanistan."

"Yes, but who will come after them?" Yar Mohammad's father replied. "I don't think we'll see peace in my lifetime. For my children and my family, I hope for peace. But I think maybe God chose this way of life for us."

Yar Mohammad gave me this shy look. "I will always remember you, *Madar-jan.*"

"How will you remember me?" I asked.

"I am a man. Men do not talk to women. But you and I did talk, and together we helped the people. That I will never forget."

It was on the tip of my tongue to say: *And I'll remember you too, because you are the one who killed the American.* But I knew Yar Mohammad wouldn't want to be remembered that way.

"I'll remember you because you're a very handsome boy," I told him.

He laughed. "You don't talk to me like that, *Madar-jan.*"

I flew back to America confused and traumatized. This had been the most difficult mission of my life. I reached Washington Dulles Airport and joined the queue for U.S. citizens. As I neared the front it suddenly occurred to me that the immigration officer was bound to ask me where I'd just come from. I hesitated, scanning the line of booths. I was trying to time it so I could get a woman and preferably an ethnic minority. I figured maybe they wouldn't be as angry about 9/11 as your average white American male.

"Excuse me, are you going?" someone in the queue asked.

I stepped aside. "No, no. You go. I'm kind of waiting for someone. . . ."

Finally I heard a voice call me from the front. "Ma'am, go to booth number five."

I stepped forward, and there was the biggest, chunkiest white American guy squeezed into booth number five, complete with a sawn-off blond crew cut. As I gazed at him a voice in my head said: *that's it—you're done for.* He reached out to take my passport with huge hands and the bulging forearms of a bodybuilder.

I tried my sweetest-ever smile. "Good afternoon."

"Good afternoon," the guy replied. "Where've you just been, ma'am?"

"Afghanistan."

"You've been to *Afghanistan?*"

"Yes."

"What were you doing there, ma'am?"

"I was delivering humanitarian aid."

"To whom?" he asked.

"To IDPs. Internally Displaced People. Like refugees."

"From Afghanistan?"

"Yep. Afghan refugees."

He flicked through my passport. "Ma'am, do you have a card or somethin' to show which aid group you're with?"

"Yes, I do." I pulled out my HTAC card.

He looked at it. "Help the Afghan Children?"

"That's right."

"Did you put this organization together? When was it formed?"

"I did. In 1993."

He started punching some data into his computer. I presumed it was a note to whoever was going to interrogate me. He checked my passport under the light to see if it was genuine. Then he glanced at me again. In the West if you are honest you look people in the eye; in the East if you look people in the eye it's considered rude. I forced myself to hold his gaze. For a long moment he stared at me, and I at him.

Then he handed me my passport. "Welcome home." He smiled.

"Excuse me?"

"Welcome home. You're sure doing good work out there, ma'am."

I stepped past him, like I was floating on air. America—it defied all clichés and prejudices. Welcome home.

In spite of the trauma of the recent mission, my focus was clearer than perhaps it ever had been now. Once the Taliban were gone, HTAC was going to start building schools to provide a proper education for girls and boys—those like Yar Mohammad and Naqibullah, who, deprived of knowledge and hope, could so easily go over to the dark side. In post-Taliban Afghanistan, that was going to be the focus of our efforts.

Randall's documentary film—entitled *Inshallah: Diary of an Afghan Woman*—aired on the Oxygen Channel in the spring of 2002. She had done a superb job, and I understood now why she'd kept sticking the camera in my face when things were really hard for me during the last mission. She was able to show the pain that I had felt in those refugee camps as the bombs fell all around us.

Her film portrayed the reality of Afghanistan under the Taliban, and the liberation of the country. It showed how we had helped some forty-five thousand people during our post-9/11 aid trip, and that in turn led to a huge groundswell of support for HTAC's work. One afternoon a few weeks after the broadcast, I got a phone call at the office.

"Hi, I'm calling from *The Oprah Winfrey Show*," a voice announced. "Are you Suraya Sadeed?"

"Right, you know, it's really not very funny!" I hung up. "Goddamn pranksters!"

It wasn't that unusual to be getting prank calls. A guy had made one recently: "We're calling from the Ford Foundation to give you five million dollars so that the Taliban can go and blow themselves up. Ha-fucking-ha!"

I'd grown suspicious of any unsolicited calls, but five minutes later the phone rang again.

"Ms. Sadeed, I really am calling from *The Oprah Winfrey Show*," the voice announced. "As a result of the documentary that was made of your work, Oprah wants you to be on the show."

"Okay, look, can I have your phone number so I can call you back?" I suggested. "Then I can be sure." I called, and I did get through to Oprah's switchboard, which meant it was genuine.

Being on *Oprah* was a great opportunity to publicize our work and to talk about our future plans. I went on the show alongside several others, most notably a couple who had lost their daughter on 9/11. They had reacted in the most amazing way imaginable, by taking aid to help Afghan women in need. I saw something of my earlier self in them: they had lost a loved one and were in search of a mission to bring meaning to their suffering.

We sat in the front row, with the audience ranged behind us, and a giant TV screen broadcasting the image live. Oprah spoke first to the husband and wife, whose work in Afghanistan had given them a real understanding of the hell the Afghan people had been put through over the last few decades. Then Oprah showed some scenes from Randall's documentary and turned to speak with me.

"Suraya, it's wonderful to have you with us today. I watched the documentary, part of which was filmed during the time of the Taliban. I think you're doing amazing work. What do you want to do next?"

"You know, my heart has always been set on education," I told her. "Education with a few innovative programs, and especially for girls who were barred from going to school under the Taliban. So my main focus now is going to be education."

"I couldn't agree more." Oprah smiled.

Oprah spoke about the importance of education for girls in Afghanistan, and then she thanked everyone who'd been on the show. Finally she announced that she had a small gift for me.

She called me onto the stage, hugged me tightly, and handed me an envelope. "It's $250,000," she whispered in my ear. "It's for girls' education, okay?"

"Oh my God!" I exclaimed. "Oh my God! $250,000!"

I couldn't believe it. It was the last thing that I'd ever been expecting, especially having shared the show with the couple who'd lost their daughter. I didn't think my story was particularly special, and I was overwhelmed and at a loss for words.

In the car en route to the airport I felt as if I were in a trance. I kept thinking: *whoa—$250,000! The things we can do with this money!* I told myself I wasn't going to phone the HTAC office and tell them. I'd do so myself, in person, and surprise them all.

In addition to Omar and Aziz, there were two others working in the HTAC office now. One was Aman, an Afghan-American man who was raising funds for HTAC from other foundations. The other was my daughter, Mariam, who was working for HTAC part-time while trying to complete her B.A. in business administration. I couldn't wait to see their reactions. But as soon as I stepped through the office door I knew that *they knew.*

"You guys watched the show, didn't you?" I challenged them.

Omar tried not to laugh. "No, we didn't."

"How did it go?" Mariam asked, feigning ignorance.

"You guys know about it!" I accused them. "Just stop it!"

They gathered around, and we laughed and hugged. It turned out that someone from Oprah's office had called to tell them the good news. I sat down at my desk right away to write Oprah a note of heartfelt thanks. HTAC had never had such a healthy bank balance—yet still there was a mountain to climb. Over 80 percent of the schools in Afghanistan had been destroyed during three decades of fighting—first against the Soviets, then among the Mujahideen, and now to drive out the Taliban. Rebuilding the education system was going to be a daunting challenge.

Oprah's support was a huge boost, and it meant far more than just the money itself. During our happy lives together Dastagir had asked me many times: *how much is ever enough?* Back then there was never enough, for I always wanted more. But I would now use that same drive to educate the Afghan people.

The time was ripe to see my dream come true—the dream of providing a decent education and life skills to every girl and boy across the country.

TWENTY-ONE

The Gift of Learning

B Y THE END OF NOVEMBER 2001 THE TALIBAN HAD BEEN DRIVEN out of Kabul. The U.S. bombing campaign coupled with the offensive by the Northern Alliance seemed to have defeated them across much of the country. It was now that HTAC went about opening an office in Kabul, and Sekander started recruiting former teachers. With a transitional government in place I planned to launch our school-building program shortly. Labor was cheap in Afghanistan, and I figured one school would cost no more than $10,000.

I decided to take $100,000 on my first school-building trip. I'd use existing HTAC funds that we had earmarked for schools—the money we'd raised in the flood of donations immediately after 9/11—and I wouldn't need to touch the Oprah money. I'd scope out what was possible, and then I'd use Oprah's $250,000 to really get our schools program going.

I called my bank and asked them to prepare $100,000 in cash for me. The day prior to my departure I went to collect it. I went to see Mandy, the banker with whom I usually dealt. She took me into the side room we always used for cash handovers and asked me to wait just a moment. I sat there with my briefcase on the desk in front of me. I presumed that Mandy was counting the money or something. The door opened, but it wasn't Mandy. Instead there were these two large guys in dark suits.

"Good afternoon, ma'am," one of them started. "Can we have a seat?"

"Sure." I smiled. I knew exactly who these guys were without anyone doing the introductions.

"Ms. Sadeed, where are you taking this money?" the other one asked.

"Just a minute, guys. Who are you?"

They pulled out their IDs: "We're with the FBI."

I took their badges and glanced over them. "Okay, so, I'm taking the money to Afghanistan."

"What are you planning to do with it?" the first guy asked.

"I'm going to build schools."

"That's a wonderful thing to be doing. So how long have you been doing this kind of work?"

"You know what, guys, I'm sure you did your homework before you got here. So you must know who I am and what I do and probably even my shoe size. So let's cut to the chase: what exactly do you guys want?"

I'd done dozens of trips carrying cash into Afghanistan and never had a problem before, so I wasn't exactly worried. I've never been one to mince words, and I figured these guys had a specific reason for being here, so why didn't they get to it.

"Well, because of what happened with 9/11 we gotta check, 'cause there's a lot of money laundering goin' on."

"Well, I'm not one of them," I interjected. "Do you have any idea how hard it is to raise funds for the kind of work I do?"

The guys glanced at each other. "No, we don't."

"Believe me, it is very, very difficult. If you really think I'm that much in love with Osama bin Laden to work so hard to raise this money and give it all to him, then you're mistaken, guys. 'Cause I am not. I really am not."

They smiled. "No, of course we know you're not."

"Well, I guess that answers your questions, doesn't it?"

"Okay, one final thing. Why cash? Why don't you do a wire transfer?"

"Well, you probably know this anyway. I mean, you're the FBI, right, so you should. There's no banking relationship between the United States and Afghanistan. So until there is, I have to take cash."

"Well, Ms. Sadeed, how do you intend to take this cash with you?" one of them asked.

I looked him in the eye. "It's like this: if I tell you, I'm no longer safe, am I?"

In spite of themselves, they laughed. "We thought we were the good guys—kind of protecting people."

"I'm sure you are. But it's need-to-know, gentlemen, and there's no need for you to know exactly how I take this money."

"Fair enough." They stood and we shook hands. "It's wonderful what you're doing. Good luck and stay safe. Here—our business cards in case you hear anything interesting."

Once they were gone a sheepish-looking Mandy returned. "Suraya, I am so sorry. You've been our customer for so long, but we have to enforce these new rules. Anything over nine thousand dollars we have to report."

"No problem, Mandy," I told her. "You do what you have to do. No harm done."

I took my $100,000, counted it, and left for home.

Two days later I flew into a Kabul recently liberated from the Taliban, and there was the unmistakable figure of Sekander. I could see instantly how he had changed. The last time I'd seen him was in June of 2001, when the Taliban were beating the crap out of him over our filming. He looked relaxed and happy now, wearing a suit of smart new clothes and a neatly trimmed beard. We glanced around the grungy airport building and laughed.

"Remember the last time we were here?" I remarked. "With those crazy American girls and their tapes stuffed down their . . ."

"Who can ever forget?"

"I'm glad those times are over, Sekander."

"Yep. Me too."

We'd rented an office in the Wazir Akbar Khan district, one of the few areas with functioning water and electricity. Sekander had identified three construction companies that we could use for our schools-building program, and he'd hired the one with the most reasonable prices. He'd also found me an accountant to run the financial side of things, and an experienced teacher-trainer to get the staff organized.

I asked Sekander to make contact with Sabera and get her over. With these new schools we'd be building, our secret Kabul girls' schools were no longer needed, and I wanted to find a way to wrap Sabera into all the stuff that we were planning. She strolled into our office dressed in this smart business suit—a totally transformed woman.

"Where's the burka?" I joked as I flung my arms around her. "God, you've changed so much. I can't believe it's you!"

She grinned. "Yeah, it's me."

"You know, I'm just so excited," I told her. " 'Cause you know what we're going to do? HTAC's going to build schools! All over Afghanistan— wherever people need them! And I'd love you to work with us on all of this. Can you manage that?"

Sabera said she'd love nothing more than to help us build those schools. It was great to have her on board.

We had a meeting scheduled with the interim government's Ministry of Education. None of us had ever set foot inside the building before, for under the Taliban our schools hadn't existed. On the drive there I soaked up the ambience in Kabul. There were no white pickups full of the Vice and Virtue thugs anymore. The streets were thronged, and some of the men were clean-shaven, while others had gotten seriously creative with little goatee beards, or plaited ones. Doing so was a simple, joyful statement that the Taliban were gone.

I told the minister for education that we'd like to build our first school in Paghman District, which was in easy driving distance of Kabul. This would be our pilot project, and if it went well I promised there would be more to follow. The minister allocated one of his staff to show us where there was government land available for school building. I thanked him warmly, then added a small cautionary note.

"Mr. Minister, please understand we did not come here with millions of dollars. But we'd like to build as many schools as we can afford."

He smiled. "I understand. And I want to give you the best choice of where to build."

On a gloriously warm and sunny morning I laid the foundation stone of that first school. Sekander had chosen well, and the construction company he'd hired had done a superb job, finding rock that could be quarried locally. That first, rough-hewn boulder was laid in the foundation trench, to signify that construction had started on HTAC's first school. Sekander, Sabera, and several of our new staff were there, as was the entire population of the village. There was no school surviving here, for everything had been laid waste during the war; local kids had taken what lessons they could in the open, scattered among the rubble of what once had been their homes.

I gave a short but emotional speech. "This is the happiest day of my life. I hope it is for you, also. It is so wonderful that here in Paghman, we are taking the first step toward a better future. Education is the future. You can rest assured that this is going to be a foundation for generations to come, those who will bring hope and prosperity to our nation, and all the things that we Afghan people have been craving for so long."

Sekander was standing right beside me, and he could see how watery-eyed I'd become. Over the years that we had worked together he'd witnessed my tears of anger, sadness, and despair, but now I was crying tears of pure happiness. He led me to one side so I could have a quiet moment while others—teachers, the school principal, the guy from the Ministry of Education, and some students—gave their own speeches. He didn't know quite what to say, but I could see the happiness written all over his features.

"You know, I hope one day we may have a HTAC school in the village where I was born," he remarked.

"*Insh'allah*—God willing," I replied. It was the least that Sekander, my loyal right-hand man, deserved.

The following day I was at the HTAC office when Sabera came to see me. I guessed what was on her mind.

"Do you remember that promise you made me?" she asked.

"About building a school in your home province? How could I ever forget? We still don't have a lot of money, but I promise the day will come when we will build you your school."

Sabera looked crestfallen. "Well, perhaps there is something you can do right now," she suggested. "There are no computers in the schools here in Kabul. So could you put them in for the twelfth graders?"

"Yes," I told her. "That I think we can do."

It was almost inconceivable, but here we were at the dawn of the twenty-first century, and there wasn't a single computer in any school in the country. Everything was done with chalk, blackboards, and exercise books, and most Afghan children didn't have a clue what a computer was.

Using his Kabul networks, Sekander managed to find a teacher, Farid, who had completed his computer studies in Peshawar. We purchased ten computers in a local Kabul market, which Farid installed in the first Afghan school ever to have them.

Sabera was overjoyed. "Ten computers and a teacher! Amazing! Can you imagine it—those kids'll be the first school pupils ever to be taught computing in Afghanistan."

It was amazing what we could achieve here, even with the limited funds HTAC had available. The day before I was scheduled to leave Kabul, I was sitting in our office when the door opened. In walked this guy in a smart Afghan army uniform. For a second I didn't recognize him.

"*Salam alaikum*, Suraya-*jan*," he greeted me.

"Oh my God!" I exclaimed. "Sekander! Is that you?"

He saluted me. "Yes, ma'am. I was in the army before. I am joining the army again."

I laughed. "But, Sekander, that means you're no longer going to be working with us. What will I do without you?"

"True." He smiled. "But I will always come to see you whenever you are here in Kabul."

We shook hands. "You've been wonderful, Sekander," I said. "You know, I've always admired your courage and sincerity, and your belief in what we were doing."

"It's been my honor to be a part of your organization," Sekander replied, in that soldierly way that he often spoke. But his voice was choked with emotion. "And it's been a joy to work alongside you, Suraya-*jan*."

In my heart I'd always known Sekander would return to the army. And I didn't need him now as I had before. The dangers of this kind of work were fading, and we all had to move with the changes that were coming to Afghanistan.

I N THE SPRING OF 2003, NEARLY A YEAR AFTER LAYING THE FOUNDA-
tion stone for the Paghman school, I paid a follow-up visit. It was a hot
and breathless April day, and I was burning with curiosity to see HTAC's
first school in action. Local kids had seen the new school rise from the
ashes of the village, and now it was finally open. The strong, whitewashed
walls rose from the rough surroundings like a symbol of hope. Inside were
the rows of desks, the blackboards, the textbooks, and the pens and pencils
that offered those children the promise of education and a future that was
so rare here. At every desk hands clutched at notebooks, heads bent in study,
as now and then a pupil stole a curious glance at me—the strange, "foreign"
visitor.

Guljan, the teacher, introduced me. A row of eyes, curious and fired by
learning, flashed at me.

"Freshta, you have something to read for Ms. Sadeed," the teacher
prompted.

A young girl barely in her teens rose to her feet. Her head was covered
in a snow-white *chadar*, her jet-black curls fingering out from the edges in
unruly confusion.

"I am the top student in the class," she began. "Once we lived in Kabul, but
the war drove us out of the city. We had no house to live in. We built a hut
from branches and sticks under a tree. My father had no work and life was terrible. But we managed, all thirteen of us in the family, and now we have a new
school." Freshta paused, darting a shy smile toward me. "I love mathematics
and sports, and my best game is volleyball. And I like growing the vegetables. I want to become a doctor in the future, so I can serve my country."

"Thanks for reading me your wonderful story," I told her. "It's great that
you want to be a doctor. It's a noble aspiration and I'm sure you'll get there."

"Freshta?" the teacher prompted. "Something else?"

Freshta's dark eyes glowed with pleasure. "This story is only a short one,
but it is in *English*, Miss Sadeed. It is called 'Homeland,' and it reflects how
everyone loves their place of birth."

She cleared her throat and held her head high. "One day Hamid and his father were sitting in their yard watching some beautiful birds flitting between the flowers. The birds flew around and were singing. Hamid asked his father: where do the birds live? They have sweet songs and are so happy. His father answered: my son, those birds are like people. Like us, they love their home."

Her classmates gave a round of applause. I joined them, as a blushing Freshta took her seat. I wiped at my eyes and made a gesture, as if the construction dust that still hung thinly in the air was irritating me. In reality I was crying: tears of happiness, tears of joy, tears at seeing my dream of education becoming a reality.

The teacher asked Ayesha to read next. Ayesha gave a quick bow before announcing that her own essay, entitled "Humor," was intended to be a short but funny one.

"There was a very lazy boy," she began. "He disliked going to school so very much. One rainy day the road was very muddy, and he asked his father to write a letter excusing him from lessons, because he couldn't get to school through the mud. His father asked him: but who will take the letter to school? The boy answered: I myself will."

A ripple of laughter went around the class. Ayesha glanced at me. "Another?"

I bobbed my head—*yes*—as a sea of young faces did likewise.

She smiled radiantly: "Poem for Kabul."

> *Oh, my Kabul,*
> *Every part of you burned,*
> *Your people roasted like coals.*
> *No moon or stars in your sky,*
> *Tears of my eyes fall,*
> *My heart pains and weeps,*
> *For you, oh my Kabul-jan.*

I smiled. "What a lovely, moving poem." Then, to the class in general: "I hope you'll continue to work hard and make your dreams come true. You're the future. You're the new promise of Afghanistan."

The bell rang for the end of class, and all of a sudden I was surrounded by laughing voices and eager, grasping hands. The teacher tried to rescue me from the crush, but I didn't want saving. I bent to speak to one especially eager girl.

"Do you like your new school?"

"Of course I do." She took hold of my hand. "Last year we had lessons under a walnut tree. There was rubble everywhere and it was so hot. No notebooks or pencils even. My father used to tell me he couldn't afford to buy any. Now we have chairs to sit on, desks, books galore, and lots of writing things. Now we have a real, proper school!"

I felt such a sense of accomplishment, of achieving my dream—and I felt so pleased for this lovely, innocent little girl. I felt joy, happiness, and a sense that you can achieve what you want, if you refuse to give up and keep on trying.

After visiting the Paghman school, I traveled north to a town called Jamal Agha, in Kapisa Province. The roads were checkpoint free and the country secure, so traveling around had never been easier. HTAC had spent nearly all of Oprah's money by now, building "real, proper schools" like the one at Paghman. I wanted to check on the last of them prior to the official opening. As I was finishing looking around, I noticed a line of heads poking shyly through the window. It was the local girls, and they started to giggle and laugh as they pointed out to one another where they wanted to sit in class.

"They're so excited, they're going to sleep here tonight," one of the girls' mothers told me. "That way they can be the first in line tomorrow, for the school opening."

"We said they shouldn't and that it's not right," another mother added, "but they're determined. So we said we'd accompany them. I mean, when was the last time we had a girls' school in Jamal Agha?"

People here were so desperate for education. I knew that. I'd seen it so many times over the years. But seeing this just brought it home to me. How was it that a movement like the Taliban had arisen on the promise of banning young people from education, this most basic of human needs? It was inconceivable. Yet it was so recent. And part of me worried that the threat of the Taliban had only faded into the background and was far from having gone away.

That evening I drove back to Kabul and stopped to drop off a friend's passport at the U.S. Embassy. The entire area was heavily guarded, with Afghan troops forming an outer cordon and U.S. troops inside. As I was leaving I passed through a barrier, and the soldier nearest me caught my eye. He was a young white guy half-buried in sandbags. It was baking hot, and he raised his water bottle at me in a tired salute.

"So, where are you going?" he called out.

"I'm going back home," I told him. "Virginia."

"Virginia, huh?" I could see the longing in his eyes. "Boy, are you lucky."

"One of these days, you know, you'll go home too."

"Uh-huh? I'm not so sure. With what's comin' in Iraq we might be away for some time."

I left the embassy feeling sorry for that young American boy who had no idea where he was next going to war. Having worked with the Taliban for years, I felt certain they weren't simply going to disappear. The Taliban had melted away before the U.S. bombing, but they were bound to launch a bloody resistance. Yet another battle for Afghanistan was coming.

A purely military solution had never worked here, and any war effort would have to be combined with diplomacy. For the sake of that young American soldier, and the Afghan people, we needed to talk. And if necessary, we needed to talk with some elements of the Taliban. I had worked with the Taliban over many difficult years. Some were ignorant thugs with whom no compromise was possible, but there were moderate, educated individuals with whom negotiations could bear fruit.

That night I drove to the Intercontinental to make use of the fast Internet connection at their café. I sent an e-mail to Karen Yanes at the Oprah Winfrey Foundation, giving her a quick update on our schools program.

Dear Karen, we are so pleased to inform you that tomorrow we're having the opening of school no 3; with the money from Oprah we've now built 3 schools that serve over 7,000 girls and boys. Thank you. I wish there was a way for the Foundation to see how happy and eager these girls are; they were waiting there 24 hours before the opening with all these colorful outfits they have made . . . It is so sad that at this time when people are very hopeful, Washington seems poised to divert all its attention to Iraq, and Afghanistan is being put on the back burner. We will be sending you the final report with pictures, as before. Thanks again, Yours, Suraya.

The next day the Jamal Agha school opening went like clockwork, and all the young girls seemed so happy. I was late returning to Kabul, and I needed to check my e-mail. I headed for an Internet café, ordered coffee and cream, and settled down to the job at hand. I had a lot of e-mails, and a long queue was building up behind me.

As I deleted the junk mail, I was half wondering what HTAC would do next, now that Oprah's three schools were finished. I noticed an e-mail from the Oprah Winfrey Foundation. I guessed it was a reply from Karen Yanes. I clicked on it. Unusually, it was from Oprah herself. I scanned it quickly, and almost fell off my chair in shock.

My friend, you are doing God's work. I am so happy. In honor of the education and freedom that you are spreading, I am giving you 1,000,000 dollars to build more schools. God bless, and keep doing what you're doing!

I just stared at the message. My mind had gone quite numb. How many zeros was that? I kept counting and recounting the zeros, but no matter how many times I counted there were still six. That was one million dollars. One million dollars!

"Oh my God!" I yelled. "Oh my God! Oh my God!"

Everyone was staring at me, but I didn't really give a damn. All I kept thinking was: *one million dollars! Just imagine how many schools we can build with that!*

That evening I got Sabera to come by the office. She sat with me to take tea, and I couldn't suppress a smile.

"What? What is it?" Sabera asked me. "I know you're up to something."

"I think I can make good on my promise! I think we can build you that school in your home town!"

Sabera started to cry. "God is kind. He answered my prayers."

By the summer of 2005, about a year and a half after Oprah's donation, we had finished work on not one, but four schools in Sabera's home of Samargan. I made sure that she had pride of place at the joint opening ceremony.

"I can't believe we have eighteen thousand students in HTAC schools," I remarked to her. "You remember how we started with those underground classrooms in Kabul? A few dozen here and a few dozen there?"

Sabera nodded and smiled. "Yes, I do. And do you remember how I once said: drop by drop a river forms."

I T WAS THE SPRING OF 2006, BARELY A YEAR AFTER I'D MADE GOOD on my promise to Sabera, and much had changed in the interim. On the upside, Aziz Qarghah had finally presented me with an ultimatum. He'd come around to my apartment dressed in a smart suit and tie, bearing a bunch of flowers. He'd told me that as he'd failed to win me all those years ago in Kabul, it was high time we gave it a go now.

I'd kind of laughed at the way he put it. He was right, of course, and I was actually happy. Really happy. I was very comfortable with Aziz, and I figured we'd be good for each other. And maybe it was time for me to settle down again. I agreed to his proposal, and we'd gone ahead and gotten married.

But just as I'd found love and happiness with Aziz, things were taking a turn for the worse in Afghanistan. The Taliban were on the rise again, and their war against knowledge was resurgent. Aziz felt this threat as painfully as I did. His family had suffered terribly under the previous totalitarian regime—that of the Afghan Communists and the Soviets. He'd lost six of his brothers during that haunting time, and he knew full well that the last thing Afghanistan needed was the Taliban back.

Late one night, I awoke in our Virginia home to the trilling of a phone. I flailed around for the receiver in the darkened bedroom. Due to the time difference between Afghanistan and the United States, the calls with the worst news always tended to come in the middle of the night.

I grabbed the telephone with a sinking feeling. "This is Suraya. Who is it?"

"It's Sabera. There's been an incident at one of the schools. . . ."

Sabera sounded worried. A note had been pinned to the door of one of HTAC's classrooms. It threatened death to any pupil or teacher who continued to attend lessons, and that the school would be burned down. With the rise of the Taliban such threats were becoming more commonplace. Increasingly village communities were being forced to mount guards, and we seemed to be spending more funds on fortifying schools than on teachers and textbooks.

I replaced the receiver and stared at it for a few seconds. It was horrible. By now we had a dozen HTAC schools up and running, and there were plans for still more. We couldn't let the Taliban's war against knowledge triumph. I reached out and woke Aziz. I knew that I shouldn't, but I needed someone to talk to. In any case, I didn't think he'd mind.

"What is it?" he asked, sleepily.

"They've threatened to burn down another of our schools."

As the Taliban's insurgency gained momentum, more schools were being threatened and more wounded American, British, Canadian, and other NATO soldiers kept coming home. Yet as the casualties mounted, all I ever seemed to hear in the news were calls to "send more troops." In truth, few Afghans wanted the American and allied soldiers to leave Afghanistan, for then it would descend into anarchy, as it had done after the Soviet withdrawal. What we did want was the same kind of effort and resources being put into rebuilding the peace as were going into fighting the war.

At the same time the world had to recognize that not all Taliban are

bad. In my years working in Afghanistan, I'd met some who were approaching reasonable. And during the Taliban's rule there was peace in Afghanistan, albeit an imperfect one. As the Taliban's presence has become ever
more visible, I've been asked to appear at various high-level venues to discuss what we should do about them. At one I listened to an American intelligence expert outline how we would defeat the Taliban, and how doing so
was the front-line battle in the war on terror.

"I just want you to clarify—who exactly is your enemy?" I'd asked him.

"Well, ma'am, the Taliban are our enemy."

"But who are the Taliban? They don't wear uniforms. They don't have a
membership list. They dress like Afghan villagers. Half of them are Afghan
villagers. So you can't really say who your enemy is. You're fighting a ghost
war, and sooner or later—and the sooner the better in Afghanistan—you
have to start talking."

"No, ma'am. We never negotiate with terrorists."

"You're always negotiating with terrorists. Look at Iraq. The only difference is you call them 'tribal sheiks' when you start talking to them, but it's
still the same people you were fighting yesterday. And in any case, most of
the Taliban aren't terrorists. They're just simple villagers who don't like a
foreign country invading theirs."

"So you think negotiations are good, ma'am?"

"Of course negotiations are good. You have to start talking sometime,
especially in a conflict like this one, otherwise you are never going to finish
this war."

A ND SO I AM TORN. I LIVE IN AMERICA, A LAND THAT I LOVE, BUT
I know that the means by which America and her allies are fighting
in Afghanistan—the bullet and the bomb—are not enough. Alone, the
soldiers will achieve nothing, and the bullets and bombs will sow a legacy of
hatred and anger among the Afghan people that will last for generations.
We in the West must do more—much more—to win the hearts and minds
of the Afghan people. We will not win hearts and minds by humiliating the

Afghan people, or by ignoring their cultural values and trying to impose our own on theirs.

We cannot presume that American-style democracy is one-size-fits-all, and that it can be imposed on Afghanistan. First, we must concentrate on investing in education and the economic advancement of the Afghan people, producing hope and positive, visible changes in their daily lives. We can do so much more to defeat the blind prejudices of the hard-line Taliban with education than we ever will achieve with military muscle alone.

As for me, I still have a mountain to climb with Help the Afghan Children. Eighteen years ago I lost Dastagir—*the one who is always helping others.* But in losing him, I became that person myself. In his dying I was gifted my mission in life, and still it feels as if it's only just beginning.

EPILOGUE

◇⟨⊂⟩◇

Drop by Drop a River Forms

TODAY, HTAC HAS OVER 100,000 STUDENTS, 27,000 OF WHOM ARE in Kandahar Province, the birthplace of the Taliban. Those 27,000 students are studying peace education and reconciliation, which is a sequence of teaching encounters that may be defined as the process of acquiring the values and developing the attitudes and behaviors to live in harmony. We believe that this is very important for a new generation, so that they may enable Afghanistan to heal.

HTAC continues to expand our program of education across Afghanistan, security permitting. I believe that having a sound education policy today will determine what Afghanistan is going to be in ten years, and for generations to come. It is a long-term investment and requires resources, patience, and collective effort, but the outcome will be the peaceful coexistence that we all want to achieve in Afghanistan.

My goal is to work increasingly with Afghanistan's Ministry of Education to incorporate a peace education program—one that HTAC has helped develop—into the national schools curriculum, so as to have maximum impact across Afghanistan. To help me achieve that goal, I'm completing a master's degree in Conflict Transformation and Peace-building, and feeding knowledge and experience from that directly into my work with HTAC and across Afghanistan.

We at HTAC move ahead with hope and resolve, but our progress is tinged with fear. We worry about the resurgence of the Taliban, which endangers all that we have achieved. If their war on knowledge triumphs, it will be a disaster for a new generation. The world community must hold its resolve in Afghanistan, for the sake of the country's children.

We hold our resolve. We take it one day at a time, and sure enough we keep making progress. For as Sabera once told me, drop by drop a river forms.

Afterword

This is not a political book. I'm a humanitarian, and HTAC is a humanitarian organization. However, I do have views on how Afghanistan's political deadlock can be broken, views formed by decades of working in the country and experience on the ground. First, the Afghan people need to know that America will continue to stand by them as they chart their own course of action and governance into the future. To underline this commitment, I believe that America should develop a long-term cooperation agreement with the Afghan state. In the shorter term, a solution to the conflict must be vested in Afghanistan, leading to a broad-based government free of foreign influence. The international community can be a facilitator and guarantor but should not be in control.

Afghans must be allowed to regenerate their traditional methods of contestation of power, within the traditional cultural context, and to negotiate their coexistence within that cultural context. And Afghanistan must utilize its natural resources to rebuild the country's destroyed economic and social infrastructure. However, in the short term and with the security challenges facing the country, the majority of Afghanistan's resources will be spent on obtaining military equipment to defend its sovereignty. Therefore, it's vital that Afghanistan adopt a neutral political status while the international community signs an accord to protect Afghanistan's borders, in case of outside aggression—similar to Switzerland's political status within Europe. That would free up scarce resources in the country, which could fund development, social advancement, and education. In that direction peace lies, for if you give people those opportunities in life, then they will be far less inclined to go to war.

You can make a difference in the life of a child. Your donation to Help the Afghan Children helps provide the gift of education to the children of Afghanistan. For further information please log on to www.HTAC.org.